T0212492

Lecture Notes in Artificial Intelligence   9872

Subseries of Lecture Notes in Computer Science

LNAI Series Editors

Randy Goebel
University of Alberta, Edmonton, Canada
Yuzuru Tanaka
Hokkaido University, Sapporo, Japan
Wolfgang Wahlster
DFKI and Saarland University, Saarbrücken, Germany

LNAI Founding Series Editor

Joerg Siekmann
DFKI and Saarland University, Saarbrücken, Germany

More information about this series at http://www.springer.com/series/1244

Matthias Klusch · Rainer Unland
Onn Shehory · Alexander Pokahr
Sebastian Ahrndt (Eds.)

Multiagent System Technologies

14th German Conference, MATES 2016
Klagenfurt, Österreich, September 27–30, 2016
Proceedings

 Springer

Editors

Matthias Klusch
DFKI
Saarbrücken
Germany

Rainer Unland
Institute for Computer Science
University of Duisburg-Essen
Essen
Germany

Onn Shehory
IBM Haifa Research Lab
Haifa
Israel

Alexander Pokahr
University of Hamburg
Hamburg
Germany

Sebastian Ahrndt
Distributed Artificial Intelligence
Technical University of Berlin
Berlin
Germany

ISSN 0302-9743 ISSN 1611-3349 (electronic)
Lecture Notes in Artificial Intelligence
ISBN 978-3-319-45888-5 ISBN 978-3-319-45889-2 (eBook)
DOI 10.1007/978-3-319-45889-2

Library of Congress Control Number: 2016950388

LNCS Sublibrary: SL7 – Artificial Intelligence

Printed on acid-free paper

This Springer imprint is published by Springer Nature
The registered company is Springer International Publishing AG Switzerland

Preface

These are the proceedings of the 14th German conference on Multiagent System Technologies, which was held on September 27–30, 2016, in Klagenfurt, Austria. The MATES 2016 conference was organized in cooperation with the Distributed Artificial Intelligence (DAI) chapter of the German Society for Informatics (GI), and sponsored by the GI. Moreover, it was co-located with the 46th Annual Symposium of the German Society for Informatics (INFORMATIK 2016) and the 39th German AI Conference (KI 2016).

The set of regular MATES 2016 conference talks covered a broad area of topics of interest including MAS engineering and modeling, issues of human-agent interaction, collaboration and coordination, agent-based adaptation and optimization, and applications of MAS, in particular in the smart energy domain. In keeping with its tradition, MATES 2016 also offered four excellent invited keynotes by well-known, reputed scientists in the domain, covering relevant topics of the broad area of intelligent agent technology. Elisabeth André from the University of Augsburg, Germany, described various computational approaches to implementing empathic behavior in a robot. Besides analytic approaches that are informed by theories from the cognitive and social sciences, she discussed empirical approaches that enable a robot to learn empathic behavior from recordings of human-human interactions or from live interactions with human interlocutors. Peter Palensky from the Technical University of Delft, The Netherlands, addressed the design of agent systems for power grids, and what we can expect from agents in cyber-physical energy systems in the future. Ryszard Kowalczyk from Swinburne University of Technology, Australia, presented selected research results in the areas of agent-based decision support systems in various application domains including traffic control, cloud computing, and micro-grids. Finally, Ulrich Furbach from the Unviersity of Koblenz, Germany, (who was this year's joint keynote speaker of MATES and KI) discussed the use of first order automated reasoning in question answering and cognitive computing, and its relation to human reasoning as investigated in cognitive psychology.

Additionally, the MATES doctoral consortium (DC) program, chaired by Alexander Pokahr, offered PhD students a platform to present and to discuss their work in an academic professional environment. Students presented their PhD projects in joint sessions receiving feedback and suggestions from their peers and experienced researchers. Moreover, each PhD student was assigned a mentor offering the student the opportunity to interact with an expert in the field on an individual basis. The mentors gave personalized feedback on the students' work and provided advice for their (academic) career development.

Overall, we received 28 submissions, each of which was peer-reviewed by at least two members of the international Program Committee. Ten papers were accepted for long presentation, and five papers were accepted for short presentation at the main conference.

This volume includes selected and revised contributions from the MATES 2016 conference and its DC program, and an invited paper. The MATES 2016 conference issued a best paper award and a best system demonstration award, which were sponsored by the DAI Lab at TU Berlin.

As co-chairs and in the name of the MATES Steering Committee, we are very thankful to the authors and invited speakers for contributing to this conference, the Program Committee members and additional reviewers for their timely and helpful reviews of the submissions, as well as the local organization team around Heinrich C. Mayr at the University of Klagenfurt for their help in making MATES 2016 a success. Besides, we are indebted to Alfred Hofmann and the whole Springer LNAI team for their very kind and excellent support in publishing these proceedings and for their continuous support of the MATES conference over the past 14 years.

Finally, we hope you enjoyed the MATES 2016 conference and drew some inspiration and helpful insights from attending it!

July 2016   Matthias Klusch
                                                          Rainer Unland
                                                           Onn Shehory
                                                      Alexander Pokahr
                                                      Sebastian Ahrndt

Organization

General Chairs

Matthias Klusch   German Research Center for AI (DFKI), Germany
Onn Shehory   IBM Research, Israel
Rainer Unland   University of Duisburg-Essen, Germany

Honorary Chairs

Michael N. Huhns   University of South Carolina, USA
Yves Demazeau   CNRS Grenoble, France
Toru Ishida   University of Kyoto, Japan

Doctoral Consortium Chair

Alexander Pokahr   University of Hamburg, Germany

Local Organizing Chair

Heinrich C. Mayr   University of Klagenfurt, Austria

MATES Steering Committee

Matthias Klusch   German Research Center for AI (DFKI), Germany
Winfried Lamersdorf   University of Hamburg, Germany
Jörg P. Müller   TU Clausthal, Germany
Sascha Ossowski   Universidad Rey Juan Carlos, Madrid, Spain
Paolo Petta   University of Vienna, Austria
Ingo J. Timm   University of Trier, Germany
Rainer Unland   University of Duisburg-Essen, Germany

Program Committee

Karl Aberer   EPF Lausanne, Switzerland
Thomas Agotnes   University of Bergen, Norway
Sebastian Ahrndt   DAI Lab, Berlin University of Technology, Germany
Bernhard Bauer   University of Augsburg, Germany
Olivier Boissier   ENSM de Saint-Etienne, France
Vicent Botti   Polytechnical University of Valencia, Spain
Nils Bulling   Delft University of Technology, Netherlands
Longbing Cao   University of Technology Sydney, Australia

Georgios Chalkiadakis	Technical University of Crete, Greece
Liana Cipcigan	Cardiff University, UK
Mehdi Dastani	University of Utrecht, Netherlands
Paul Davidsson	University of Malmo, Sweden
Jörg Denzinger	University of Calgary, Canada
Frank Dignum	University of Utrecht, Netherlands
Jürgen Dix	Technical University of Clausthal, Germany
Johannes Fähndrich	DAI Lab, Berlin University of Technology, Germany
Klaus Fischer	DFKI, Germany
Maria Ganzha	University of Gdansk, Poland
Maria Gini	University of Minnesota, USA
Vladimir Gorodetsky	Russian Academy of Sciences, Russia
Axel Hahn	University of Oldenburg, Germany
Koen Hindriks	Delft University of Technology, Netherlands
Yasuhiko Kitamura	Kwansei Gakuin University, Japan
Franziska Klügl	University of Oerebro, Sweden
Ryszard Kowalczyk	Swinburn University of Technology, Australia
Winfried Lamersdorf	University of Hamburg, Germany
Arndt Lüder	University of Magdeburg, Germany
Lars Mönch	Fernuniversität Hagen, Germany
John-Jules Meyer	University of Utrecht, Netherlands
Jörg P. Müller	Technical University of Clausthal, Germany
Tim Norman	University of Aberdeen, UK
Ingrid Nunes	Federal University of Rio Grande do Sul, Brazil
Eugenio Oliveira	Universidade do Porto, Portugal
Andrea Omicini	University of Bologna, Italy
Nir Oren	University of Aberdeen, UK
Sascha Ossowski	University King Juan Carlos, Spain
Terry Payne	University of Liverpool, UK
Mathias Petsch	Technical University of Ilmenau, Germany
Paolo Petta	University of Vienna, Austria
Wolfgang Renz	HAW Hamburg, Germany
Valentin Robu	Heriot-Watt University Edinburgh, UK
Juan Antonio Rodriguez Aguilar	IIIA-CSIC, Spain
Michael Rovatsos	University of Edinburgh, UK
Alessandro Ricci	University of Bologna, Italy
Jordi Sabater Mir	IIIA-CSIC, Spain
David Sarne	Bar Ilan University, Israel
Carles Sierra	IIIA-CSIC, Spain
René Schumann	HES-SO Western Switzerland, Switzerland
David Sislak	Czech Technical University, Czech Republic
Michael Sonnenschein	University of Oldenburg, Germany
Katia Sycara	Carnegie Mellon University, USA
Andreas Symeonidis	Aristotle University of Thessaloniki, Greece
Matthias Thimm	University of Koblenz-Landau, Germany

Huaglory Tianfield	Glasgow Caledonian University, UK
Ingo J. Timm	University of Trier, Germany
Adelinde Uhrmacher	University of Rostock, Germany
Francesca Toni	Imperial College London, UK
Leon van der Torre	University of Luxembourg, Luxembourg
Birgit Vogel-Heuser	Technical University of Munich, Germany
George Vouros	University of Piraeus, Greece
Gerhard Weiss	University of Maastricht, Netherlands
Michael Weyrich	University of Siegen, Germany
Michael Winikoff	University of Otago, New Zealand
Franco Zambonelli	University of Modena, Italy
Ning Zhong	Maebashi Institute of Technology, Japan

Additional Reviewers

Merlinda Andoni
Vahid Yazdanpanah

Doctoral Consortium PC Members

Bernhard Bauer	University of Augsburg, Germany
Jan Ole Berndt	University of Trier, Germany
Nils Bulling	Delft University of Technology, The Netherlands
Maria Ganzha	University of Gdansk, Poland
Vladimir Gorodetsky	St. Petersburg Institute for Informatics and Automation, Russia
Axel Hahn	University of Oldenburg, Germany
Franziska Klügl	Örebro University, Sweden
Jörg P. Müller	TU Clausthal, Germany
Andrea Omicini	Alma Mater Studiorum - Università di Bologna, Italy
Sascha Ossowski	University Rey Juan Carlos, Spain
Paolo Petta	Austrian Research Institute for AI, Austria
Jordi Sabater Mir	IIIA-CSIC, Spain
Jürgen Sauer	University of Oldenburg, Germany
René Schumann	University of Applied Sciences Western Switzerland, Switzerland
Matthias Thimm	University of Koblenz, Germany
Ingo J. Timm	University of Trier, Germany
Rainer Unland	University of Duisburg-Essen, Germany
Michael Weyrich	Universität Siegen, Germany

Contents

MAS Modeling, Engineering, and Coordination

Commonsense Reasoning Meets Theorem Proving

Ulrich Furbach and Claudia Schon[✉]

Universität Koblenz-Landau, Mainz, Germany
{uli,schon}@uni-koblenz.de

Abstract. The area of commonsense reasoning aims at the creation of systems able to simulate the human way of rational thinking. This paper describes the use of automated reasoning methods for tackling commonsense reasoning benchmarks. For this we use a benchmark suite introduced in literature. Our goal is to use general purpose background knowledge without domain specific hand coding of axioms, such that the approach and the result can be used as well for other domains in mathematics and science. Furthermore, we discuss the modeling of normative statements in commonsense reasoning and in robot ethics (This paper is an extended version of the informal proceedings [9] and [10]).

1 Introduction

Commonsense reasoning aims at creating systems able to simulate the human way of rational thinking. This area is characterized by ambiguity and uncertainty since it deals with problems humans are confronted with in everyday life. Humans performing reasoning in everyday life do not necessarily obey the rules of classical logic. This causes humans to be susceptible to logical fallacies but on the other hand to draw useful conclusions automated reasoning systems are incapable of. Humans naturally reason in the presence of incomplete and inconsistent knowledge, are able to reason in the presence of norms as well as conflicting norms, and are able to quickly reconsider their conclusions when being confronted with additional information. The versatility of human reasoning illustrates that any attempt to model the way humans perform commonsense reasoning has to use a combination of many different techniques. Such techniques can also be subsumed under the keyword 'cognitive computing' which was coined by IBM after the success of their Watson-System in the Jeopardy! quiz show.

In this paper we describe the progress we made so far in creating a system able to tackle commonsense reasoning benchmarks. We start in Sect. 2 with a short description of a natural language question answering project, from which we learned a lot about implementing commonsense reasoning. Namely to combine and to apply techniques from automated theorem proving, natural language processing, large ontologies as background knowledge and machine learning.

Work supported by DFG FU 263/15-1 'Ratiolog'.

M. Klusch et al. (Eds.): MATES 2016, LNAI 9872, pp. 3–17, 2016.
DOI: 10.1007/978-3-319-45889-2_1

In Sect. 3 we discuss the use of automated reasoning in cognitive computing. We introduce several benchmarks for the area of commonsense reasoning and describe the techniques which we combine therein. In order to find the more plausible answer to the benchmark problems, machine learning techniques come to use and we present first experimental results from this area. In a final Sect. 4 we discuss the modeling of normative rules in commonsense reasoning and in robot ethics.

2 Automated Reasoning in the Question Answering System LogAnswer

This section introduces the Loganswer project, which was finished only recently and from which we learned some valuable lessons for the topic of this paper. This project [6] researched a system for open domain question answering from a snapshot of the German Wikipedia. The user enters a question in natural language and the LogAnswer system provides answers together with highlighted textual sources. Opposed to other question answering systems, the LogAnswer system does not rely solely on shallow linguistic methods but uses the automated theorem prover Hyper to compute the answers. For this process possible answer candidates are determined by syntactic keyword search and ranked by machine learning techniques. For the 200 best answer candidates from this process Hyper is invoked with the semantic contents of the answer candidate represented in predicate logic together with the query and background knowledge. The whole process of answering a question is time critical, since users are not willing to accept slow respond times. It is not surprising that Hyper is not always able to construct a proof when confronted with an answer candidate for the question under consideration in reasonable time. If no proof can be found within a certain time limit, a technique called relaxation is used. This techniques allows to weaken or drop subgoals of the question in order to enable Hyper to find a proof within the time limit. Of course, this technique comes at the expense of accuracy. In the last step, all proofs are ranked by machine learning techniques and for the three best proofs a natural language answer is presented to the user.

One finding which can be seen as an especially interesting insight from the LogAnswer project is the following fact: When combined with suitable background knowledge and machine learning techniques, automated theorem provers can be successfully applied even in domains where exact yes or no answers cannot be expected.

In the sequel we suggest to use first-order logic automated reasoning techniques to tackle commonsense reasoning tasks. It is reasonable to question the choice of first-order logic since there are many other logics, like defeasible logic and other non-monotonic logics, which seem to be a much better choice. Using first-order logic, however, has the crucial advantage that it allows the usage of highly optimized theorem provers. In our case we use the Hyper theorem prover [2] to solve the reasoning tasks occurring in commonsense reasoning problems. At first glance it seems to be a drawback of first-order logic theorem provers that they are only able to answer yes or no (or sometimes even don't answer at all). However, our experiences in the LogAnswer project demonstrated that the combination of background knowledge, a theorem prover with its proof objects like (partial) proofs or (partial) models and machine learning techniques is able to come to impressive conclusions. We are convinced that the combination of the afore described techniques leads to a result which is much more than the sum of its parts.

3   Automated Reasoning in Cognitive Computing

The previous section demonstrated that for natural language question answering several different techniques and knowledge sources have to be combined in a cooperative and efficient manner. This fits nicely under the term 'cognitive computing' which was coined by IBM research in order to describe such 'Watson-like' systems [5]. We consider commonsense reasoning as an area which perfectly fits the prerequisites to be tackled by cognitive computing.

3.1   Benchmarks for Commonsense Reasoning

For a long time, no benchmarks in the field of commonsense reasoning were available and most approaches were tested only using small toy examples. Recently, this problem was remedied with the proposal of various sets of benchmark problems. There is the Winograd Schema Challenge [17] whose problems have a clear focus on natural language processing whereas background knowledge has an inferior standing. Another example is the Choice Of Plausible Alternatives (COPA) challenge[1] [26] consisting of 1000 problems equally split into a development and a test set. Each problem consists of a natural language sentence describing a scenario and a question. In addition to that two answers are provided in natural language. The task is to determine which one of these alternatives is the most plausible one. Figure 1 presents two problems from this benchmark suite. Like in the two presented examples, the questions always ask either for the *cause* or the *result* of an observation.

Even though for the COPA challenge capabilities for handling natural language are necessary, background knowledge and commonsense reasoning skills are crucial to tackle these problems as well, making them very interesting to evaluate cognitive systems. All existing systems tackling the COPA benchmarks focus on linguistic and statistical approaches by calculating correlational statistics on words.

Another set of benchmarks is the Triangle-COPA challenge[2] [19]. This is a suite of one hundred logic-based commonsense reasoning problems which was developed specifically for the purpose of advancing new logical reasoning

---

[1] Available at http://people.ict.usc.edu/~gordon/downloads/COPA-questions-dev.txt.

[2] Available at https://github.com/asgordon/TriangleCOPA/.

```
1: My body cast a shadow over the grass. What was the CAUSE of this?

   1. The sun was rising.
   2. The grass was cut.

13: The pond froze over for the winter. What happened as a RESULT?

   1. People skated on the pond.
   2. People brought boats to the pond.
```

Fig. 1. Example problems 1 and 13 from the COPA challenge.

approaches. The structure of the problems is the same as in the COPA Challenge, however, the problems in the Triangle-COPA challenge are not only given in natural language but also in first-order logic.

Figure 2 depicts a problem from this benchmark suite consisting of a natural language description as well as first-order logic representation of a situation, a question, and two alternative answers.

```
The triangle opened the door, stepped outside and started to shake. Why
did the triangle start to shake?
```
$exit(e1, lt) \land shake(e2, lt) \land seq(e1, e2)$

```
   1. The triangle is upset.
```
$unhappy(e3, lt)$
```
   2. The triangle is cold.
```
$cold(e4, lt)$

Fig. 2. Narrative and formalization of an example problem no. 44 from the Triangle-COPA challenge.

Until now only one logic based system is able to tackle the Triangle-COPA benchmarks: [19] and more recently [11] use abduction together with a set of hand-coded axioms. Furthermore, there is a preliminary approach using deontic logic to address the problems given in these benchmarks [7]. We refrain from using hand-coded knowledge and suggest to use knowledge bases containing commonsense knowledge like OpenCyc [16], SUMO [24,25], ConceptNet [18] and Yago [27] together with a theorem prover instead.

3.2   Combination of Techniques

As described afore, the creation of a system for commonsense reasoning requires cognitive computing, in particular the combination of techniques from different areas. Even gathering appropriate background knowledge for a specific benchmark problem requires the use of different techniques. Figure 3 depicts the different steps necessary to gather suitable background knowledge for a given COPA problem. When combining an example problem with background knowledge, several problems have to be solved:

Fig. 3. Gathering background knowledge for a benchmark problem. The starting formulae are generated by transforming the natural language problems of COPA into first-order logic using the Boxer system.

1. If the problem is given in natural language it has to be transformed into a logical representation.
2. The predicate symbols used in the formalization of the example are unlikely to coincide with the predicate symbols used in the background knowledge.
3. The background knowledge is too large to be considered as a whole.

The first problem can be solved using the Boxer [4] system which is able to transform natural language into first-order logic formulae. We assume that this is done before the techniques given in Fig. 3 are applied. Please note that this step is not necessary when benchmarks given in first-order logic are considered, like it is the case for the Triangle-COPA challenge.

We address the second problem by using WordNet [20] to find synonyms and hypernyms of the predicate symbols used in the formalization of the example. Note that the formalization of the example consists both of the formulae describing the situation as well as the formulae for the two alternatives. In the next step, predicate symbols used in OpenCyc [16], which are similar to these synonyms and hypernyms are determined. With the help of this information a connecting set of formulae is created. In this step, it is also necessary to adjust the arity of predicate symbols which is likely to differ, since Boxer only creates formulae with unary or binary predicates.

The third problem is addressed using selection methods. For this, all predicate symbols occurring in the formalization of the example and in the connecting set of formulae are used. As selection methods, SInE as well as k-NN as they are implemented in the E.T. metasystem [15] come to use. The selected axioms are combined with the connecting set of formulae and the resulting set of formulae constitutes the background knowledge for the example at hand.

The COPA challenge contains two different categories of problems. In the first category, a sentence describing an observation is given and it is asked for the *cause* of this observation. Probem no. 1 given in Fig. 1 is an example for a question in this category. In this case, the task is to determine which of the two provided alternatives is more likely to be the cause of the observation described in the sentence. We call this category the *cause category*.

In the other category a sentence describing an observation is given and it is asked about the *result* of this observation. In this case, the task is to decide which of the two alternatives is more likely to result from the situation described in the sentence. We call this second category the *result category*. Even though

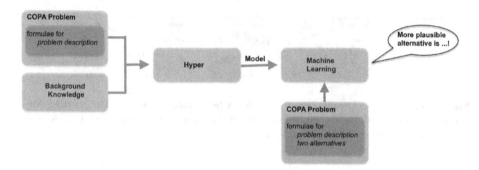

Fig. 4. Addressing a problem in the *result* category: Using the selected background knowledge together with Hyper and machine learning.

the category does not influence the way the background knowledge is selected, it is necessary to use different approaches for the two categories when combining this background knowledge with automated reasoning methods.

Figure 4 depicts how to tackle a problem from the result category in order to determine the more plausible alternative result. Please note that the selected background knowledge does not only consist of axioms stemming from the knowledge base used as a source for background knowledge but also contains the connecting formulae which were created as depicted in Fig. 3. First, this background knowledge is combined with the logical formulae representing the description of the benchmark problem. The resulting set of formulae serves as input for a theorem prover, in our case the Hyper prover. Hyper constructs a model for the set of formulae which, together with the logical representation of the two alternatives, is used by machine learning techniques to determine which of the two alternatives is more plausible. In the remainder of this paper, we focus on problems belonging to the result category.

3.3 Lessons Learnt so far

We created a prototypical implementation of the workflow depicted in the previous section. Our implementation is able to take a problem from the COPA or Triangle-COPA challenge, it selects appropriate background knowledge, generates a connecting set of formulae and feeds everything into Hyper. The machine learning component inspecting the generated model is in an experimental phase and is addressed in Sect. 3.4 below.

Issues with Inconsistencies

COPA challenge. We performed a very preliminary experiment to test this workflow. From the COPA benchmark set we selected 100 problems. Feeding these examples into the workflow resulted finally in 100 proof tasks for Hyper and we learned a lot — about problems which have to be solved. Hyper found 37 proofs and 57 models; the rest are time-outs. One problem we encountered is that some contradictions leading to a proof are introduced by selecting too general hypernyms from WordNet. E.g. the problem description of example 1 given in Fig. 1 is transformed into the following first-order logic formula by Boxer:

$$\exists A(ngrassC(A) \wedge \exists B, C, D(rover(B, A) \wedge rpatient(B, C) \wedge ragent(B, D)$$
$$\wedge\, vcast(B) \wedge nshadow(C) \wedge nbody(D) \wedge rof(D, C) \wedge nperson(C)))).$$

From WordNet the system extracted the information, that 'individual' is a hypernym of 'shadow' and 'collection' is a hypernym of 'person' leading to the two connecting formulae:

$$\forall X(nshadow(X) \rightarrow individual(X))$$
$$\forall X(nperson(X) \rightarrow collection(X)).$$

The selection from OpenCyc resulted among others in the axiom

$$\forall X \neg(collection(X) \wedge individual(X)).$$

These formulae together lead to a closed tableau—a proof of unsatisfiability—which has nothing to do with one of the alternatives that the sun was rising or the grass was cut.

To remedy this problem, we use a tool called KNEWS[3] [1] to disambiguate Boxer's output. This tool calls the Babelfy[4] [21] service to link entities to BabelNet[5] [23]. Babelfy is a multilingual, graph-based approach to entity linking and word sense disambiguation. BabelNet is a multilingual encyclopedic dictionary and a semantic network. Since the BabelNet entries are linked to Wordnet synsets, this tool provides the suitable Wordnet synset for predicate names generated by Boxer. In a second run of the experiment we only used the disambiguated results to construct a bridging set of formulae and to select background knowledge. It turned out that the selected background knowledge is much more focused on the problem under consideration. Furthermore, only one of the 100 COPA problems we tested, was inconsistent. So we solved this first problem by disambiguating Boxer's output.

The one contradiction which still occurred in the second experiment stems directly from inconsistencies in the knowledge base used as source for background knowledge (in our case OpenCyc). E.g. the two formulae

$$\forall X \, speed(fqpquantityfnspeed(X))$$
$$\forall X \neg speed(X)$$

were selected immediately leading to a contradiction which again does not have to do anything with the two alternatives about the sun rising or the grass being cut. This illustrates that we have to find a way to deal with inconsistent background knowledge.

---

[3] Many thanks to Valerio Basile for being so kind to share KNEWS. (Available at: https://github.com/valeriobasile/learningbyreading).

[4] Available at: http://babelfy.org.

[5] Available at: http://babelnet.org.

Triangle-COPA challenge. We used the workflow depicted in Fig. 3 for the 100 problems given in the Triangle-COPA challenge with a timeout set to 1000 s. Due to the structure of the problems, we treated all problems in the Triangle-COPA challenge as problems belonging to the afore-described result category. In our first experiments, Hyper constructed 12 models, 65 proofs and 17 timeouts. The remaining 6 problems caused an error. Inspection of the 65 proofs revealed that 38 were caused by the following formula selected from Cyc:

$$\forall X \neg action(X) \tag{1}$$

As soon as $action(i)$ can be derived for an individual i, this formula leads to a contradiction. Since the topic of all Triangle-COPA problems are interpersonal relationships, it is reasonable that instances of the *action* predicate are derived in many examples. Formula (1) itself does not provide interesting information for our scenario which is why we removed it from our version of OpenCyc.

We restarted the workflow for the modified background knowledge. This resulted in 15 models, 42 timeouts, 37 proofs and 6 errors. It is remarkable that the major part of the 22 examples which were unsatisfiable due to Formula (1) in the first experiment, led to timeouts in our second experiment. Only 3 of these problems led to models. We are planning to further improve these results by adding new sources for background knowledge as described in the next section.

Insufficient Background Knowledge

COPA challenge. Another challenge when combining problems with background knowledge is the lack of appropriate background knowledge. Consider the example number 13 from the COPA challenge which we presented in Fig. 1. The background knowledge selected for this example contains formulae on iceskating:

$$\forall X(iceskate(X) \rightarrow isa(X, c\_iceskate)).$$

However, the information that freezing of a pond results in a surface suitable for skating, is missing. This explains, why not enough inferences were performed and the constructed model does not contain information on ice skating.

One explanation for the lack of inferences is the fact that we are currently only using OpenCyc as a source of background knowledge. We are planning to remedy this situation by including different other sources of background knowledge like ConceptNet [18], the Suggested Upper Merged Ontology (SUMO) [24,25], the Human Emotion Ontology (HEO) [12] and the Emotion Ontology (EMO) [14].

ConceptNet is a semantic network containing large amounts of commonsense knowledge. This graph consists of labeled nodes and edges. The nodes are also called concepts and represent words or word senses. The edges are relations between these concepts and represent common-sense knowledge that connect the concepts. Relating to the COPA problem described afore, ConceptNet contains very helpful knowledge like the fact that in winter one likes to skate.

$$winter{-}CausesDesire \rightarrow skate$$

SUMO is a very large upper ontology containing knowledge which could be helpful as background knowledge. For example, SUMO contains the knowledge that *icing* is a subclass of *freezing* which could be helpful for our benchmark problem. One very interesting point is that there is a mapping from SUMO to WordNet synsets. This will be very helpful during the creation of formulae bridging from the vocabulary of the benchmark problem and the synonyms and hypernyms to the vocabulary used in SUMO.

Triangle-COPA challenge. When testing the workflow depicted in Fig. 3, experiments produced 15 models. Please note that, since our background knowledge does not contain eventualities, we remove the eventuality from the formulae describing the problem, meaning that we map $shake(e2, lt)$ to $shake(lt)$. Closer inspection of these models revealed that some helpful inferences were made. Considering the model constructed for example problem no. 44 given in Fig. 2 shows that the following ground instances were derived: $leave(lt)$, $move(lt)$, $tremble(lt)$, $judder(lt)$ and $shiver(lt)$. While these inferred ground instances look encouraging, the final step of deducing $cold(lt)$ is still missing. This situation could be remedied by the use of ConceptNet, which contains fitting additional knowledge "You would shiver because it was cold" represented as:

$$shiver-MotivatedByGoal \rightarrow it\ be\ cold$$

This is why we are planning to integrate ConceptNet as background knowledge. Another interesting source for additional background knowledge are the HEO and EMO ontology. Both these ontologies contain information on human emotions which is very suitable for the Triangle-COPA challenge since its problems consist of descriptions of small episodes on interpersonal relationships.

3.4   Ranking of Proofs and Proof Attempts

When using the automated reasoning system Hyper within the LogAnswer system we already had to tackle the problem that the prover nearly never found a complete proof of the given problem. In order to find a best answer of the system we had to compare several proofs, or rather proof attempts. For this ranking we used machine learning to find the best proof rsp. answer. We are planning to use a similar approach for the commonsense benchmarks.

In the sequel we describe how to use machine learning techniques for problems of the result category and present first experimental results. In the workflow depicted in Fig. 4, we construct a tableau for $P \cup BG$, where P is the problem description and BG is the background knowledge. This tableau may contain open and closed branches. The closed branches are parts of a proof and the open branches either represent a model (and hence no closed tableau exists) or they are only open because of a time-out for this branch. With the help of this tableau, we try to decide which of the two alternatives $E1$ and $E2$ is 'closer' to a logical consequence of $P \cup BG$.

In the LogAnswer system we gave the two answers to humans to decide which is closer to a logical consequence and we then used this information to train a machine learning system. For the scenario of the COPA and Triangle-COPA benchmarks we designed a preliminary study, which aims at using the information about the tableau created for $P \cup BG$ together with information from formulae of the problem and the background $P \cup BG$ to generate examples for training.

We restricted our preliminary study to propositional logic and analyzed tableaux created by the Hyper prover for randomly created sets of clauses. For each pair of propositional logic variables p and q occurring in a clause set, we were interested in the question if p or q is 'closer' to a logical consequence. We reduced this question to a classification problem: for each pair of variables p and q, the task is to learn if $p < q$, $p > q$ or $p = q$, where $p < q$ means, that q is 'closer' to a logical consequence than p and $p = q$ means that p's and q's 'closeness' to a logical consequence is equal. Consider the following set of clauses:

$$p0$$
$$p4 \rightarrow p2 \vee p3 \vee p7$$
$$p0 \rightarrow p4$$
$$p3 \wedge p5 \rightarrow p6$$
$$p3 \wedge p5 \wedge p8 \rightarrow p1$$
$$p2 \rightarrow \bot$$

Clearly, $p0$ and $p4$ are logical consequences of this clause set. Therefore $p0 = p4$ and $p0 > q$ for all other variables q. On the other hand, from $p2$ it is possible to deduce a contradiction, which leads to $p2 < q$ for all other variables q. Comparing $p6$ and $p1$ is a little bit more complicated. Neither of these variables is a logical consequence. However, assuming $p3$ and $p5$ to be true, allows to deduce $p6$ but not $p1$. In oder to deduce $p1$ it is necessary to assume not only $p3$ and $p5$ to be true but also $p8$. Therefore $p1 < p6$.

To use machine learning techniques to classify this kind of examples, we represent each pair of variables (p, q) as an instance of the training examples and we provide the information, which of the three relations $<, >, =$ is correct for p and q. Each of these instances contains 22 attributes. Some of these attributes represent information on the clause set like the proportion of clauses with p or q in the head as well as rudimentary dependencies between the variables in the clause set. In addition to that, we determine attributes representing information on the hypertableau for the set of clauses like the number of occurrences of p and q in open branches. Furthermore, we determine an attribute mimicking some aspects of abduction by estimating the number of variables which have to be assumed to be true in order to deduce p or q respectively. This allows us to perform comparisons like the one between $p1$ and $p6$ in the above example. Of course, we also take into account whether one of the two variables is indeed a logical consequence.

For the first experiments, 1,000 sets of clauses each consisting of about 10 clauses and containing about 12 variables were randomly generated and used to create a training set. For each pair of variables occurring in one of the clause sets,

Table 1. Confusion matrix for classifying the test set with the learnt decision tree. The numbers occurring in the diagonal represent all correctly classified instances, whereas the other cells list incorrectly classified instances.

	< (predicted)	> (predicted)	= (predicted)
< (actual)	5,595	78	33
> (actual)	90	5,589	27
= (actual)	9	5	772

an instance was generated. All in all this led to 123,246 examples for training purposes. In these examples, the classes < and > each consists of 57,983 examples and the class = of 7,280 examples. We used the J48 tree classifier implemented in the Weka [13] system to construct a decision tree for the training set. This classifier implements the C4.5 algorithm. We tested the generated decision tree with a test set which was generated from 100 randomly generated sets of clauses different from the clause sets used for the training examples. This resulted in a test set consisting of 12,198 instances. The learnt decision tree correctly classified 98.02 % instances of our test set. Table 1 provides information on correctly and incorrectly classified instances of the different classes.

We are aware that automatically classifying the test set might introduce errors into the test set and therefore tampers the results. Since it is very labor-intensive to manually generate test data, we only created test instances from two clause sets manually. For this much smaller test set the generated decision tree was able to correctly classify 80 % of the instances.

In the next step, we are planning to expand our experiments to clause sets given in first-order logic. When creating the instances of the training examples for first-order logic, attributes different from the ones in the previous experiment have to be considered, since unification has to be taken into account.

4   Normative Statementes

When considering commonsense reasoning problems, normative statements can be very useful as well. In this section we discuss the presentation of normative rules in commonsense reasoning and in multi-agent systems.

Norms in Commonsense Reasoning. In [8] we introduced some ideas how to add normative statements to the background knowledge used to tackle the Triangle-COPA challenge. The main idea of these normative statements was to express information about met and unmet expectations. To formalize these statements, standard deontic logic was used. Standard deontic logic (SDL) corresponds to the well-known modal logic K together with a seriality axiom $\mathsf{D} : \Box P \to \Diamond P$. In this logic, the $\Box$-operator is interpreted as 'it is obligatory that' and the $\Diamond$ as 'it is permitted that'. The $\Diamond$-operator can be defined by

$\Diamond P \equiv \neg \Box \neg P$. The seriality axiom in SDL states that, if a formula has to hold in all reachable worlds, then there exists such a world. With the deontic reading of $\Box$ and $\Diamond$ this means: Whenever the formula P ought to be, then there exists a world where it holds. In consequence, there is always a world, which is ideal in the sense that all the norms formulated by 'the ought to be'-operator hold.

Considering the Triangle-COPA challenge, it sounds reasonable to formalize the fact that one should defend friends if they are under attack. This can be accomplished by a set of deontic logic formulae which are the set of ground instances of the following statement:

$$friend(X, Y) \wedge attack(Z, X) \rightarrow \Box defend(Y, X). \tag{2}$$

Since formula (2) contains variables, it is not a SDL formula. However, we use it as an abbreviation for its set of ground instances. In the same way we could formalize that a person is disappointed if she is under attack and a friend does not hurry to her defense.

Deontic logic is not only the logic of choice when formalizing knowledge about norms in interpersonal relationships but also for the formalization of ethical codes for agents.

Norms in Robot Ethics. In multi-agent systems, there is a challenging area of research, namely the formalization of 'robot ethics'. It aims at defining formal rules for the behavior of agents and to prove certain properties. As an example consider Asimov's laws, which aim at regulating the relation between robots and humans. In [3], the authors depict a small example of two surgery robots obeying ethical codes concerning their work. These codes are expressed by means of MADL, which is an extension of standard deontic logic with two operators. In [22], an axiomatization of MADL is given. Further, it is asserted, that MADL is not essentially different from standard deontic logic. This is why we use SDL to model the example.

In the example, there are two robots $ag1$ and $ag2$ in a hospital. For the sake of simplicity, each robot can perform one specific action: $ag1$ can terminate a person's life support and $ag2$ can delay the delivery of pain medication. In [3], four different ethical codes J, $J^\star$, O and $O^\star$ are considered:

- "If ethical code J holds, then robot $ag1$ ought to take care that life support is terminated." This is formalized as:

$$J \rightarrow \Box act(ag1, term) \tag{3}$$

- "If ethical code $J^\star$ holds, then code J holds, and robot $ag2$ ought to take care that the delivery of pain medication is delayed." This is formalized as:

$$J^\star \rightarrow J \wedge J^\star \rightarrow \Box act(ag2, delay) \tag{4}$$

- "If ethical code O holds, then robot $ag2$ ought to take care that delivery of pain medication is not delayed." This is formalized as:

$$O \rightarrow \Box \neg act(ag2, delay) \tag{5}$$

- "If ethical code $O^\star$ holds, then code O holds, and robot $ag1$ ought to take care that life support is not terminated." This is formalized as:

$$O^\star \rightarrow O \wedge O^\star \rightarrow \Box \neg act(ag1, term) \tag{6}$$

Further we give a slightly modified version of the evaluation of the acts of the robots, as stated in [3], where $(+!!)$ denotes the most and $(-!!)$ the least desired outcome. Note that terms like $(+!!)$ are just propositional atomic formulae here.

$$act(ag1, term) \wedge \quad act(ag2, delay) \rightarrow (-!!) \tag{7}$$
$$act(ag1, term) \wedge \neg act(ag2, delay) \rightarrow (-!) \tag{8}$$
$$\neg act(ag1, term) \wedge \quad act(ag2, delay) \rightarrow (-) \tag{9}$$
$$\neg act(ag1, term) \wedge \neg act(ag2, delay) \rightarrow (+!!) \tag{10}$$

These formulae evaluate the outcome of the robots' actions. It makes sense to assume, that this evaluation is effective in all reachable worlds. This is why we add formulae stating that formulae (7)–(10) hold in all reachable worlds. For example, for (7) we add:

$$\Box(act(ag1, term) \wedge act(ag2, delay) \rightarrow (-!!)) \tag{11}$$

Since our example does not include nested modal operators, the formulae of the form (11) are sufficient to spread the evaluation formulae to all reachable worlds. The normative system $\mathcal{N}$ formalizing this example consists of the formalization of the four ethical codes and the formulae for the evaluation of the robots actions.

A possible query would be to ask if the most desirable outcome $(+!!)$ will come to pass if ethical code $O^\star$ is operative. This query can be translated into a satisfiability test. If $\mathcal{N} \wedge O^\star \wedge \Diamond\neg(+!!)$ is unsatisfiable, then ethical code $O^\star$ ensures outcome $(+!!)$.

Since Hyper is able to decide the description logic $\mathcal{SHIQ}$ and standard deontic logic formulae can be translated into description logic knowledge bases, we can use Hyper for this satisfiability test. We obtain the desired result namely that (only) ethical code $O^\star$ leads to the most desirable behavior $(+!!)$.

5   Conclusion

We presented an approach to tackle benchmarks for commonsense reasoning. This approach relies on large existing ontologies as a source for background knowledge and combines different techniques like theorem proving and machine learning with tools for natural language processing. With the help of a prototypical implementation of our approach, we conducted some experiments with problems from the COPA challenge. We presented our experiences made in these experiments together with possible solutions for the problems occurring in the examples considered.

Future work aims at the integration of additional sources of background knowledge as well as improving the bridging between the vocabulary used in the benchmarks and the background knowledge.

References

1. Basile, V., Cabrio, E., Gandon, F.: Building a general knowledge base of physical objects for robots. In: The Semantic Web. Latest Advances and New Domains (2016)
2. Bender, M., Pelzer, B., Schon, C.: System description: E-KRHyper 1.4 -extensions for unique names and description logic. In: Bonacina, M.P. (ed.) CADE 2013. LNCS, vol. 7898, pp. 126–134. Springer, Heidelberg (2013)
3. Bringsjord, S., Arkoudas, K., Bello, P.: Toward a general logicist methodology for engineering ethically correct robots. IEEE Intell. Syst. **21**(4), 38–44 (2006)
4. Curran, J.R., Clark, S., Bos, J.: Linguistically motivated large-scale NLP with C&C and boxer. In Proceedings of the ACL 2007 Demo and Poster Sessions, pp. 33–36, Prague, Czech Republic (2007)
5. Ferrucci, D.A.: IBM's Watson, DeepQA. SIGARCH Computer Architecture News, vol. 39, no. 3, June 2011
6. Furbach, U., Glöckner, I., Helbig, H., Pelzer, B.: Logic-based question answering. KI - Künstliche Intelligenz, 2010, Special Issue on Automated Deduction, February 2010
7. Furbach, U., Gordon, A., Schon, C.: Tackling benchmark problems for commonsense reasoning. In: Proceedings of Bridging - Workshop on Bridging the Gap between Human and Automated Reasoning (2015)
8. Furbach, U., Pelzer, B., Schon, C.: Automated reasoning in the wild. In: Felty, A.P., Middeldorp, A. (eds.) CADE-25. LNCS, vol. 9195, pp. 55–72. Springer, Heidelberg (2015)
9. Furbach, U., Schon, C.: Commonsense reasoning meets theorem proving. In: Proceedings of the 1st Conference on Artificial Intelligence and Theorem Proving AITP 2016, Obergurgl, Austria (2016)
10. Furbach, U., Schon, C.: Commonsense reasoning meets theorem proving. In: Proceedings of Bridging-20016 - Workshop on Bridging the Gap between Human and Automated Reasoning (2016, to appear)
11. Gordon, A.S.: Commonsense interpretation of triangle behavior. In: Schuurmans, D. Wellman, M.P. (eds.) Proceedings of the Thirtieth AAAI Conference on Artificial Intelligence, 12–17 February 2016, Phoenix, Arizona, USA, pp. 3719–3725. AAAI Press (2016)
12. Grassi, M.: Biometric ID Management and Multimodal Communication: Joint COST 2101 and 2102 International Conference, BioID_MultiComm 2009, Madrid, Spain, 16–18 September 2009, Proceedings, Chapter Developing HEO Human Emotions Ontology, pp. 244–251. Springer, Heidelberg (2009)
13. Hall, M.A., Frank, E., Holmes, G., Pfahringer, B., Reutemann, P., Witten, I.H.: The WEKA data mining software: an update. SIGKDD Explor. **11**(1), 10–18 (2009)
14. Hastings, J., Ceusters, W., Smith, B., Mulligan, K.: The emotion ontology: enabling interdisciplinary research in the affective sciences. In: Beigl, M., Christiansen, H., Roth-Berghofer, T.R., Kofod-Petersen, A., Coventry, K.R., Schmidtke, H.R. (eds.) CONTEXT 2011. LNCS, vol. 6967, pp. 119–123. Springer, Heidelberg (2011)
15. Kaliszyk, C., Schulz, S., Urban, J., Vyskocil, J.: System description: E.T. 0.1. In: Felty, A.P., Middeldorp, A. (eds.) CADE-25. LNCS, vol. 9195, pp. 389–398. Springer, Heidelberg (2015)
16. Lenat, D.B.: Cyc: a large-scale investment in knowledge infrastructure. Commun. ACM **38**(11), 33–38 (1995)

17. Levesque, H.J.: The winograd schema challenge. In: Logical Formalizations of Commonsense Reasoning, Papers from the 2011 AAAI Spring Symposium, Technical report SS-11-06, Stanford, California, USA, 21-23 March 2011, AAAI (2011)
18. Liu, H., Singh, P.: ConceptNet – a practical commonsense reasoning tool-kit. BT Technol. J. **22**(4), 211–226 (2004)
19. Maslan, N., Roemmele, M., Gordon, A.S.: One hundred challenge problems for logical formalizations of commonsense psychology. In: Twelfth International Symposium on Logical Formalizations of Commonsense Reasoning, Stanford, CA (2015)
20. Miller, G.A.: WordNet: a lexical database for English. Commun. ACM **38**(11), 39–41 (1995)
21. Moro, A., Raganato, A., Navigli, R.: Entity linking meets word sense disambiguation: a unified approach. Trans. Assoc. Comput. Linguist. (TACL) **2**, 231–244 (2014)
22. Murakami, Y.: Utilitarian deontic logic. In: Proceedings of the Fifth International Conference on Advances in Modal Logic AiML 2004, pp. 288–302 (2004)
23. Navigli, R., Ponzetto, S.P.: BabelNet: the automatic construction, evaluation and application of a wide-coverage multilingual semantic network. Artif. Intell. **193**, 217–250 (2012)
24. Niles, I., Pease, A.: Towards a standard upper ontology. In: Proceedings of the International Conference on Formal Ontology in Information Systems, vol. 2001, pp. 2–9. ACM (2001)
25. Pease, A.: Ontology: A Practical Guide. Articulate Software Press, Angwin (2011)
26. Roemmele, M., Bejan, C.A., Gordon, A.S.: Choice of plausible alternatives: an evaluation of commonsense causal reasoning. In: AAAI Spring Symposium: Logical Formalizations of Commonsense Reasoning (2011)
27. Suchanek, F.M., Kasneci, G., Weikum, G.: Yago: a large ontology from Wikipedia and WordNet. Web Semant. **6**(3), 203–217 (2008)

Personality and Agents: Formalising State and Effects

Sebastian Ahrndt[✉], Frank Trollmann, Johannes Fähndrich,
and Sahin Albayrak

DAI-Laboratory of the Technische Universität Berlin,
Faculty of Electrical Engineering and Computer Science,
Ernst-Reuter-Platz 7, 10587 Berlin, Germany
sebastian.ahrndt@dai-labor.de

Abstract. Personality is one of the central elements determining the behaviour of humans. It influences other cognitive mechanisms such as emotions and moods and thus effects attention and actions. However, in the literature about cognitive agents, work that investigates the effects of personality is rare and somewhat disconnected. Bridging this gap represents one step towards conceptualising human behaviour in software agents, e.g. for resource-bounded agents in highly-dynamic environments or for virtual humans with realistic behaviour. The integration of personality in agents also requires its integration into reasoning processes used in agent-based systems. In this paper, we propose a formalisation that enables reasoning about the effects and state of personality. This formalisation is integrated into the '$\mathcal{L}$ogic $\mathcal{O}$f $\mathcal{R}$ational $\mathcal{A}$gents' ($\mathcal{LORA}$) and is the foundation for reasoning about the personality of other agents and the influence of personality on the action selection process.

Keywords: User/machine systems · Human factors · Software psychology · Cognitive models · Logic-based approaches and methods

1 Introduction

While reading about cognitive characteristics in agent-based system, one will soon recognise several approaches that bring emotions to artificial agents. Available work reaches from modelling and applying emotions [10,11] to (completely axiomatised) logics of emotions [1,7,18]. The latter enable discussion and analysis of the effects of emotions on decision-making in a use-case independent and principle manner.

The integration of personality has not been studied in as much detail (*cf.* Sect. 2). However, following [14], personality is a significant factor for human behaviour and determines the outcome of essential behavioural processes, e.g., cognition and emotional reactions. Furthermore, it influences other affective phenomena such as moods and thus should be a central element in the reasoning and deliberation process of cognitive agents. The foundation of these processes

© Springer International Publishing Switzerland 2016
M. Klusch et al. (Eds.): MATES 2016, LNAI 9872, pp. 18–26, 2016.
DOI: 10.1007/978-3-319-45889-2_2

is a formalism that can represent personality and can be integrated into existing formalisms used in the reasoning processes of cognitive agents. Within this work, we propose a formalisation of personality that enables reasoning about the state and effects of personality.

We begin our discussion by reviewing existing approaches that integrate personality in agent-based systems in Sect. 2 and comparing them to approaches for formalising emotions. Afterwards, we discuss the objectives of this work in detail. In Sect. 4 we first describe $\mathcal{LORA}$ in an abstract manner to provide the necessary information to comprehend the remaining parts of the work and further present our integration of personality. Section 5 provides final remarks and insights into future work.

2 Related Work

Excursus – Personality Theories: Human factor psychology describes a human's personality by means of traits or types. What these approaches have in common is that traits or types are characteristic features of human beings, and that the human's behaviour and motives can be explained along behavioural patterns. Today, there are two well-established theories about human personality, namely: the *Five-Factor Model* of personality and the *Myers-Briggs Type Indicator*. We discussed the differences between both approaches and showed that the former is more suited for the integration of personality in agents in [2].

The representation of cognitive characteristics has a long tradition in agent-based systems and reaches from individual characteristics such as emotions, moods and personality to complex behavioural influences such as the cultural background. The areas of interest include next to virtual agents, virtual humans and personal assistants also (multi)agent-based simulations in different domains (e.g. traffic simulation, or crowd simulation). Another branch of research focuses on modelling and examining the effects of personalities on interactions between agents and their environments. In particular, the effects of personalities in cooperative settings. We have published a comprehensive analysis of available state of the art in prior work [3] that shows that the implemented effects of personality are often specific for the considered use-case and not applicable in general.

Most approaches define the effects/influences of personality in a rule-based or scripted manner. Unfortunately, personality traits are not inherently good or bad; their influence is context-dependent. This makes reasoning about personality influences a problem which is hard to solve by rule-based approaches. [17] presents a more advanced agent-based model of personality based on MBTI. In [2,3], we showed how this can be achieved for the FFM, extending [8] to the complete set of personality traits.

Although these approaches consider personality in isolation, the overall objective is to build an agent-model that brings together all cognitive characteristics. This is discussed in some work, for example: [11] presents an architecture for artificial characters with personality, emotions, and moods based on the BDI model; [10] proposes an extension of the BDI model introducing information about the personality, emotions and the physiology of a human; [5] introduces a concept for virtual characters that include specific personalities and emotional reactions. These approaches discuss architectural considerations from the software engineering perspective and provide first steps towards the integration of more than one cognitive characteristic.

A variety of approaches formalise emotions in agents. The PhD project of *Carole Adam* [1] provides an in-depth analysis of this topic and proposes a logic of emotions in agents. The formalisation is based on the OCC model and realised by expressing emotions based on the modalities beliefs, desires, and intentions. For instance, joy is defined as a feeling that happens when an agent is pleased about a desirable event.[1] Analogously, [7] presents an approach that formalises the intensity of emotions using the concept of graded modalities. The PhD project of *Bas R. Steunebrink* [18] describes a complete framework that formalises the emotional reactions from appraisal to coping.

Comparing the work on emotion and personality in agents reveals a gap with respect to theoretical and practical maturity. Our long-term goal is to bridge this gap. Our first step is a formalisation of the concept of personality. In contrast, to logic of emotions, this can not be done by using combinations of existing modalities, but via a new modality (*cf.* Sect. 4.1).

3   Objective: Reasoning About Personality

The objective of our work is to enable (1) reasoning about the influence of personality on the behaviour of an agent and (2) to derive the characteristics of personality of an agent from observations of its' behaviour. These two aspects requires a formalism that is able to represent (a) the effect of personality on the behaviour of an agent and (b) the state of personality of an agent. The representation of this formalism is the main contribution of this paper.

Reasoning about the influence of personality and deriving personality characteristics requires an underlying representation of personality, its effect and its state. Representing the effect of personality requires the ability to formulate that sth. is derived from the agents personality. Using commitment-strategies as example we could make the following informal statement:

1. Due to its personality agent i tends towards open-minded commitment.

This statement specifies that the cause for the open-minded commitment is the agents personality (as opposed to other factors such as incomplete knowledge). Such statements can be used to reason about consistent behaviour that is explained by the agents' personality.

Further necessary statements take into account the reasoning about personalities and the comparison of personalities of agents. Here statements of the following form are interesting:

---

[1] Using the syntax of $\mathcal{LORA}$ this could be formalised as $(Joy\ i\ \varphi) = (Bel\ i\ \varphi) \wedge (Des\ i\ \varphi)$ [1, pp. 100–101].

2. Agent i is conscientious.

In addition to discrete classes of personality it can be usefull to talk about the extent of personality traits:

3. The agent i is more conscientious than agent k.
4. The agent i is very conscientious.

Finally, both kinds of statement can be combined to formulate dependencies between the personality of an agent and its behaviour:

5. If agent i is very conscientious then due to its personality agent i tends towards open-minded commitment.

This statement is an implication built from statements 1 and 4. It can be used to derive the agents' behaviour, when the personality state is known (1). In the example it would be possible to derive that the agent is likely to be open-minded when it is conscientious. The statement can also be used to derive information about personality traits from the agents behaviour (2). In the example, an agent that does not exhibit open-minded commitment is less likely to be conscientious.

4   Formalisation of Personality

This section presents our integration of personality into $\mathcal{LORA}$ [20]. We start with a short introduction into the logic. $\mathcal{LORA}$ is a logic developed to enable reasoning about the behaviour of agents using the modality operators *Belief*, *Desire*, and *Intention*. The vocabulary is based on the sorts Ag – agents, Ac – actions, Gr – groups of agents, and U – other individuals. For these sorts constants and variables can be defined and used in first-order predicate logic formulas together with additional domain-specific formulas. A model in the logic contains a domain description $D = \langle D_{Ag}, D_{Ac}, D_{Gr}, D_U \rangle$, specifying the available entities for each sort. A temporal dimension is added by a set of time points T and a branching, temporal relation $\mathcal{R} \subseteq T \times T$. As the logic follows a possible world semantic, a set of worlds W is defined. Worlds are related to temporal structures. The operators $\mathcal{B}$, $\mathcal{D}$ and $\mathcal{I} : D_{Ag} \to \wp(W \times T \times W)$ represent the modalities. They map an agent to a set of triples, each of which assigns a possible world and a time point to another world. To reason about belief accessible worlds the shortcut function $\mathcal{B}_t^w(i) = \{w' | \langle w, t, w' \rangle \in \mathcal{B}(i)\}$ is defined. It denotes that agent i beliefs that w' is a possible world state at time point t. Shortcut functions for $\mathcal{D}$ and $\mathcal{I}$ are defined analogously. The elements in the sets $\mathcal{B}/\mathcal{D}/\mathcal{I}_t^w(i)$ represent i in world w at time point t.

Based on the possible world definition of these three modalities reasoning about the fulfilment of formulas is implemented. For $\mathcal{B}$ this can be done via $(Bel\ i\ \varphi)$ stating that an agent i believes φ. These state formulas are evaluated with a specific world w and a specific time point t. The formula *Bel* is defined as: $\langle w, t \rangle \models (Bel\ i\ \varphi)$ iff $\forall w' \in \mathcal{B}_t^w(\llbracket i \rrbracket), \langle w', t \rangle \models \varphi$, where $\llbracket i \rrbracket$ is the evaluation of term i under a variable assignment. Intuitively, this statement states that an agent i believes a statement φ if this statement holds in all worlds that are accessible via its beliefs.

4.1   Representing the Effects of Personality

In this section, we discuss how to extend $\mathcal{LORA}$ to enable reasoning about the influence of personality on the behaviour of an agent. This is done by introducing personality as new modality. This design decision was made based on the observation that the influence of emotions is frequently represented by combinations of the existing modal operators (Believes, Desires and Intentions) (cf. [1,7,18]). However, personality is different from emotion as it "...is the coherent patterning of affect, behavior, cognition, and desires (goals) over time and space" [16]. In contrast, the effects of emotions are bounded to a particular time and object [13]. In fact, emotions always occur relative to something (object, event, action) [12]. "A helpful analogy is to consider that personality is to emotion as climate is to weather" [16]. Thus, psychologist consider personality to be (to some extent) a time and space independent cognitive mechanism; that influences each stage of the decision-making process of humans [16]. To substantiate this statement the interested reader is referred to work that shows that we as humans have a relatively stable personality over our lifespan as adults (*cf.* [6,9,19]).

The conclusion we draw from these findings is that personality is per se independent of the *Beliefs*, *Desires*, and *Intentions* at specific times. Therefore, our approach is to represent personality as dedicated modality. We have presented an extension of the syntax and semantics of $\mathcal{LORA}$ introducing a personality modality in prior work [4]. The effects of personality of each agent are given by the modality operator $\mathcal{P} : D_{Ag} \to \wp(W \times T \times W)$. The operator $\mathcal{P}$ is named personality-accessibility relation. It defines all worlds that are in line with the personality of an agent $i \in D_{Ag}$ given a specific situation $\langle w, t \rangle$, where $w \in W$ and $t \in T$. Analogous to the other modalities the shortcut function $\mathcal{P}_t^w(i) = \{w' | \langle w, t, w' \rangle \in \mathcal{P}(i)\}$ can be used to reason about personality in a specific world and time. Reasoning about the fulfilment of formulas is enabled by a state formula (Per $\langle ag\text{-}term \rangle$ $\langle state\text{-}fmla \rangle$). The semantics of this state formula is defined based on an agent i and a state formula φ. We assume that the statements are usually evaluated in the context of a fixed model and variable assignment and omit them for the sake of brevity. Consequently, the semantic of *Per* is defined as $\langle w, t \rangle \models (Per\ i\ \varphi)$ iff $\forall w' \in \mathcal{P}_t^w(\llbracket i \rrbracket), \langle w', t \rangle \models \varphi$. The formula (Per $i\ \varphi$) verbalises the fact that agent i tends to φ. Here *tends to* refers to the influence of personality and not to other preferences, e.g., in terms of emotions and moods. Indeed, *tends to* is a placeholder for a personality-descriptive verb that must be used in a specific situation [15]. In a general manner it can be interpreted as φ being aligned with the personality of agent i, as this formula holds in all worlds which are accessible with the personality of i.

This operator can now be used to describe the first statement from our objectives. We can say that due to its personality agent i tends towards open-minded commitment via the state-formula:

$$(Per\ i\ hasOpenMindedCommitment(i))$$

Here, $hasOpenMindedCommitment(i)$ is a predicate describing that an agent i has open-minded commitment.

4.2   Representing the State of Personality

Reasoning about the state of personality of an agent requires having a notion to represent this state. As described in Sect. 2, we consider the FFM to be most suited for the integration of personality in agents. In FFM each personality trait is represented by a continuous scale.[2] Hence, one personality consists of a real number value for each trait. These values are interpreted with respect to a maximum and minimum (e.g., 1 and -1), where the maximum means that the factor is fully developed, the minimum means that the factor is not developed, and the average means that the factor is balanced. For example, a value of 1 for extraversion denotes that the person is considered extroverted while a value of -1 means the person is introverted and a value of 0 means that neither a strong tendency towards introversion nor extravorsion can be observed.

To include this model into $\mathcal{LORA}$ we first need to enable handling real numbers to express and compare the extent of personality traits. For this purpose the comparison functions $=, <$ and $>$ can be used. These are integrated as additional state formulas comparing two real number expressions: $\mathbb{R} = \mathbb{R}$; $\mathbb{R} < \mathbb{R}$; $\mathbb{R} > \mathbb{R}$. For further use cases other real-valued expressions (e.g., addition or multiplication) may be relevant. These can be integrated analogous to the statements above.

For the formalisation, we assume that the personality only depends on the agent itself and is stable over time. Thus, the personality does not depend on the world or the time point but solely on the agent. To represent the state of personality we define one function per personality factor that maps the agent to the value representing the extent of the respective personality trait: $O, C, E, A, N : Ag \rightarrow \mathbb{R}$. The numbers derived from personality traits usually need to be interpreted in some way. For instance, on the scale presented above (-1 to 1) it could make sense to exclude personalities between -0.3 and 0.3 as they may be considered to be roughly balanced. For the trait extraversion the two extremes of the scale can be interpreted as introversion and extroversion. Here we could consider agent i to be introverted if $E(i) < -0.3$ and extroverted if $E(i) > 0.3$ and neither of those if $-0.3 < E(i) < 0.3$. This enables discrete reasoning about personality categories as in MBTI but allows for the definition of more nuanced subclasses. Constants and variables representing real numbers are required to express such statements. Those can be integrated into $\mathcal{LORA}$ analogously to the variables and constants of other sorts, e.g., variables denoting agents. For readability we denote constants by their actual values, e.g., 0.3 is a constant of value 0.3 whose name is "0.3".

These statements now enable expressions that refer to personality traits of agents and interpret them, either in the context of personality traits of other agents or in the context of variables or constants. They are sufficient to express statements 2 to 4. Statement 2 denotes that an agent i is conscientious. It could be expressed as $C(i) > 0.3$. Comparing two agents conscientiousness, e.g., to state that an agent i is more conscientious than an agent k (statement 3) can be

---

[2] We will use the following abbreviations next: openness to experience (O), conscientiousness (C), extraversion (E), agreeableness (A) and neuroticism (N).

expressed as follows: $C(i) > C(k)$. Intervals in the continuous personality scale can be used to express more fine-grained personality trait distinctions. Here, we could consider an agent to be very conscientious when it has a higher trait than 0.8. Using this (arbitrary) line we can formulate statement 4 as $C(i) > 0.8$.

5   Discussion and Future Work

The goal of our formalisation is to enable reasoning about the interdependencies of personality and behaviour of a natural agent. Section 4 describes how $\mathcal{LORA}$ can be extended to represent the effects and state of personality. Both extensions can be combined to express how specific personality types (*i.e.*, the state of personality) influence the agent. An example is given in the fifth statement in Sect. 3, which expresses that a very conscientious agent tends towards open-minded commitment. This can be expressed as follows:

$$C(i) > 0.8 \rightarrow (\text{Per } i \; hasOpenMindedCommitment(i)).$$

Such statements represent the relation between state and effects of personality and can be used for reasoning, e.g., along the implication operator. The extension of $\mathcal{LORA}$ can also be used for further discussions about the relation of the formal representation of personality to other parts of the logic.

Integrating personality as own modality provides the fundamentals for a comprehensive analysis of the properties that are useful to characterise an agent with personality. From a purely logical aspect there is no reason to do that, as we have build a formal system enabling us to use all possible combinations of the formulas and operators available. However, that would mean to ignore the semantic of the properties, *i.e.*, to not discuss how the properties influence the behaviour of an agent and which influences are meaningful/reasonable for analysing personality driven behaviour of agents. A full discussion of these relations will be done in future work.

Another relation that could be beneficial to observe is the relation between formalisations of emotions and our formalisation of personality. Several authors represent emotions via formulas over the believe, desire and intention modalities. Personality also influences the way in which we react to situations emotionally, *i.e.*, the occurrence, intensity, and duration of emotions. The representation of personality presented in this paper provides a foundation for considering such relations between personality and emotions.

Although our extension enables the integration of personality into the reasoning process in general, it does not enable to derive relation between personality and behaviour directly. Doing so in a general way requires formalising findings from psychology in the form of statements that can be used for reasoning among multiple approaches. Our formalisation provides a vocabulary to express those statements.

References

1. Adam, C.: Emotions: from psychological theories to logic formalization and Implementation in a BDI agent. L' Institute National Polytechnique de Toulouse (2007)
2. Ahrndt, S., Aria, A., Fähndrich, J., Albayrak, S.: Ants in the OCEAN: modulating agents with personality for planning with humans. In: Bulling, N. (ed.) EUMAS 2014. LNCS, vol. 8953, pp. 3–18. Springer, Heidelberg (2015)
3. Ahrndt, S., Fähndrich, J., Albayrak, S.: Modelling of personality in agents: from psychology to implementation. In: Bordini, E., Weiss, Y. (eds.) Proceedings of the HAIDM 2015, Co-located with AAMAS 2015. pp. 1–16. IFAAMAS (2015)
4. Ahrndt, S., Fähndrich, J., Lützenberger, M., Albayrak, S.: Modelling of personality in agents: from psychology to logical formalisation and implementation. In: Bordini, E., Weiss, Y. (eds.) Proceedings of the AAMAS 2015, pp. 1691–1692. IFAAMS (2015)
5. Bevacqua, E., de Sevin, E., Pelachaud, C., McRorie, M., Sneddon, I.: Building credible agents: behaviour influenced by personality and emotional traits. In: Lèvy, B., Yamanaka, A. (eds.) Proceedings of the KEER 2010, pp. 1–10 (2010)
6. Caspi, A., Roberts, B., Shiner, R.: Personality development: stability and change **56** 453–484 (2005)
7. Dastani, M., Lorini, E.: A logic of emotions: from appraisal to coping. In: Conitzer, L., Winikoff, M., Padgham, L., van der Hock, W. (eds.) Proceedings of the AAMAS 2012. IFAAMAS (2012)
8. Durupinar, F., Allbeck, J., Pelechano, N., Badler, N.: Creating crowd variation with the OCEAN personality model. In: Padgham, P., Müller, P. (eds.) Proceedings of the AAMAS 2008, pp. 1217–1220. IFAAMAS (2008)
9. Hampson, S.E., Goldberg, L.R.: A first large-cohort study of personality-trait stability over the 40 years between elementary school and midlife **91**, 763–779 (2006)
10. Jones, H., Saunier, J., Lourdeaux, D.: Personality, emotions and physiology in a BDI agent architecture: the pep ->> BDI model. In: Proceedings of IAT 2009, pp. 263–266. IEEE (2009)
11. Bressane Neto, A.F., Corrêa da Silva, F.S.: On the construction of synthetic characters with personality and emotion. In: da Rocha Costa, A.C., Vicari, R.M., Tonidandel, F. (eds.) SBIA 2010. LNCS, vol. 6404, pp. 102–111. Springer, Heidelberg (2010)
12. Oatley, K., Jenkins, J.M.: Understanding Emotions. Blackwell Publishing, Oxford (1996)
13. Ortony, A., Norman, D., Revelle, W.: Affect and proto-affect in effectivefunctioning. In: Fellous, J.M., Arbib, M.A. (eds.) Who Needs Emotions?. Series in Affective Science, pp. 173–202. Oxford University Press, New York (2005)
14. Ozer, D.J., Benet-Martínez, V.: Personality and the prediction of consequential outcomes. Annu. Rev. Psychol. **57**, 401–421 (2006)
15. de Raad, B., Mulder, E., Kloosterman, K., Hofstee, W.K.: Personality-descriptive verbs. Eur. J. Pers. **2**, 81–96 (1988)
16. Revelle, W., Scherer, K.R.: Personality and emotion. In: Sander, D., Scherer, K. (eds.) The Oxford Companion to Emotion and the Affective Sciences. Series in Affective Science, p. 512. Oxford University Press, New York (2010)
17. Salvit, J., Sklar, E.: Modulating agent behavior using human personality type. In: Proceedings of the HAIDM at AAMAS 2012, pp. 145–160 (2012)
18. Steunebrink, B.: The Logical Structure of Emotions. Utrecht University, The Netherlands (2010)

19. Wilks, L.: The stability of personality over time as a function of personality trait dominance. Griffith Univ. Undergraduated St. Psy. J. **1**, 1–9 (2009)
20. Wooldridge, M.: Reasoning about Rational Agents. Intelligent Robotics and Autonomous Agents. The MIT Press, Cambridge (2000)

An Ontology-Driven Approach for Modeling a Multi-agent-Based Electricity Market

Geovanny Poveda[✉] and René Schumann

University of Applied Sciences Western Switzerland (HES-SO VS),
Rue de Technopole 3, 3960 Sierre, Switzerland
{geovanny.poveda,rene.schumann}@hevs.ch
http://silab.hevs.ch

Abstract. Model Driven Development has prompted domain experts to use high-level languages for specifying, testing, verifying and code final application. While Model Driven Development has had a significant contribution to the development of Multi-Agent-Based Simulation, it becomes more and more important to develop appropriate means for representing and integrating the knowledge of domain experts into auto-generated simulation agent-based models. This paper proposes an approach for modeling and simulating agent-based models on the basis of an Ontology-Driven Conceptual Modeling approach in a quite generic scenario for modeling electricity markets. The contribution of this paper is focused on the creation of set of methods, mechanisms and tools to support the design, implementation and experimentation of agent-based models from the instantiation of an ontology-based conceptual modeling.

Keywords: Model driven · Ontology driven · Simulation · Conceptual model · Multi agent based simulation

1 Introduction

Over the last years, several lines of research have allowed deregulated electricity markets to be studied. Among others, Multi-Agent Based Simulation (MABS) has been one of the most prominent approach for simulating decentralized electricity markets. While MABS has had a significant contribution to the deeper understanding of complexity in the electricity market, it becomes more important to develop appropriate means for creating a single and integrated formalism to define the MABS dimensions. Model-Driven Development (MDD) has become an important approach in software discipline to link design and code. It is a software engineering paradigm which uses models as a mean for specifying, testing, verifying and *generating* code for a final application [13].

While MDD has enabled modelers to support the creation of agent-based models from a conceptual design, it becomes more and more important to develop appropriate means for representing and integrating the domain knowledge expertise of experts in simulation models. Ontology-Driven Conceptual

© Springer International Publishing Switzerland 2016
M. Klusch et al. (Eds.): MATES 2016, LNAI 9872, pp. 27–40, 2016.
DOI: 10.1007/978-3-319-45889-2_3

Modeling (ODCM) uses ontologies to drive the creation of simulation models and in doing so makes use of an agreed upon set of terms and relationships that are shared by domain experts, modelers, and model development tools. Most importantly, ontologies provide foundations for enabling the extension of structural changes on models, as well as, their automated extension.

In this article we introduce an integrated solution for modeling and simulating agent-based models on the basis of an ODCM approach. The contribution of this paper is focused on the creation of a model to support the automatic implementation of agent-based models from the instantiation of an ontology-based conceptual modeling. The structure of this paper is as follows: Sect. 2 provides an overview of MDD approach for Multi-Agent System technologies. Section 3 introduces our proposed ODCM approach by describing the conceptual model and simulation design phases. Section 4 describes the organizational architecture of the MABS model. Next, Sect. 5 illustrates the advantages of the contribution presented by a proof of concept. Finally, Sect. 6 concludes and gives possible future research directions.

2   Background

Several studies for modeling Multi-Agent Systems by using Model Driven Development have been already proposed [5–7,14]. A comprehensive comparison of these studies is out of the scope of this paper. However, a short overview on most representative related works is given in the remainder of this section. In [7] Garro and Russo have presented easyABMS, a full-fledged methodology for the agent-based modeling and simulation of complex systems. The approach of such study relies on both Agent-Oriented Software Engineering (AOSE) modeling techniques and simulation tools for ABMS. easyABMS is focused on system modeling and simulation analysis rather than details related to programming and implementation as it exploits the model-driven paradigm, making it possible the automatic code generation from a set of (visual) models of the system. In [6], the authors propose the jointly exploitation of both Platform-Independent Meta-models and Model-Driven approaches to define a Model-Driven process named MDA4ABMS. The stated process is conforms to the OMG Model-Driven Architecture (MDA) and enables the definition of Platform-Independent simulation models from which simulation models and their code can be automatically obtained.

In [14] Candelaria and Pavón propose a high-level conceptual modeling abstraction for simulation development, it includes transformation tools that facilitate the implementation of simulations on different simulation platforms. The framework presented is based on the MDA pattern by means of a platform-independent modeling language, a code generation process and templates, and specific simulation platforms. In [5] the authors have present a model to bridge the gap between the design and the application of Agent oriented systems. They demonstrated how the MDA could be used to derive practical applications of

Agents from Agent oriented design. Their major contributions were in the definition of a common, agent-neutral model that applies to all the concepts required by the FIPA-compliant agent platform.

Another line of research has highlighted the importance of using ontologies for supporting the implementation of agent-based simulation through the designing of conceptual model. In [16] Ying et al. describe MOMA, a methodology for ontology-based multi-agent application development which focuses on the development of an ontology as driving force of the development of Multi Agent Systems for experimentation in the financial domain. MOMA consist of two main development phases: Ontology Development and Agent Development. In the first stage concepts and relations in the domain are identified and they are modeled for a specific application, then code that can be used in the agent development phase is generated.

3   An Ontology-Driven Modelling Approach for Agent-Based Simulations

Following the approach mentioned in Sect. 1, an ontology-based model driven development approach has been designed. The proposed model employs a single and integrated formalism to define the MABS dimensions, in particular, the design of conceptual modeling and the generation of agent-based models from instances of a conceptual model. The basis of the stated model includes two major phases: (i) conceptual modeling; and (ii) simulation design.

3.1   Conceptual Modelling Phase

In this phase, a set of high level abstraction of concepts and relations have to be created for describing the domain in which MABS models will be defined. The basis of the proposed conceptual modeling includes an ontology which describes the agent organizational structure of the simulated models (capabilities, behaviors, beliefs, actions), as well as, the vocabulary for describing the set of fundamental concepts around the domain to be described.

3.2   Simulation Design Phase

The simulation design phase enables mechanisms for the automated construction of agent-based models from instances of the ontology-based conceptual modeling. In this phase, a set of transformation rules, directives and templates have been created to transform the axioms from the ontology-based conceptual modeling (classes, object properties, properties, properties restrictions) to elements of a MABS model (classes, attributes, associations, roles, plans, etc.), and deploy it as an agent model. Figure 1 shows the components of the stated phase. To derive agent models from the ontology-based conceptual modeling, two activities have to be performed:

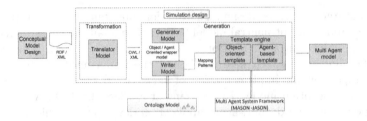

Fig. 1. Simulation design phase overview

– Transformation Activity: In this model, axioms from the conceptual model are classified into classes, object properties, and data properties and then, the OWL API [8] is used for translating Resource Description Framework (RDF) subjects into OWL classes that relate predicates and objects as property restrictions. The set of transformation rules used for keeping the dependence between subjects and their properties are: (i) objects are considered as part of a `<owl:Restriction>` property through the use of the `OWLObjectSomeValuesFrom` interface; and (ii) predicates are considered as a restriction of subjects through the use of the `getOWLSubClassOfAxiom` interface. Listing 1.1 shows a section of the algorithm used for transforming the model.

Listing 1.1 A section of the algorithm used for defining the transformation model.

```
String subLabel = subject.toString();
OWLClass owlclass1 = owlfact.getOWLClass(IRI.create(subLabel));

createOWLDeclarationAxiom(owlclass1);
OWLClass owlclass2 = owlfact.getOWLClass(IRI.create(objLabel));
createOWLDeclarationAxiom(owlclass2);
OWLObjectProperty hasRelation = owlfact.getOWLObjectProperty(IRI.create(predicate.toString()));

//create OWL Pattern
OWLClassExpression hasRelationSome = owlfact.getOWLObjectSomeValuesFrom(hasRelation, owlclass2);
OWLSubClassOfAxiom axiomPattern = owlfact.getOWLSubClassOfAxiom(owlclass1, hasRelationSome);
owlmanager.addAxiom(ont, axiomPattern);

public void createOWLDeclarationAxiom(OWLClass owlclass){
OWLDeclarationAxiom declarationAxiom = owlfact.getOWLDeclarationAxiom(owlclass);
owlmanager.addAxiom(ont, declarationAxiom);
}
```

– Code Generation Activity: In this activity, a set of operations are used to write the program structure of the agent-based model in terms of their organizational structure. The basis of the stated activity includes the model preparation and writing activities.

Model Preparation Activity. This activity provides mechanisms for defining the high level structure of artifacts (packages, classes, functions and relations) to be involved in the serialization of files. It uses the transformed OWL-based conceptual modeling and executes a set of mapping rules for representing the ontological axioms into an internal model named Jmodel. A Jmodel is an intermediate programmatic representation created to perform the expressiveness of OWL axioms into Java oriented models. Among others, multiple inheritance, properties without type and inverse properties are the most important. A Jmodel consist of a set of instanced Java classes and Java objects assigned to specific packages instances.

In order to build the instances of Java classes, resources from the Jena data structure [3] are located, and for all instances of that class, Java interfaces and their respective implementing Java class are generated. In order to express the multiple inheritance of OWL axioms, interfaces are embedded inside their corresponding Java classes and they are enabled to be included into an object-oriented hierarchy composed of sub and supper-class relations. Once classes are defined, both, object and data properties are retrieved from resources and they are translated into object-oriented artifacts depending on the type of property. In the case of object properties, that is, relation of a class to another class, instantiated object-oriented methods are created recursively. Given that OWL properties can be of multiple types, a list of multiple generic objects have to be created for ensuring that object properties can be used in the specified range. When annotation properties come from a <rdf:datatype> property, that is literals, they are transformed as global object-oriented attributes with accessors methods (get and set) on the related OWL class.

Afterwards, subclasses from the Jena data structure resource are identified and their cardinalities and values restrictions are checked. To be ensure constraints are satisfied, the range of the object properties acting as <owl:OnProperty> property are associated to a Java interface named RestrictionManager to be exposed to the classes acting as <owl:OnClass> property. Thus, classes acting as restrictions can be instanced though a synchronized getByName() method that use the Java reflection mechanism. Figure 2 shows the mechanisms involved in the generator model.

Writing Activity. To perform the process of writing the program code of the model (skeleton, constructor, methods, and headers) a rule-based template engine is involved. Template files use a set of high level programming structures that describe the syntactic and semantic structure to be used for serializing the model. Syntactic descriptions are used for describing the skeleton structure of classes and headers. Semantic structures are used for describing the methods and functions by using global identifiers from the stated Jmodel. The use of templates files help to keep the transformation rules out of the application code. Thus, new templates can be added and existing ones can be customized without modifying the application code.

Listing 1.2 shows how syntactics and semantics structures are used for describing the content of Java classes. Syntactic structures are created by using pre-defined language expressions for the Java identifiers and modifiers. Note that semantic structures are created by using global identifiers variables that use the Java reflection mechanism to create methods dynamically from values

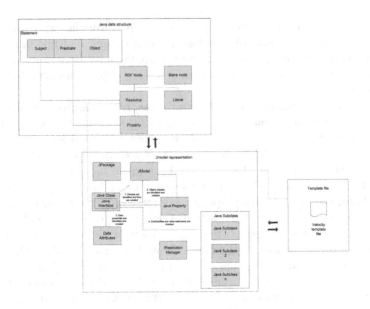

Fig. 2. Generator model overview

of the Jmodel. In the case of object properties, a `for-each` velocity[1] statement enable the creation of Java object iterators and lists by using the global
`jmodel.listclasses` variable, which contains the set of transformed classes
from the conceptual model.

Listing 1.2 A section of a template file used for the generic-object oriented model.

```
public class \$cName extends IndividualImpl implements \$iName {

    // syntactic structure
    public static void main(String[] args)
    {

    }
    // semantic / syntactic structure
#foreach (\$cls in \$jmodel.listJClasses())
                #set(\$clsName = \$cls.getJavaClassName())
                    List<\${clsName}> \${clsName} = new ArrayList<\${clsName}>();
            \${clsName} temp\${clsName} = new \${clsName}();
            Iterator<\${clsName} > \${clsName}Itr;
```

As stated before, the conceptual model provides a vocabulary that describes
the set of organizational agent building blocks and their relations with the fundamental concepts around the simulated domain. To provide the object-oriented
model the ability to be described in terms of their capabilities, behaviors, plans,
beliefs, interactions, protocols and communication mechanisms, a set of transformation rules based on the previously mentioned template engine have been
involved. To describe how classes can be controlled and scheduled to access to

---

[1] http://velocity.apache.org/.

the resources and services of the model, a velocity template file is used to include the set of fundamental functions and methods from the MASON API [11]. The stated file describes syntactic structures that include the `Stepabble` interface [11] as well as, its hook method named `Step` [11]. Thus, agents are able to reason at runtime the changes and updates on the environment.

To provide a more understandable approach to enable the communication among agents, the `SimState` object [10] has been involved to represent the overall model. The `SimState` object is created to communicate agents in the model via `getter` methods of the stated `step` method. The model object serves as a communication device by holding information need by other agents. Finally, to describe the behavioral, belief and capabilities descriptions, classes and interfaces from the JASON API [2] are included. There is a template file which specify the structure of the agent model in terms of its communication model. Listing 1.3 shows how the agent organization is included. Note that an interface has been created for providing classes the ability to extend the overall agent architecture of the JASON API.

Listing 1.3 A section of a template file used to involve agent capabilities

```
package \$testcasePkg;
    import java.util.Iterator;
    import com.hp.hpl.jena.ontology.OntModel;import com.hp.hpl.jena.ontology.Ontology;
    import com.hp.hpl.jena.rdf.model.ModelFactory;import java.util.ArrayList;
    import java.util.List;

    public class \$electricityMarketSimulation extends \$SimState implements \$Steppable {
    private static String namePrefix = "ClassInstance";
    private static int nameCount = 0;

    public \$electricityMarketSimulation(final long seed) {
            super( seed );
    }
    @Override
    public void step(final SimState state) {

            OntModel ontModel = ModelFactory.createOntologyModel();
            Ontology ontology = ontModel.createOntology(base);

            #foreach (\$cls in \$jmodel.listJClasses())
                #set(\$clsName = \$cls.getJavaClassName())
                List<\${clsName}> \${clsName} = new ArrayList<\${clsName}>();
                \${clsName} temp\${clsName};
                Iterator<\${clsName} > \${clsName}Itr;
                Iterator<\${clsName} > \${clsName}Itr;
    }

    public JasonAgent(String id, String aslFilePath, Logger logger)
            throws SimulationException {
    this.id = id;
    this.logger = logger;
    this.message = new ArrayList<Message>();
    this.actions = new HashMap<String, Class<? extends JasonAgentAction>>();
    this.configActions();
    try {
        agent = new Agent();
        agent.init();
        agent.load(aslFilePath);
    } catch (JasonException e) {
        . . . . . . . . . . . . . . . . . .
    }
    }
}
```

4   Multi Agent System Organizational Structure

This section describes the organizational architecture of the MABS model to be generated. It describes a set of building blocks for defining the role, behaviors, capabilities and interactions of the agents on models. Such structure, has

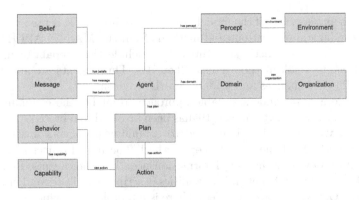

Fig. 3. Agent organizational structure of model

been defined on the basis of an agent-based interaction model, where an agent describes the capabilities that electricity market players have to perform for negotiation and the roles they play during the execution of bilateral contracts. In that structure, agents are autonomous entities able to update their negotiation knowledge by perceiving information from their market (environment) and performing actions from the organization (norm, mission, cooperation, goals). Figure 3 shows the concepts used for defining the agent organizational structure of our model.

4.1   Agent Model

The agent concept describes the capabilities agents have to perform negotiation and the roles they play during the execution of bilateral contracts. In our model, agents are autonomous entities able to update their negotiation knowledge by performing actions from the organization (cooperation, organization) and perceiving information from their market (resource). Agents update their plans by performing roles and behaviors that depends the context the agent is acting and the task to be achieved.

4.2   Role Model

The role model provides a definition of the roles and domains to be employed for modeling the electricity market. The role model involves the actor definition, a generic concept used for representing the parties that take places in the bilateral transactions. It also involves the domain definition, a concept used for delimiting the areas of negotiation for a particular purposes (consumption, distribution, retailing). Last but not least, a role describe itself the external negotiation interactions with other players/parties in relation to the goal to be achieved given a bilateral transaction.

4.3   Interaction Model

The interaction concept describes how the intercommunication among agents take place. To model agent interactions, a two-level system structure has been involved. In such structure, the highest level enables the interaction among agents each other and between agents and the environment through roles. Lowest level concerns the environment. An interaction takes place when an agent performs an action and such action is translated into an event that is notified to another agent that exhibits the specific behavior [12]. The meta model of the interaction concept is depicted in Fig. 4. It is important to note that in our model, an interaction it is not a just a *message passing*, it also includes protocol, a message scope and actor definitions. In this aspect, the actors interact with the protocol through a set of messages that are exchanged by the concerned parties.

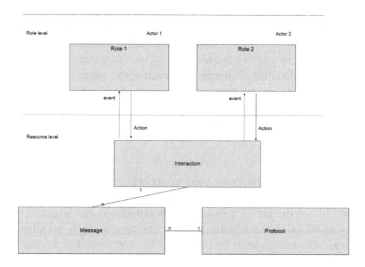

Fig. 4. Meta model of the concepts used in the interaction aspect specification.

4.4   Organization Model

The organization model describes how the system organizations of electricity retailer market is modeled and their relationships with another market system. It describes how players from the electricity retailer market can cooperate and participate in the market by considering their roles and capabilities. Organizational model also defines how the negotiation mechanisms of bilateral contracts can be defined in terms of their interactions (communication). It involves protocols, a concept used to establish a standard to interchange message during the negotiations.

4.5 Behaviour Model

The behavior concept describes how the plans are performed by players of the electricity retailer market and how the information flows among such actors. In this aspect, a behavior describes an abstract representation that connects the players with their behavioral features. Behaviors provide the basis of specifying the internal activities of players through plans. A plan is a specialization of the behaviors which defined a set of flows and activities. In this aspect, the activities represent the actions to be performed in the plans and they are linked throw flows [15].

4.6 Environment Model

The environment concept describes the resources that can be dynamically created or shared by the agents in the electricity retailer market. In this aspect, features for modeling how offers and contracts can be accessed have been considered. Environment concept is responsible of enabling and controlling the access to the market and some negotiation services by using concrete means for agents. It provides a set of inherited elements: observable and state to enable agents to have access to resources and services. Thus, agents are able to reason at run-time a new environment they are discovering [4].

5 Proof of Concept

This section presents how our proposed approach can be applied. We provide here an example for modeling a strictly simplified negotiation in the electricity retail market. In particular, a scenario for a simulated deregulated electricity market focusing on bilateral negotiations [9] between a single retailer and multiple customers. The example to be presented in that section is focused on show how the model proposed in Sect. 3 can be used for creating agent-based models from an ontology-based conceptual model. In this scenario, customers negotiate a time of use tariff [1] under a set of specified terms and conditions, including energy price, energy quantity and duration. Note that the proposed proof of concept provides the foundations for showing how generic agent-based models explained in Sect. 3 can be generated rather than fully agent-based models. In the following subsections, the processes involved in each phase are presented.

Conceptual Modelling Phase. In this step, we specify the concepts in the target of the scenario previously detailed and describe it in the in the ontology-based conceptual model. In a first stage, the conceptual model is explored and high hierarchy classes are identified to perform the correspondence between the conceptual model definitions and the concepts distinguished by domain experts during the analysis stage. By using the Protégé tool[2], domain experts describe the classes, properties, data properties and individuals to be involved in the agent-based electricity model. Such description includes participants, market features and strategic descriptions. The following types of participants have been considered:

– Retailer: represents the business units that sell energy to a retail market.
– Customer: represents the players buying energy in the retail market. It includes households, commercial, industrial and other electricity consumers.

Next, we describe some fundamental concepts around the bilateral negotiations. Concepts such as market operation, methods of negotiation, as well as strategic behavior of participants have been included:

– Bilateral negotiation methods: represents the set of negotiation methods to be used. It includes (i) request for bid, (ii) offer method and (iii) announce reward table.
– Protocol: represents the set of message flow that specify how the exchange of messages is processed. It includes stacked alternating offer protocol and monotonic conseccion protocol.
– Strategy: represents the set of strategies to be used. It includes logrolling and compensation.

Simulation Design Phase. In this step, the agent-based electricity model is generated from instances of the previously designed conceptual model. To transform the conceptual model into an agent-oriented generic model, we created a software utility to use the functions and methods proposed in the simulation design phase (see Sect. 3.2). Listing 1.4 shows the main two activities executed during the transformation model. In a first stage, the RDF model is transformed into OWL axioms and rewritten to RDF/XML syntax. Next, methods from the generator model are instanced and the RDF/XML model is transformed into a object-oriented generic model. Finally, the generated classes should be placed in the corresponding package and directory.

Figure 5 shows how the generic object-oriented model is generated automatically after the execution of the stated class. Note that concepts and objects properties from the conceptual modeling haven been transformed into JAVA classes. Note that created classes do not involve the organizational structure of agents since the writing activity of the model has been based on the object-oriented template. Next section shows how the agent-oriented model is created.

---

[2] http://protegewiki.stanford.edu/wiki/.

Listing 1.4 A class to create the generic object-oriented model.

```
public class ElectricityMarketSimulation {

public static void main(String[] args) {
try {
      File file = new File(''emordfinstances.rdf'');

      String fileName = file.getName();
      System.out.println(fileName );

      ConvertRDFtoOWL convert= new ConvertRDFtoOWL();
      convert.transformRDFtoOWL(fileName );

      File source = new File(''emordfinstances.owl/'');
      File dest = new File(''emotransformed.owl/'');
      try {
              FileUtils.copyFile(source, dest);
            } catch (IOException e) {
              e.printStackTrace();
            }

      ConvertOWLSyntax converter = new ConvertOWLSyntax();
      converter.SyntaxRewrite(''http://silab.hevs.ch/projects/simulation/testing/emotransformed.owl&format=RDF/XML'');

            OntModel ontModel = OntologyUtils.loadOntology(''file:emo.owl'');
            JenaArtefacts artefacts = new JenaArtefacts();
            artefacts.generate(ontModel, ''src'', ''ch.hevs.silab.swisselectric.simulation.demo.emo.ns'');
            }
       }
}
```

```
.va  ElectricitySimulation.java ×  SILAB.java ×  ElectricitySimulation.java ×  Protocol.java ×  UtilityCompany.java ×  SilabGui.java ×

Source  History

14   /**
15    *
16    * @author geo
17    */
18   public class UtilityCompany {
19
20       protected double maxPrice;
21           protected double expenses = 0;
22
23           List<ElectricityOrder> buyOrders = new ArrayList<ElectricityOrder>();
24           List<ElectricityOrder> sellOrders = new ArrayList<ElectricityOrder>();
25
26           public UtilityCompany(double price) {
27                   super();
28                   maxPrice = price;
29           }
30
31           public double getMaxPrice() {
32                   return maxPrice;
33           }
34
35           public double getExpenses() {
36                   return expenses;
37           }
38
39           public void updateExpenses(double change) {
40                   expenses += change;
41           }
42
43
44           public void orderTrades(AuctionMarket market) {
45
46                   double surplus;
47
48                   }
```

Fig. 5. A class of the generated generic object-oriented model.

Agent System Organizational Structure. In this step the generic agent-oriented model is created. The stated model is created from the set of transformation rules previously explained in the writing activity section. Agent-based model is generated in terms of the application programming interface of the MASON framework. Figure 6 shows how the main class of the package generated is expressed in terms of the MASON API. The figure also shows how the

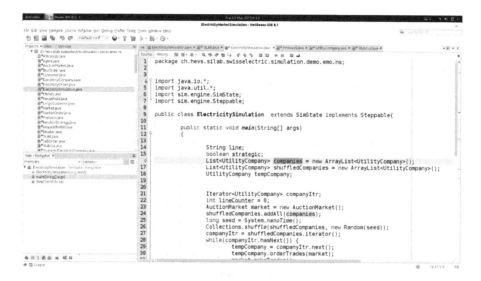

Fig. 6. The generated agent-based model.

concepts and relations previously defined in the conceptual model, they have been created in the agent model.

6 Summary

In this article we have introduced an integration solution for modeling and simulating agent-based models on the basis of an ODCM approach. The proposed solution has been envisaged to facilitate the creation of agent-based electricity market simulations by using ontologies as the driving force of a MDD approach. We have proposed a model which merge MDD and ODCM approaches to offer a set of methods able to generate automatically agent-based models from the design of a conceptual model. We have presented and explained the phases of the model by distinguishing three main stages: (a) a conceptual model transformation; (b) an organizational agent architecture adaption; and (c) agent-based generic code generation. The model is still under development, it is currently focused to generate generic agent-oriented structures for the agent system. Future research efforts will be devoted to: (i) improving the algorithms used for translating the object-oriented generic model into agent-based simulation models. We plan to include mapping strategies that involves the automatically generation of object oriented methods from the annotation properties defined in the conceptual model. (ii) our research will also provide techniques for supporting the design and experimentation of the agent-based models by involving semantic-based rules for adapting changes in the behavior of the agent model, in such a way that conditional structures can be included on the generic agent-based model and it can generate executable agent-based models.

References

1. Algarvio, H., Lopes, F., Santana, J.: Multi-agent retail energy markets: bilateral contracting and coalitions of end-use customers. In: 2015 12th International Conference on the European Energy Market (EEM), pp. 1–5. IEEE (2015)
2. Bordini, R.H., Hübner, J.F.: A Java-based interpreter for an extended version of agentspeak. University of Durham, Universidade Regional de Blumenau (2007)
3. Carroll, J.J., Dickinson, I., Dollin, C., Reynolds, D., Seaborne, A., Wilkinson, K.: Jena: implementing the semantic web recommendations. In: Proceedings of the 13th international World Wide Web conference on Alternate track papers and posters, pp. 74–83. ACM (2004)
4. Dikenelli, O., Gleizes, M.-P., Ricci, A. (eds.): ESAW 2005. LNCS, vol. 3963. Springer, Heidelberg (2006)
5. Elammari, M., Issa, Z.: Using model driven architecture to develop multi-agent systems. Int. Arab J. Inf. Technol. 10(4), 349–355 (2013)
6. Garro, A., Parisi, F., Russo, W.: A process based on the modeldriven architecture to enable the definition of platform-independent simulation models. In: Pina, N., Kacprzyk, J., Filipe, J. (eds.) Simulation and Modeling Methodologies, Technologies and Applications. Advances in Intelligent Systems and Computing, vol. 197, pp. 113–129. Springer, Heidelberg (2013)
7. Garro, A., Russo, W.: easyABMS: a domain-expert oriented methodology for agent-Based modeling and simulation. Simul. Model. Pract. Theor. 18(10), 1453–1467 (2010). Simulation-based Design and Evaluation of Multi-Agent Systems
8. Horridge, M., Bechhofer, S.: The OWL API: a Java API for OWL ontologies. Semant. Web 2(1), 11–21 (2011)
9. Lopes, F., Ilco, C., Sousa, J.: ilateral negotiation in energy markets: strategies for promoting demand response. In: 2013 10th International Conference on the European Energy Market (EEM), pp. 1–6. IEEE (2013)
10. Luke, S.: Multiagent simulation and the mason library. George Mason University (2011)
11. Luke, S., Cioffi-Revilla, C., Panait, L., Sullivan, K., Balan, G.: Mason: a multiagent simulation environment. Simulation 81(7), 517–527 (2005)
12. Meersman, R., Tari, Z., et al.: On the Move to Meaningful Internet Systems 2004: CoopIS, DOA, and ODBASE. LNCS. Springer, Heidelberg (2002)
13. Pavón, J., Gómez-Sanz, J.J., Fuentes, R.: Model driven development of multi-agent systems. In: Rensink, A., Warmer, J. (eds.) ECMDA-FA 2006. LNCS, vol. 4066, pp. 284–298. Springer, Heidelberg (2006)
14. Sansores, C., Pavón, J.: Agent-based simulation replication: a model driven architecture approach. In: Gelbukh, A., de Albornoz, A., Terashima-Marín, H. (eds.) MICAI 2005. LNCS (LNAI), vol. 3789, pp. 244–253. Springer, Heidelberg (2005)
15. Wooldridge, M.: An Introduction to Multiagent Systems. Wiley, New York (2009)
16. Ying, W., Ray, P., Lewis, L.: A methodology for creating ontology-based multi-agent systems with an experiment in financial application development. In: 2013 46th Hawaii International Conference on System Sciences (HICSS), pp. 3397–3406. IEEE (2013)

Design and Use of a Semantic Similarity Measure for Interoperability Among Agents

Johannes Fähndrich$^{(\boxtimes)}$, Sabine Weber, and Sebastian Ahrndt

DAI-Laboratory, Department of Electrical Engineering and Computer Science,
Technische Universität Berlin,
Ernst-Reuter-Platz 7, 10587 Berlin, Germany
johannes.faehndrich@dai-labor.de

Abstract. The capability to identify the sense of polysemic words, *i.e.* words that have multiple meanings, is an essential part of intelligent systems, e.g. when updating an agent's beliefs during conversations. This process is also called Word Sense Disambiguation and is approached by applying semantic similarity measures. Within this work, we present an algorithm to create such a semantic similarity measure using marker passing, that: (1) generates a semantic network out of a concepts used e.g. in semantic service descriptions, (2) sends markers through the networks to tag sub-graphs that are of relevance, and (3) uses these markers to create a semantic similarity measure. We will discuss the properties of the algorithm, elaborate its performance, and discuss the lifted properties for the algorithm to be used in WSD. To evaluate our approach, we compare it to state of the art measures using the *Rubinstein1965* dataset. It is shown, that our approach outperforms these state of the art measures.

1 Introduction

In a recent work [23], it was argued that the applicability of agent technologies to real world problems is limited. Part of the conclusion that was drawn by the authors is that interoperability between agent-based systems and other more frequently used paradigms such as service oriented architectures (SOA) [10] is a key factor for the acceptance of agent technology. Among others, the authors inferred that capability descriptions, matching techniques (e.g., ontology matching), and planning approaches provide significant challenges when facing the need of interoperability in heterogeneous software landscapes.

Bridging the gaps between AOSE and SOA would enable agents to use a vast amount of web services as additional sensors and actors. In fact, the agent-community identified this opportunity long ago. However, many approaches use a static combination of web services that is determined during design time [23]. *But is it not that autonomous agents should decide which capabilities to use during runtime?* To enable this, there is the need to extend the capability of available planning techniques towards the ability to use semantic service descriptions. One key-factor in this circumstance is the ability to identify the meaning of a

© Springer International Publishing Switzerland 2016
M. Klusch et al. (Eds.): MATES 2016, LNAI 9872, pp. 41–57, 2016.
DOI: 10.1007/978-3-319-45889-2_4

description and with that the concepts making up this description, which is in the focus of our research.

This paper approaches the problem of ontology matching on service descriptions as basis of a learning mechanism for new concepts. Here each concept used to describe a service (semantically) has to be matched to the concepts known to the agent (its beliefs). Since the known concept are used to describe a service request. The concepts used to describe an service might be embedded into a ontology or they might not.

If, for example, an agents' goal description includes a statement like *"arrange a meeting at noon"* and a provided service has the description *"parking cost estimates for midday parking"*, noon needs to be mapped to midday. This is especially of interest to description parts where no additional ontological information is given. Here the first task is to identify the sense of a word, which is also known as the Word Sense Disambiguation (WSD), *i.e.* the process of identifying the sense of polysemic words. Research on this area so far has identified WSD as a main problem of language understanding. In [2] an overview about the area and available approaches is given. WSD itself is a sub-area of natural language understanding and an AI-complete problem [18,43]. In the state of the art ontology matching approaches words only have one meaning, which simplifies the problem to comparing the words properties and its structural place in the ontology [37].

For the sake of an example, we refer to the beliefs of an agent. By integrating new concepts into its beliefs the agents is able to extend the actions available to it by becoming able to search, identify, and use new services. Here our example is that an agent knows the concept *"noon"* and learns the new concept *"midday"*. The first hurdle to overcome is the need to identify whether the new concept represents something the agent already knows or not and, further, in which relation the new concept stands to older ones. This establishes a common ground which allows communication with other agents.

Representing meaning as a graph is one of the two ways AI, cognition and linguistic researchers think about meaning (so-called connectionist view). Logicians and formal representation of meaning, on the other side, include the symbolic representation, where description logics is used to describe the language and the meaning of symbols and their references. This *neats* vs. *scruffy* discussion is lasting for 40 years, now [28]. The approach proposed here combines those two views by integrating symbolic information into a connectionist approach.

For the remainder of this work, we first look at the state of the art of semantic similarity measures (Sect. 2). Then we describe how knowledge is represented in a graph structure that serves as foundation for the representation of meaning. Upon this graph marker passing[1] is used to create the dynamic part of meaning representing thoughts [9]. The marker passing algorithm uses node and edge interpretation to guide its markers. The node and edge interpretation models the symbolic influence of certain concepts [7]. To evaluate the resulting artificial representation of meaning an experiment is presented in which the parameters of

---

[1] Sometimes referred to as Activation Spreading or Token Passing.

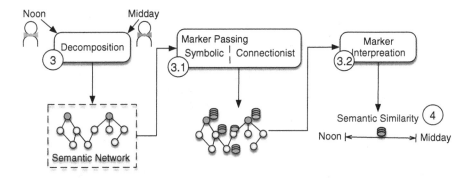

Fig. 1. Overview of the algorithm to measure semantic similarity of two concepts.

the marker passing are evaluated through finding semantic similarities between concepts [29]. We finally compare the reached results to state of the art measures using the *Rubinstein1965* dataset. It is shown, that our approach outperforms the state of the art measures and, further, is able to adapt to different contexts.

Figure 1 depicts our abstract approach, from the input of two concepts, which are decomposed into a semantic graph (Sect. 3). Then we use marker passing to identify relevant sub-graphs (Sect. 3.1) and describe the parameters used to interpret the marker information (Sect. 3.2). The whole concept is used to create a semantic similarity measure that is experimentally evaluated (Sect. 4).

2   Related Work

The research literature on word similarity metrics ranges from thesaurus based approaches (*cf.* [19]) to neuronal networks (*cf.* [26]). These approaches can be classified into groups based on the used data structure. Most commonly the differentiation is made between *knowledge-based* and *corpus-based* approaches [25]. *Zhang et al.* [48] use the same classification in their survey, further subdividing the domain of knowledge-based approaches into *taxonomies* and *ontologies*. Taxonomies are organised by the generalisation-specialisation relationship only, while ontologies are taxonomic structures enriched with other semantic relationships. Based on this classification we selected three state of the art approaches, using them as a baseline during our evaluation. We selected the *Electronic Lexical Knowledge Base* [19] (taxonomy-based), the *Bidirectional One-Step* approach [8] (ontology-based), and the *Word2Vec* [26] (corpus-based) approach as typical representatives of their group. *Lastra-Diaz et al.* [20] has not been selected as it mixes corpus-based and ontology-based approaches. The approach of *Mikolov* [26] has been selected as it provides a better performance than the algorithm of *Baroni* [4]. Bringing the categories and approaches together, Fig. 2 shows the development of the most prominent word similarity metrics on a time scale, starting with the work of *Rada et al.* [32] and ranging to the latest work, which was presented by *Lastra-Diaz et al.* [20]. We compare our approach to all

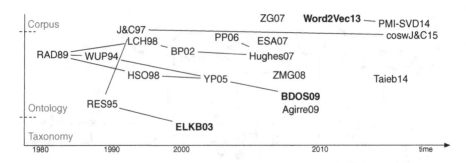

Fig. 2. Overview of the state of the art of semantic similarity measures.

measures within the same performance range of the state of the art according to the surveys of *Pilehvar et al.* [31], *Lastra-Díaz, García-Serrano* [20], and *Zesch and Gurevych* [47]. Excluding the approach of Yang [44] (denoted as YP05) because it has been performed on a subset of the dataset.

In conclusion, all these approaches are not context dependent and, thus, lack the ability to select a semantic similarity specific to a given context. This context can be the knowledge of the agent or some additional information which is specific to the time of execution.

3   Semantic Similarity Measures

To create a semantic similarity measure our approach utilises a lexical decomposition approach to extract relevant information from a set of heterogeneous information sources. A detailed description of the decomposition can be found in a prior work [11]. The semantic graph is enriched with all available information from the following sources: *WordNet, Wiktionary, Wikidata,* and *Babel-NET.* Here the graph is created by lexical decomposition that breaks each concept semantically down until a set of semantic primes is reached [12,35]. This approach is based on the linguistic theory named Natural Semantic Metalanguage (NSM) [15,40]. NSM states that all natural languages have a semantic core consisting of 65 semantic primes in which each word can be decomposed. In the created graph, nodes and edges are no longer disjoint since a word can appear as a relation or as a concept. With this lexical decomposition the beliefs of an agent are used as initial knowledge for building a semantic graph representing the believed facts of the agent. The abstract decomposition is shown in Algorithm 1[2].

Figure 3 shows a simplified depiction of the result graph of Algorithm 1 for our example task of analysing the concepts *"midday"* and *"noon"*. If edges are symmetric they are shown without direction, further, some of the edges have been removed to increase readability. Building a bigger network in this way allows us

---

[2] Implementation available at: https://gitlab.tubit.tu-berlin.de/johannes_faehndrich/ semantic-decomposition. For access contact the first author.

Algorithm 1. Lexical Decomposition

Name: Decompose **Input:** Concept, PRIMES **Output:** Concept

  1: Concept ← Normalisation(Concept)
  2: Relations ← getRelations(Concept)
  3: Definitions ← lookUpDefinitions(Concept)
  4: **if** Concept ∈ PRIMES **then return** concept
  5: **end if**
  6: **for all** r ∈ Relations **do**
  7:     **if** r ∈ PRIMES **then**
  8:         AddRelation(Concept, r, getPrimOfConcept(r))
  9:     **else**
10:         AddRelation(Concept, r, r.target)
11:         decompose(r,PRIMES)
12:         decompose(r.target, PRIMES)
13:     **end if**
14: **end for**
15: **for all** *definition* in Definitions **do**
16:     **for all** *def* in *definition* **do**
17:         AddRelation(Concept,"definition", *def*)
18:         **if** *def* in PRIMES **then continue**
19:         **else**
20:           decompose(*def*,PRIMES)
21:         **end if**
22:     **end for**
23: **end for**
24: **return** Concept
25:

---

to broaden the context in which we can interpret concepts (e.g., *"arrange a meeting at noon for lunch"*). A semantic graph is built for each new concept, and is merged into one graph extending the beliefs of the agent. The outcome is used in the next step, which is the marker passing. Here the task is to compare two concepts regarding their semantic similarity. The marker passing uses these concepts as starting points to activate relevant sub-graphs. This algorithm will be explained next.

3.1   Marker Passing in Context

The marker passing algorithm (See footnote 2) can be subdivided into four phases. These are depicted in Fig. 4: (1) the *pre-processing* for preparing the graph; (2) the *selection of the pulse size*, which defines which nodes will pass markers within the pulse; (3) the *pulse* itself, where all spreading nodes are activated and pass on their markers (each pulse consists of an *activation step* for each active node) including the *post-processing* step, were e.g. the results are normalised and (4) the checking of the termination condition. The input parameters for the marker-passing algorithm are the node interpretations, the termination condition and the underlying graph.

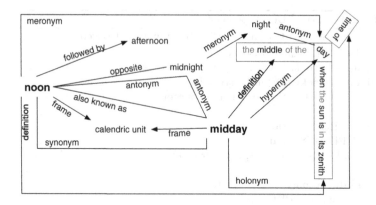

Fig. 3. Example graph for the words midday and noon.

A marker here is a datatype which hold the information needed by the marker passing and the interpretation functions. In our example a marker holds a double value called "activation" and an node id called "origin". The activation of a node thus is the cumulated activation of all markers present on this node. The origin is the node id of the node the marker has been placed at the beginning of the marker passing.

For our example, we put start markers on the two nodes c_1 = "noon" and c_2 = "midday", in addition to some contextual concepts denoted with C. Staring the marker passing "noon" e.g. passes markers in the first pulse to each concept of its definition "time of day where the sun is in its zenith". Midday on the other hand amongst others edges activates its holonym "time of day" where now at the concept "day" markers from both concept meet. In addition "meeting", "parking" and "lunch" could be chosen as contextual concepts which are activated as well. From one pulse the active concept passes markers to its outgoing edges depending on its interpretation function $N.out()$ and the interpretation of the in-function $N.in()$.

Generalising the graph used by Thiel and Berthold [39] the marker passing can be abstracted to a multi-graph $G = (V, E, w)$ where the nodes (V), the edges (E) which can have multiple sources and targets and their weights w represent a pulse at time t. In each pulse all spreading nodes pass their markers to their neighbours over connecting edges. The activation of a node consists of a set of all markers passed to the node. The activation step can then be formalised as follows:

$$\hat{a}_t(e) = \sum_{u \in e.source} N(u).out(a_{t-1}(u), e) \tag{1}$$

$a_{t-1}(u)$ is the activation of node u after pulse $t - 1$ with $t > 0$ and $\hat{a}_t(e)$ is the activation step, where all active nodes pass markers regarding to their out-function of the node interpretation function $N()$. The node interpretation N allows us to define different node types, like for example a negation node which activates differently then other nodes to reflect negation during the marker

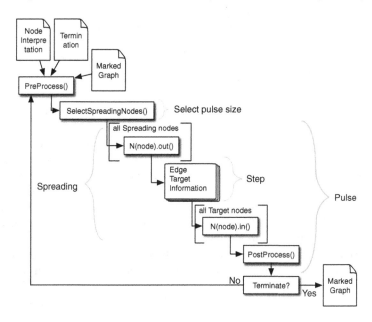

Fig. 4. Overview of the algorithm to measure semantic similarity of two concepts.

passing. The sum on markers is defined as sum of activation per origin. The markers are removed from the active node and passed to their destination. Here they are interpreted by the in-function of the node:

$$\hat{a}_t^*(v) = \hat{a}_{t-1}^*(v) + \sum_{v \in e.target} N(v).in(\hat{a}_t(e), e) \qquad (2)$$

where $\hat{a}_t^*(v)$ represents the activation of the node after all the markers passed over the edges connected to v are incorporated by the in-function into its current activation. This is repeated until the termination condition is reached.

After the termination condition has been positively evaluated the activation can then be used to calculate the semantic similarity between our example nodes $c_1 =$ *"noon"* and $c_2 =$ *"midday"* in the context C in many ways. After the marker passing step, the graph contains markers which must be interpreted. In Fig. 1 this step is called marker interpretation. The idea is that closer concepts will have more markers on the same nodes compared to concepts at greater distances. We tried multiple interpretations (e.g. maximum, averages, final activation, with and without normalisation) and the following one yield the best results:

$$d_{sim}(c_1, c_2, C) = \left\| \frac{\sum_{v \in V} \sum_{t=0}^{t_{max}} \Phi(\hat{a}_t^*(v), c_1, c_2)}{\sum_{\forall w \in V} a^0(w)} \right\|_{c_1}^{c_2} \qquad (3)$$

where C is a set of concepts describing the context and $\| \cdot \|_{c_1}^{c_2}$ is the total amount of activation of origin c_1 and c_2. Remember that the concepts in C are activated to influence the activation of concepts closer to the given context. Here:

$$\Phi(\hat{a}_t^*(v), c_1, c_2) = \begin{cases} \hat{a}_t^*(v) & \text{, if } \exists m_{1,2} \in \hat{a}_t^*(v) : m_1.origin = c_1 \wedge m_2.origin = c_2 \\ \emptyset & \text{, else} \end{cases}$$

$$(4)$$

filters all nodes which have not been activated by at least two of the start markers. In this way, if we activate two concepts (in our example "noon" and "midday") at the beginning, this set contains all nodes which have been activated by markers of both starting concepts or the context. The context here helps to select to word sense out of multiple definitions for "noon" and "midday" since "meeting" activates "time" and "parking" as well which gives more activation to definitions of "noon" and "midday" having to do with time. The result is normalised by the amount of start activation to obtain the semantic similarity. Here the devision divides the activation of each marker by origin. For example the activation of the markers of "noon" making up the $\Phi(\hat{a}_t^*(v))$ are divided by the amount of start activation put on $c_1 =$ "noon" at the beginning. t_{max} is defined by the termination condition of the marker passing. The resulting similarity of this algorithm of "noon" and "midday" is 0.9 where humans in the test dataset guess a similarity of 0.985.

How the marker passing is configured e.g. how the weights of the edges are selected and how the in- and out-functions are defined, is subject to the next section.

3.2   Parameters of the Marker Passing to Create a Semantic Similarity Measure

The novelty in this marker passing algorithm is the node and edge interpretation function denoted by $N()$ in Fig. 4. This interpretation functions allow each node and edge to react distinctively to markers passed from ($N.out$) or to ($N.in$) them. With this symbolic information each node can interpret each marker independently and thus can have a individual threshold. The behaviour of each node is specified within these two functions, whereas the in-function specifies what to do with incoming markers and the out-function specifies how markers are passed to other nodes. The size of the pulse can be chosen by the *SelectSpreadingNodes* function, which selects those nodes which activate during the next pulse from the set of *active nodes*. Active nodes are those nodes which reach some node specific threshold. This threshold and the in- and out-function is part of the node interpretation. After each pulse a given termination condition is checked. This termination condition prevents the markers to be equally distributed over the network [5].

In the experiment carried out two words are given without context, part of speech information or word sense. In our approach the two words are given to the decomposition which creates a semantic graph based on the information sources used by the decomposition. The result is a semantic graph for each word. Here in our example of *"noon"* the sending agent could talk about a time of day, whereas the receiving agent could talk about a "the highest point" of a story[3].

As information on the marker we chose a numeric activation level and a marker "origin" encoding the starting node of the marker. We chose this symbolic information since it seams minimalistic without reducing the marker passing to a triviality.[4] The activation level is used to measure the distance to the origin node. We use the "origin" of the marker to react to cases in which a node is activated by at least two different concepts.

The underlying graph consists of nodes, where each node represents one concept of the decomposition. The edges of the graph represent the relations of the decomposition. Each edge has a edge type corresponding to its semantic relation in the decomposition and a numerical weight — for example, an antonym relation creates a antonym edge with a specific weight. All semantic relations known to the decomposition are weighted edges. The following edge types have been specified:

- **Semantic relations** are relations we derive from the dictionaries used during the decomposition. Here we take the following relations into account: synonyms (semantically similar in some contexts), antonyms (the opposite of something), hyponyms (specialisation), hypernyms (generalisation) and meronyms (part-of relations).
- **Others** are relations that are not specified in the dictionaries used in the decomposition but are taken from the domain ontology of the agent. Here relations like *"is uncle of"* or *"is owned by"* could be introduced into the decomposition. There edges in the resulting graph are weighted with 1.0.

Similar to the edge type, the graph consists of different types of nodes. The following node types have been specified:

- **Concept nodes** represent a concept and hold the markers passed to it. The threshold of a concept node is reached if one of the marker origin reaches the numeric activation threshold τ.
- **Stop word nodes** represent words which are ignored. Those are taken form natural language processing theory [41]. Those nodes can not be activated.
- **Prime nodes** represent semantic primes from NSM, which act as leave nodes and collect markers without passing them on.

Furthermore, there are infinite specialisation methods for the marker passing. We have made the following design decisions to build our semantic similarity measure:

- There is neither a pre- nor a post-processing step.

---

[3] Even with contextual information such concepts are not always easy to identify, as shown by Bar-Hillel [3], e.g. *"The box is in the pen"*.

[4] With less symbolic information the marker passing becomes activation spreading, which in the special case of artificial neuronal networks is subject to research.

- Start Marker are put on the two initially decomposed concepts. The start marker declares the origin of the marker. All start markers specifies a equal activation level.
- The threshold τ is a selected marker value, that is checked against the total amount of markers of a node. The τ might differ with each node interpretation. Here we chose a numerical upper limit as τ for a threshold of activation collected by the markers.
- The in-function of a node collects the markers at the "marker passing step", which the current node is the target of. Markers of all edges are sorted by their origin. Furthermore, the in-function sums-up the activation of all origins to update the activation level of the node.
- The Pulse size was selected in a way that all active nodes are spreading nodes instead of having, e.g., each node activated in an own pulse. This has been done since the activation is collected additively in our in-function and does not decay (i.e. does not reduce over time) in a node.
- The out-function propagates markers with the total amount of activation to all edges weighted with the appropriate edge weight. Additionally the markers at the moment of activation are held in an activation history for later analysis. After an activation the node has no markers of any origin.
- The termination condition is set to the maximum step count one marker can achieve in the graph and a maximum amount of markers of different origins which have crossed a concept.
- Context C is left empty since the test dataset does not provide context.

Next we will introduce the configuration of those parameters we used to create our results. The symbolic information is used in the following way: The marked graph is analysed for nodes which have passed markers of multiple origins. The activation of all markers that were passed to this node (independent of the origins) is summed up. To do so, the node history is used to look-up the total activation the node has experienced over time. Thus nodes which have a throughput of markers of multiple origins contribute more activation to the final marker count. Additionally the node type allows us to ignore stop words and stop the activation if a semantic prime is reached.

4 Evaluation

Evaluating is done on linguistic datasets where word similarity is measured. No ontology matching dataset is used, since ontology matching datasets manly focus on structural matching. This can be seen as facilitation of the task of finding a semantic similarity measure, where additional information is provided.

To evaluate the presented approaches we selected widely-used datasets. The most frequently used is the one published by Rubenstein and Goodenough 1965 (RG65) [36]. It consist of 65 noun pairs. The semantic similarity of these pairs were rated on a scale of zero to four by ten test subjects. Most papers dealing with metrics for semantic similarity use this dataset, which makes it suitable for the verification of claimed results and comparison between different metrics. Other datasets that were applied are the WordSimilarity-353 Test collection [13], the Miller and Charles dataset [27], the MTurk dataset [33], the MEN dataset [6], and the Stanford Rare Word Similarity dataset [24]. We selected these datasets to assure that the selection of words compared to each other is as big as possible. Moreover we wanted to make sure, that not only the similarity between nouns, but between all different word types is evaluated. Nevertheless, since most of the related work found is compared using the RG65 [36] dataset, we compare our results as well on this dataset. We normalised the dataset RG65 to contain similarity values between 0 and 1.

4.1 Parameter Selection

The parameters selected in Table 1 depend on design decisions during the creation of the marker passing. Here many combinations of parameters can yield the same or better results and we do not claim that our parameters yield the optimal result. However, later it can be seen that our approach can keep up with the state of the art.

Table 1. Parameters of the marker passing for our semantic similarity measurement.

Parameter	RG-65		
	Min	Max	Best
StartActivation	0	100	3.30
Threshold	0	1	0.32
DefinitionLinkWeight	−1	1	0.25
SynonymEdgeWeight	−1	1	−0.94
AntonymEdgesWeight	−1	0	−0.11
HypernymEdgesWeight	−1	1	0.30
HyponymEdgesWeight	−1	1	0.11
TerminationPulsCount	1	100	99
DoubleActivationLimit	0	1	0.53
DecompositionDepth	1	2	2

To come up with an estimate of the best value for the parameters, we have used an evolutionary algorithm. Here the individual's DNA of an initial population is made up of random values of the parameters described in Table 1. The individual evaluation is done with a n-fold cross-validation using the RG65 [36] dataset with 65 folds. Evolution is done by mutating the best individual in all parameters randomly. One exception is the custom relations out of the domain ontology, which are weighted 1.0.

The best result was yielded by the parameters shown in column 'best' of Table 1. Interesting for this result is that the parameters are interdependent.

Having synonym edges with negative weights seams not intuitive. Also that the weights of antonym edges are less negative than the ones of synonyms. This can be explained with the frequency of the relation types. WordNet includes more synonym relations then antonym relations. Additionally the dataset RG65 consist solely of nouns, where antonyms are infrequent. The decomposition depth has been limited to 2 because of computational resources, which were not able to handle decomposition of deeper levels. The parameter selection is significant, since the results from one example learning run reaches correlation from 0.008 to 0.832 in 45.253 generations. Additionally the parameters are specially trained for the properties of the example dataset. Here the learning needs to be repeated for each new dataset with different properties.

4.2   Evaluation Results

The experiment has been implemented in Java using the WordNet 3.1 and the MIT Java Wordnet Interface (JWI)[5]. For the Wiktionary implementation the Java-based Wiktionary Library (JWKTL)[6] has been used with a Wiktionary dump[7]. With the above introduced parameter selection, we were able to reach the results shown in Table 2. The other results are taken from [31, p. 116, Table 9] and from [20, p. 148, Table 4] and present the state of the art in this experiment.

Table 2. Comparison of Spearman's ρ and Pearson's r correlation coefficients of different approaches with our approach (**Marker Passing, number 2.**) in descending order with respect to ρ. Anything but our results are taken from [31, p. 116, Table 9] and from [20, p. 148, Table 4].

#	Approach	RG-65		#	Approach	RG-65	
		ρ	r			ρ	r
1.	coswJ&C [20]	0.876	–	11	Rad89 [32]	0.79	0.79
2.	**Marker Passing**	**0.87**	**0.79**	12	LCH [21]	0.79	0.84
3.	Word2vec [26]	0.84	0.83	13	HSO [16]	0.79	0.73
4.	H&R [17]	0.84	–	14	WUP [42]	0.78	0.80
5.	ZMG-08 [46]	0.84	–	15	ESA [14]	0.75	0.49
6.	Lin [22]	0.834	–	16	Res95 [34]	0.74	0.81
7.	Agirre et al. [1]	0.83	–	17	PMI-SVD [4]	0.74	0.74
8.	ZG-07 [45]	0.82	0.49	18	ELKB [19]	0.65	–
9.	BDOS [8]	0.81	–	19	PP06 [30]	0.62	0.58
10.	Taieb [38]	0.80	0.80				

---

[5] http://projects.csail.mit.edu/jwi/.
[6] https://www.ukp.tu-darmstadt.de/software/jwktl/.
[7] https://dumps.wikimedia.org/ downloaded on 2015.12.19.

The spearman's ranked correlation coefficient ρ is an overall ranking measure. Together with the pearson's r Table 2 shows the performance of the state of the art semantic similarity measures in comparison to each other.

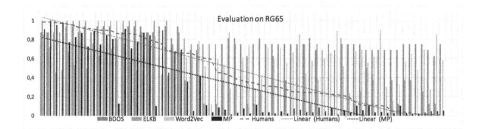

Fig. 5. Evaluation result showing the RG65 dataset.

Figure 5 illustrates an example results for the RG65 dataset, comparing our results to the three reference approaches we selected. Here, the x-axes represents the similarity of a word pair out of the RG65 dataset. The y-axis listed the 65 different word pairs ordered from semantically close concepts (synonyms in the best case) to concepts with less semantic similarity. Most of the time, the marker passing (MP, black) underestimates the similarity in contrast to our three reference measures. The underestimation gets worse the less the semantic similarity is, until at the far end the measure overestimates the similarity. But we can see that the linear progression of the MP approach is closest to the human (dotted line) guess of similarity. The best average performance of the other approaches is reached by the ELKB approach, which overestimates the similarity most of the time. BDOS and Word2Vec overestimate the semantic similarity of far concepts consistently. This happens because the general knowledge sources like WordNet or corpora always find a path between two concepts in the example of BDOS.

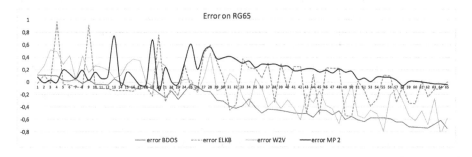

Fig. 6. Evaluation error of the similarity measures tested on the RG65 dataset

Figure 6 shows the error of the analysed approaches. Here we can identify the concepts where the approaches deliver good/bad results. For example, it can be noticed that the error of MP is greater in the mid-range of the semantic similarity and that the reference measures get worse with a declining semantic similarity. The ELKB approach has less error for distance word pairs as it returns zero if no distance is found. Thus the missing error for semantically distant word pairs here is due to failure of the approach to handle distant words. BDOS on the other hand has almost no error for close concepts. Here short paths between two concepts can be found in WordNet. But the further the distance of the words, the less accurate BDOS becomes.

4.3   Discussion and Future Work

We can see in Figs. 5 and 6 that the thesaurus based approach (ELKB) estimates well when closely related concepts are the problem, whereas the semantic similarity gets smaller the metric becomes less accurate and unable to connect two concepts. In Fig. 6 we can see that ELKB's error increases with the increases of semantic similarity of the concepts. The WordNet-Path-length approach (BDOS) on the other hand finds nearly the same similarity for close as for distend concepts.

The use of the RG65 [36] dataset seams insufficient since only nouns are compared. More complex datasets exist, which could be used in the future for comparison. Using part-of-speech independent datasets will worsen thesauri approaches like ELKB since mostly nouns are formalised in thesauri.

Furthermore, the extension to have a WSD algorithm which uses context can be created through the following steps: The contextual words are decomposed, the results are merged into the graph and markers are passed to them. Then the word sense is selected with the most semantic similarity by identifying the nodes that received the most activation from multiple origins.

In the progress of selecting actions in unknown domains, an agent needs to handle new concepts autonomously. The algorithm proposed here can be seen as a foundation for the integration of new concepts into the beliefs of an agent. Thereby, new concepts and their relations are added to an existing and ever-growing semantic graph representing the beliefs of an agent. Here concepts which have a semantic similarity bigger then a given threshold can be integrated in the belief if the relations do not contradict any prior knowledge.

The here proposed mechanism can be used to determine the semantic similarity not only super- and sub-matches of e.g. input parameters, which helps the agent to select fitting services to a given request. The reasoning on ontologies is left to another work.

Future work will include more complex datasets and extending the matching from the worst case to a less general but more informative case where addition information is given. The context dependent decomposition of the concept that is unknown to the agent, and with that a word sense disambiguation for the context of the agent will be a future challenge.

References

1. Agirre, E., Alfonseca, E., Hall, K., Kravalova, J., Paşca, M., Soroa, A.: A study on similarity and relatedness using distributional and WordNet-based approaches. In: NAACL (2009)
2. Agirre, E., Edmonds, P.G.: Word Sense Disambiguation: Algorithms and Applications. Springer, Heidelberg (2007)
3. Bar-Hillel, Y.: The present status of automatic translation of languages. In: Advances in Computers, vol. 1 (1960)
4. Baroni, M., Dinu, G., Kruszewski, G.: Don't count, predict! A systematic comparison of context-counting vs. context-predicting semantic vectors. In: Proceedings of the 52nd Annual Meeting of the Association for Computational Linguistics, (vol. 1: Long Papers) (2014)
5. Berthold, M.R., Brandes, U., Kötter, T., Mader, M., Nagel, U., Thiel, K.: Pure spreading activation is pointless. In: CIKM (2009)
6. Bruni, E., Tran, N.K., Baroni, M.: Multimodal distributional semantics. J. Artif. Intell. Res. (JAIR) **49**, 1–47 (2014)
7. Charniak, E.: A neat theory of marker passing. In: AAAI (1986)
8. Chen, D., Jianzhuo, Y., Liying, F., Bin, S.: Measure semantic distance in wordnet based on directed graph search. In: EEEE 2009 (2009)
9. Crestani, F.: Application of spreading activation techniques in information retrieval. Artif. Intell. Rev. **11**(6), 453–482 (1997)
10. Erl, T.: SOA Principles of Service Design. Prentice Hall, Upper Saddle River (2007)
11. Fähndrich, J., Ahrndt, S., Albayrak, S.: Are there semantic primes in formal languages? In: Omatu, S., Bersini, H., Corchado Rodríguez, J.M., González, S.R., Pawlewski, P., Bucciarelli, E. (eds.) Distributed Computing and Artificial Intelligence 11th International Conference. AISC, vol. 290, pp. 397–405. Springer, Heidelberg (2014). (Chapter 46)
12. Fähndrich, J., Ahrndt, S., Albayrak, S.: Formal language decomposition into semantic primes. ADCAIJ Adv. Distrib. Comput. Artif. Intell. J. **3**(8), 56 (2014)
13. Finkelstein, L., Gabrilovich, E., Matias, Y., Rivlin, E., Solan, Z., Wolfman, G., Ruppin, E.: Placing search in context: the concept revisited. ACM Trans. Inf. Syst. **20**, 116–131 (2002)
14. Gabrilovich, E., Markovitch, S.: Computing semantic relatedness using wikipedia-based explicit semantic analysis. IJCAI **7**, 1606–1611 (2007)
15. Goddard, C., Wierzbicka, A.: Semantic and Lexical Universals: Theory and Empirical Findings. John Benjamins Publishing, Amsterdam (1994)
16. Hirst, G., St-Onge, D.: Lexical chains as representations of context for the detection and correction of malapropisms (1998)
17. Hughes, T., Ramage, D.: Lexical semantic relatedness with random graph walks. In: EMNLP-CoNLL (2007)
18. Ide, N., Veronis, J.: Introduction to the special issue on word sense disambiguation: the state of the art. Comput. Linguist. **24**(1), 2–40 (1998)
19. Jarmasz, M., Szpakowicz, S.: Rogets thesaurus and semantic similarity rogets thesaurus relations as a measure of semantic distance. In: Proceedings of the International Conference on Recent Advances in Natural Language Processing (RANLP 2003), pp. 212–219 (2003)
20. Lastra-Díaz, J.J., García-Serrano, A.: A novel family of IC-based similarity measures with a detailed experimental survey on WordNet. Eng. Appl. Artif. Intell. **46**, 140–153 (2015)

21. Leacock, C., Miller, G.A., Chodorow, M.: Using corpus statistics and WordNet relations for sense identification. Comput. Linguist. **24**, 147–165 (1998)
22. Lin, D.: An information-theoretic definition of similarity. In: ICML (1998)
23. Luetzenberger, M., Kuester, T., Masuch, N., Fähndrich, J.: Multi-agent system in practice - when research meets reality. In: AAMAS 2016, Singapore (2016)
24. Luong, M.T., Socher, R., Manning, C.D.: Better word representations with recursive neural networks for morphology. In: CoNLL-2013 (2013)
25. Mihalcea, R., Corley, C., Strapparava, C.: Corpus-based and knowledge-based measures of text semantic similarity. In: AAAI (2006)
26. Mikolov, T., Chen, K., Corrado, G., Dean, J.: Efficient estimation of word representations in vector space (2013). arXiv.org
27. Miller, G.A., Charles, W.G.: Contextual correlates of semantic similarity. Lang. Cogn. Process. **6**(1), 1–28 (2007)
28. Minsky, M.L.: Logical versus analogical or symbolic versus connectionist or neat versus scruffy. AI Mag. **12**, 35–51 (1991)
29. Navigli, R.: Word sense disambiguation: a survey. Comput. Surv. **41**, 10 (2009)
30. Patwardhan, S., Pedersen, T.: Using wordnet-based context vectors to estimate the semantic relatedness of concepts. In: Proceedings of the EACL 2006 Workshop Making Sense of Sense-Bringing Computational Linguistics and Psycholinguistics Together, vol. 1501, pp. 1–8. Citeseer (2006)
31. Pilehvar, M.T., Navigli, R.: From senses to texts: An all-in-one graph-based approach for measuring semantic similarity. Artif. Intell. **228**, 95–128 (2015)
32. Rada, R., Mili, H., Bicknell, E., Blettner, M.: Development and application of a metric on semantic nets. IEEE Trans. Syst. Man Cybern. **19**(1), 17–30 (1989)
33. Radinsky, K., Agichtein, E., Gabrilovich, E., Markovitch, S.: A word at a time: computing word relatedness using temporal semantic analysis. ACM, New York (2011)
34. Resnik, P.: Using information content to evaluate semantic similarity in a taxonomy. CoRR abs/cmp-lg/9511007 (1995)
35. Riemer, N.: The Routledge Handbook of Semantics. Routledge, London (2015)
36. Rubenstein, H., Goodenough, J.B.: Contextual correlates of synonymy. Commun. ACM **8**(10), 627–633 (1965)
37. Shvaiko, P., Euzenat, J.: Ontology matching: state of the art and future challenges. IEEE Trans. Knowl. Data Eng. **25**, 158–176 (2013)
38. Taieb, M.A.H., Ben Aouicha, M., Ben Hamadou, A.: A new semantic relatedness measurement using WordNet features. Knowl. Inf. Syst. **41**(2), 467–497 (2014)
39. Thiel, K., Berthold, M.R.: Node similarities from spreading activation. In: Berthold, M.R. (ed.) Bisociative Knowledge Discovery. LNCS, vol. 7250, pp. 246–262. Springer, Heidelberg (2012)
40. Wierzbicka, A.: Semantics: Primes and Universals. Oxford University Press, Oxford (1996)
41. Wilbur, W.J., Sirotkin, K.: The automatic identification of stop words. J. Inf. Sci. **18**(1), 45–55 (1991)
42. Wu, Z., Palmer, M.: Verbs semantics and lexical selection. In: Proceedings of the 32nd Annual Meeting on Association for Computational Linguistics (1994)
43. Yampolskiy, R.V.: AI-complete, AI-hard, or AI-easy - classification of problems in AI. In: MAICS, pp. 94–101 (2012)
44. Yang, D., Powers, D.M.: Measuring semantic similarity in the taxonomy of wordnet. In: Proceedings of the Twenty-eighth Australasian Conference on Computer Science, vol. 38, pp. 315–322. Australian Computer Society, Inc. (2005)

45. Zesch, T., Gurevych, I.: Analysis of the Wikipedia category graph for NLP applications. In: Proceedings of the TextGraphs-2 (2007)
46. Zesch, T., Müller, C., Gurevych, I.: Using wiktionary for computing semantic relatedness. In: AAAI (2008)
47. Zesch, T., Gurevych, I.: Wisdom of crowds versus wisdom of linguists - measuring the semantic relatedness of words. Nat. Lang. Eng. **16**(1), 25–59 (2010)
48. Zhang, Z., Gentile, A.L., Ciravegna, F.: Recent advances in methods of lexical semantic relatedness – a survey. Technical report (2012)

Dynamic Metrics for Multi-agent Systems Using Aspect-Oriented Programming

Application to DIMA Platform

Toufik Marir[1,2(✉)], Farid Mokhati[1,2], Hassina Bouchelaghem-Seridi[3],
and Boubakar Benaissa[1]

[1] Department of Mathematics and Computer Sciences,
University of Oum El Bouaghi, Oum El Bouaghi, Algeria
marir.toufik@yahoo.fr, mokhati@yahoo.fr,
Boubakar.Benaissa@yahoo.fr

[2] Research Laboratory on Computer Science's Complex Systems (ReLa(CS)2),
University of Oum El Bouaghi, Oum El Bouaghi, Algeria

[3] LABGED Laboratory, Department of Computer Science,
University of Annaba, Annaba, Algeria
seridi@labged.net

Abstract. The measurement is an important field in the software engineering. This field studies the assignment of a value to a software attribute using metrics. In fact, the use of metrics, which are the defined measurement methods and the measurement scales, in software engineering allows among other goals to control the quality of the software products, the quality of the software processes or the evolution of the software projects. Usually, we distinct two kinds of metrics: the static and the dynamic ones. The static metrics can be obtained from the source code of the software. On the other side, the dynamic metrics requires the execution of the software. Consequently, the static metrics are the most applied because of their relative simplicity compared to the dynamic metrics. However, we think that the dynamic metrics are more appropriate in some software categories. Multi-Agent Systems (MAS) is one of these categories because of the flexible nature of the agents. Consequently, we propose in this paper the using of the Aspect-Oriented Programming (AOP) to measure the dynamic metrics of multi-agent systems. In fact, the proposed approach provides several advantages like the simplicity, the reusability and the extensibility. In order to validate the proposed approach, we developed a tool that allows measuring of some metrics of DIMA-based applications.

Keywords: Dynamic metrics · Measurement methods · Multi-agent systems · Aspect-oriented programming · DIMA platform · AspectJ

1 Introduction

The development of quality software, with the estimated costs and during the planned times are among essential goals of the software projects. However, the evaluation of these goals is not always obvious. In fact, the nature of the software products and projects

© Springer International Publishing Switzerland 2016
M. Klusch et al. (Eds.): MATES 2016, LNAI 9872, pp. 58–72, 2016.
DOI: 10.1007/978-3-319-45889-2_5

complicates the measurement task and does not give correct values. Consequently, measurement has become an active field of software engineering [1, 2]. The measurement is defined as the assignment of a value (quantitative or qualitative) to a software attribute [3]. This value (called the measure) can be served to several purposes. For example, we can use it to evaluate the quality of the software, the complexity of a project or the productivity of a development team. In order to calculate the measures, we must apply some simple or sophisticated methods. According to the ISO-9126 standard [3], the method applied to obtain the measurement and the measurement scale is called a metric.

Usually, we distinct two kinds of metrics: static and dynamic ones. The static metrics are calculated from the source code of the software [4]. In contrast, we need to execute the software in order to measure the dynamic metrics [4]. The static metrics are mostly applied because of their relative simplicity compared to the dynamic ones [4–6]. However, the dynamic metrics provides more accurate values [4].

Several programming paradigms have been emerged since the appearance of software engineering. Obviously, we must take into account the specificities of each programming paradigm, during the proposition of the software metrics. For example, specific metrics are proposed for Object-Oriented software [7], Aspect-Oriented Programming (AOP) [8] and Multi-Agent Systems (MAS) [9, 10]. In the case of MAS, we can measure some specific attributes like the autonomy, the reactivity and flexibility of agents. For example, in some contexts we need to develop high-level autonomous agents (such as, robots for exploring the space). Otherwise, in different contexts, the agents must be developed with limited autonomy (for example, agent for controlling very destructive missiles). Thus, we think that the measurement of specific attributes of MAS is very interesting. It can be used for several purposes like controlling the quality of the developed systems, choosing the most adequately agents for a giving project or evaluating existing systems in order to maintain them.

Despite the importance of the static metrics for measuring some attributes of the MAS, we think that the dynamic metrics are more appropriate for multi-agent systems because of their unpredictable evolution nature. An agent is characterized by the flexibility of its behaviors [11]. So, it can change its behavior according to its current situation. Consequently, the code of a multi-agent system cannot give us sufficient information about its future execution (for example, when an agent will reach its goal). Consequently, we cannot use only the code to measure some attributes of the multi-agent systems. As a result, we must measure the desired attributes during the execution of the system. Despite the importance of this aspect (the measurement method), the most specific metrics proposed for multi-agent systems ignored it. In this paper, we address the question: *how we can measure these dynamic metrics of the MAS?* Actually, we propose the application of the Aspect-Oriented Programming (AOP) [12] in order to measure some dynamic metrics of Multi-Agent Systems (MAS). The feasibility of this approach is validated on a well-known multi-agent platform, namely, DIMA (for Development and Implementation of Multi-Agent systems) platform [13].

The reminder of this paper is organized as the following: we present in Sect. 2 some related works followed by presentation of proposed approach. Section 4 is devoted to present the developed tool and case study. Finally, conclusion and some future works are presented in Sect. 5.

2 Related Works

The measurement is a vital task in software projects. This task allows controlling the quality of software products or projects and the evolution of software projects too. Obviously, we cannot propose metrics without taking into account the specificities of the programming paradigms. In fact, the continuous evolution of the programming paradigms requires a continuous adaptation of the metrics to those paradigms. Multi-agent paradigm, as one of the relatively recent programming paradigms, it does not make the exception. Several specific metrics for multi-agent systems are proposed since the emergence of this paradigm. Recently, the proposition of metrics to measure the different aspects of multi-agent systems keeps growing.

Lass et al. [14] presented a survey of metrics for multi-agent systems. They decomposed the measures for two categories: Measures of Performance and Measures of Effectiveness. Moreover, they cited the different levels we can apply the metrics (the agent, the framework, the platform and the host). The authors proposed a framework allowing the application of the different metrics. The proposed framework is composed of three components: the selection, the collection and the application. The First component allows determining the metrics to apply according to the evaluation goals thanks to the Goal, Question, Metric (GQM) approach [15]. The second component is used to collect data allowing the application of the metrics. Finally, we must apply the metrics in order to determine if the system meets the goal of the evaluation or not.

The authors [14] presented several interesting points in their work. We think that the decomposition of the MAS in layered system allows mastering the measurement and evaluation process. Moreover, the authors proposed a framework in order to apply the different metrics. However, the proposed framework ignored the measurement method. The authors oversimplified this aspect by proposing the instrumenting of the code or using stopwatch to record the timing information. We think that the measurement methods deserve more attention because it can influence on the obtained results. Moreover, it can be became complex and tedious task.

Sivakumar and Vivekanandan [9] proposed metrics to assess the reactivity of agents. For this purpose, they decompose this characteristic into three sub-characteristics: the interaction, the perception and the communication. Each one of these sub-characteristics is measured by a set of metrics. For example, the perception sub-characteristic is measured by the use and the update of knowledge. Despite that the proposed attributes seem dynamic (like the update of knowledge), the authors proposed static metrics to measure them. For example, the update of knowledge is defined as "*the number of statement that will update the variables in the agent*" [9]. The authors [9] developed a tool that assesses the proposed metrics for Jade platform based on a syntactic analysis.

Mahar and Bhatia [10] targeted the measure of the intelligence of agents. The authors considered that the attributes which determine the intelligence of agent are: the adaptability, the goal orientation and the learning. Then, they proposed metrics for each one of these attributes. The number of roles and the agent goals achievements are two metrics used to measure the goal orientation attribute.

Away from discussions about the proposed attributes of intelligence which are debatable because of the lack of several well-known attributes (like the reactivity [11]), we think that it is difficult to measure some metrics using only the source code of the software. The authors [10] proposed some dynamic metrics but they did not present explicitly the measurement method. It seems that the functions that calculate these metrics are being incorporated in the code of the system under analysis. This technique suffers from some major drawbacks. First, the incorporated code can influence negatively on the performance of the system under analysis. Calculating the measurement functions consumes the calculating resources. Moreover, if these functions are not optimized, it can influence negatively on the normal function of the system. Second, the incorporation of the measurement functions in the code of the system is a difficult task. In fact, we must identify exactly the adequate incorporation points and incorporate the measurement function *manually* in order to obtain correct results. Finally, despite that this method ensures the measurement of the dynamic metrics, the application of this technique requires the existence of the code of the application under analysis. In fact, in several cases we have not the possibility to access to the code of the systems but we need to measure their characteristics. Despite that we live the open source age, several firms did not distribute the code of their applications.

Instead of this approach based on the manual incorporation of the measurement function, some tools have been developed to measure automatically specific metrics of the multi-agent systems. Generally, these tools are called profiling. A profiling tool uses the execution trace of the application in order to measure the desired metrics. Despite that the profiling tools are proposed the first time forty-five years ago [16], the emergence of the multi-agent systems led to the development of several specific profiling tool for these systems [17] (like *AgentSpotter* [18]). Obviously, the profiling tools ensure the reusability characteristic because we can execute several applications using the same tool. However, each profiling tool is designed to measure some specific-metrics (generally the performance). In fact, the extensibility characteristic (the possibility of extending the existing tool to support more metrics) is generally an omitted characteristic.

It seems important to note that the *MEANDER* tool [19] attempted to be extensible. So, the developers of this tool give us the possibility of introducing our metrics and the tool integrated them in the multi-agent systems. However, it is necessary to have the code of the system under evaluation in order to using this tool.

The Table 1 gives a summary of the different methods using to measure the attributes of the multi-agent systems. Moreover, we compared these methods using the

Table 1. Summary of the measurement methods and their characteristics.

Method	Type of the metric	Simplicity	Reusability	Extensibility	Necessity of the code
Syntactic analysis	Static	Automatic (Simple)	Reusable	Extensible	Yes
Incorporating the measurement functions	Dynamic	Manual (Difficult)	Not reusable	Extensible	Yes
Profiling tools	Dynamic	Automatic (Simple)	Reusable	Generally not extensible	No

type of the metric, the simplicity, the reusability, the extensibility and the necessity of the application's code criteria.

In the next section, we will present our proposed approach to measure the dynamic metrics of the multi-agent systems.

3 The Proposed Approach

As we mentioned previously the most proposed metrics for multi-agent systems are static ones. Moreover, the proposed methods to measure the dynamic metrics suffer from several problems like, the difficulty, the not-reusability and the not-extensibility. So, we proposed an approach to ensure these characteristics. Our approach is based on the using of the Aspect-Oriented Programming paradigm (AOP) [12]. This latter is one of the recent programming paradigms. As the most of programming paradigms, this paradigm is proposed to manage the growth of software complexity. In fact, the aspect-oriented programming proposes a new way to modularizing the software. So, the *crosscutting concerns* are separated from the *core concerns*. These crosscutting concerns are developed as aspects which will be woven to the main system automatically thanks to weaver. Obviously, an aspect incorporates, in addition to the crosscutting behaviour, specification of the weaving condition in order to wave crosscutting concerns in adequate points. Figure 1 gives the principle of this programming paradigm.

Our approach is based on this idea. Hence, we must analyze the multi-agent programming language in order to determine the functions which can influence on the agent behaviour. For example, the functions allowing sending and receiving messages

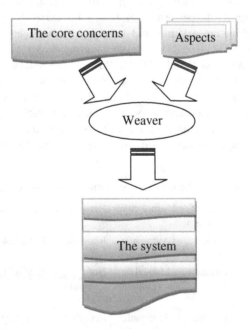

Fig. 1. The principle of the Aspect-Oriented Programming (AOP).

are examples of these functions. Then, we must develop aspects which allow capturing the execution of selected functions. Of course, aspects must save the important information of each function's execution such as, execution date, function's kind and function parameters. Therefore, we obtain a list of essential events appeared during the execution of multi-agent system. Finally, we can calculate dynamic metrics using this list of events. Figure 2 presents this approach.

Despite that it is possible to calculate the dynamic metrics simultaneously with the execution of multi-agent system (*On-The-Fly Metrics*); we recommend the optimization of the aspects used to capture execution events. Ideally, these aspects must only capture and save the event execution and the calculation of metrics must be postponed until the end of multi-agent system execution. In fact, simultaneous execution of calculating metrics and multi-agent system execution can increase the execution time of aspects. In this case, the use of Aspect-Oriented Programming shares with the incorporation of measurement functions the disadvantage of the negative influence of the measurement cited above. In other words, the execution of aspects, in this case, can influence on the normal execution of multi-agent system.

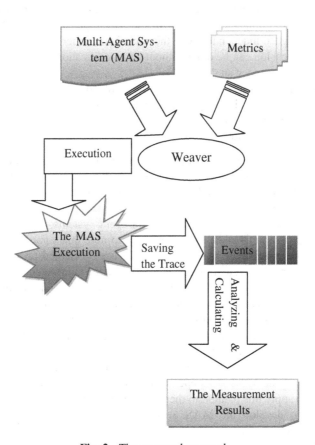

Fig. 2. The proposed approach.

It seems important to note that the influence of the execution of the metrics on the normal execution of the application under analysis is not a specific disadvantage of our approach. The almost proposed methods for the measurement of the dynamic metrics use a portion of the execution time to calculate the metrics. Naturally, the used time can influence on the execution of the multi-agent systems. We think that the only solution to this problem is to optimize the code of the metrics (as we applied in our approach).

Our approach combined the advantages of the two well known methods used to measure dynamic metrics (the incorporation of the code and profiling tool). In fact, our approach provides the following advantages:

- **The simplicity:** thanks to the weaver, the different metrics can be incorporated automatically on the application's code. In fact, the aspects specify the adequate points in which the measurement function should be inserted. The users of our approach must only execute the application under analysis using an aspect compiler. Thus, we think that this approach allows using the dynamic metrics in easy way.
- **The reusability:** in our approach, the metrics are designed as aspects. Consequently, they provide a high level of modularity. Hence, it is possible to reuse the same aspects to measure different multi-agent systems.
- **The extensibility:** the modularity of the designed metrics simplifies the eventual possibility of extending these metrics to measure more attributes. Moreover, the aspects are designed independently to the application under analysis. Consequently, the possible extension can be done without any modification of the existing metrics or the applications under analysis.
- **It is not necessary to have the code of the application.** In fact, it is possible to incorporate the aspects in the executable file of the applications thanks to the weaver (File *JAR* for example). Thus, the proposed approach allows measuring the attributes that we have not the code.

Perhaps an essential question we must respond in our approach is the feasibility of combining two different programming paradigms in the same project: aspect-oriented programming and multi-agent paradigm. We note that several programming languages support both paradigms. Especially, Java programming language is one of the wide used languages which can be used to develop multi-agent systems [20] and support the aspect-oriented programming [21]. It is important to note that some significant works attempt to develop multi-agent systems using the aspect-oriented programming. This later can be used to modeling, to design or to implement the multi-agent systems [22, 23]. Thus, the characteristics of the agents (such as the autonomy, the learning, the mobility… etc.) are designed as crosscutting concerns which are developed as aspects. By contrast to the development of the characteristics of the multi-agent systems as aspects, Mehmood et al. [24] proposed a framework that separates the performance aspect from the other functional and non-functional aspects.

Finally, we note that the use of aspect-oriented programming to measure the dynamic metrics of the MAS is independent to the approach used to develop it. The only condition to apply this method to measure the dynamic metrics is the ability of the approach used to develop the MAS to support the aspect-oriented programming. Consequently, if we use an agent oriented programming language which is an extension of the object-oriented programming language (such as Java), then we can easily using the aspect-oriented programming to develop the metrics because the most object-oriented programming languages have their extension that support aspect paradigm. Similarly, the platforms developed upon the existing programming languages that support the aspect-oriented programming (like DIMA [13] and JADE [25]) can also support our approach. In the next section, we will present a tool we developed to validate the proposed approach using the DIMA platform [13].

4   A Tool to Measure the Dynamic Metrics

In order to validate the feasibility of our approach, we developed a tool that allows the measurement of some dynamic metrics on well known multi-agent platform, namely DIMA [13]. We choose DIMA because it is a Java-based platform and it offers several advantages. We give a brief presentation of this platform in the next section. Then, we present the dynamic metrics we proposed. In the last section, we will describe how we used the developed tool to measure the proposed metrics of a real case study.

4.1   DIMA Platform

DIMA is a Java multi-agent platform built as an extension of object-oriented programming. The developers of this platform focused on modularity as one of the important software quality's attributes. Hence, this platform allows the development of open and generic agents. The openness is due to the possibility to enrich the agent with only the necessary capabilities. In fact, an agent is designed in this platform as one or more components which reflect its capabilities. For example, communication capability is developed as a separated component which is integrated only in the communicating agent. On the other hand, the generic nature is a consequence of the possibility of developing several agent architectures (reactive, deliberative and hybrid architectures).

The basic brick to build a DIMA agent is the proactive component. In fact, this component specifies the minimal agent capability that makes the difference between agents and the other software components (like objects). As is shown in Fig. 3, this component includes two specific methods: *isAlive()* and *step()*. The *isAlive()* method is used to specify the goal of the agent. By contrast, the *step()* method is used to describe the behaviour of the agent.

The DIMA platform is extended to support the fault-tolerant multi-agent systems through the development of the DIMAX platform [26].

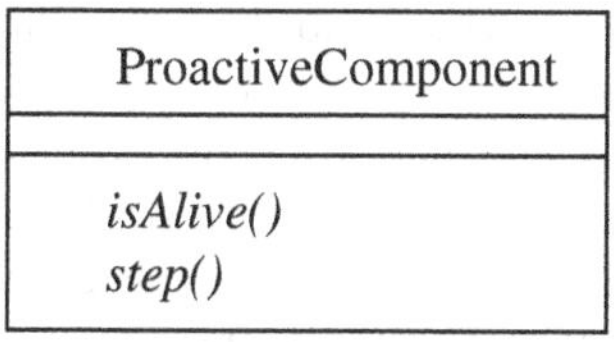

ProactiveComponent
isAlive() *step()*

Fig. 3. The proactive component of the DIMA agent.

4.2 The Proposed Metrics

As it is proposed in our approach, the proposition of metrics is based on the identification of the language constructs proposed by multi-agent platform. Hence, we have studied the DIMA platform in order to identify its specific language constructs. Therefore, the result of this step gave function that executes behaviour (*step* method), a function that specifies the agent's goal (*isAlive* method), the function allows the suspension of the agent's behaviour (*wwait* method) and the function allows the communication between agents (*sendMessage* and *sendAll* method).

The main component of the developed tool is a set of aspects used to capture the execution of the previous identified functions. We used the *AspectJ* [21] language to develop the different aspects because it is Java-based aspect-programming language (compatible with DIMA platform). As an example, Fig. 4 gives a portion of code allowing to capture the execution of *step()* method.

```
public aspect Capture_Step {
   pointcut Capture_Step(BasicReactiveAgent Agent) :
      execution (* *step()) && target(Agent);
   before(BasicReactiveAgent Agent): Capture_Step(Agent){
      // save the event's information
      }
}
```

Fig. 4. Aspect used to capture the execution of the method *step()*.

Finally, the execution trace will be analyzed to calculate the specified metrics. As an example, the developed tool allows the measurement of the following metrics:

- **The Average of Executed Behaviours (AEB):** an agent executes its behaviours in order to achieve its goals. However, the behaviour execution is not *free*. In fact, the agent uses its resources during the execution of its behaviours. Consequently, it is important to know how much the behaviours are executed in order to reach the agent's goals. This metric represents the average number of executed behaviours per agent.
- **The Average of Broken Behaviours (ABB):** the reactivity of an agent represent its ability of to perceive its environment and generate instant responses to possible occurred changes [11]. Consequently, an agent can suspend its current behaviour in order to execute another one. Thanks to this capability, an agent can react to an urgent event or suspend useless behaviour until the emergence of an important event. In both cases, an agent that suspends its current behaviour shows more reactivity. Therefore, we propose the *Average of Broken Behaviour* as a metric of the reactivity of the agent. This metric is calculated as the number of suspended behaviours against all the executed behaviours.

- **The Goal Achievement Acceleration (GAA):** the behaviour execution is not only not free, but it can be also expensive (considering the resources consummation). Sometimes, it would be sensible to cancel a goal that is seen expensive. Consequently, this metric measures the achieved goals according to the executed behaviour or the execution time.
- **The Average Communication Load (ACL):** despite that the communication is a fundamental aspect in multi-agent systems, this process is expensive. Therefore, it is important to limit the communication among agents to the appropriate level. This metric gives the average number of exchanged messages per agent.
- **The Average of Requested Services (ARS):** among the messages exchanged between agents, messages used to request services have special importance. In fact, the agents are autonomous entities. The autonomy means the ability of the agent to operate without the intervention of humans or other agents [11]. Consequently, when an agent requests a service, it means it cannot reach its goal independently. Consequently, the average requested services per executed behaviour.

The developed tool allows the graphical presentation of the calculated metrics.

It is important to note that the proposition of the metrics is outside the scope of this paper. We proposed these metrics only to validate our approach and demonstrate its advantages. It is easy to extend the proposed metrics to support more measurements as we explained above.

We used our tool to measure the above metrics on a real multi-agent system. The next section gives a brief presentation of the case study and the obtained results.

4.3   Case Study

We chose to validate the developed tool on the auction system. This latter is composed of two kinds of agents (*Seller* and *Buyer*) interacting according to the famous *Contract Net* interaction protocol. The goal of this system is to sale products or services. Hence, the seller starts its execution by sending *CFP* (*Call For Proposal*) messages to the buyer agents. Then, it passes to the wait state until the reception of the buyer's answers. When the seller receives the answers of buyers, it evaluates them and sends their answers to the corresponding buyers. The answers of the seller can be accept or reject proposal. The seller must wait the confirmation of the buyer agent before to pass to the final state.

On the other hand, the buyer agent starts its execution by waiting the *CFP* message. When it receives the latter, it evaluates the received message and gives its answers that can be proposal or refuse. Then, the buyer passes to the wait state until the reception of the seller's answer. If the received answer is an accept proposal, then it must send a confirmation and passes to the final state; else it must pass directly to the final state.

The interaction between the different agents composing this system is presented in Fig. 5 using the sequence diagram. Because of the limit space of this paper, it is difficult to present the individual behaviour of each agent.

This system is launched with a seller agent and three buyers (*Buyer1*, *Buyer2* and *Buyer3*). Thanks to *AspectJ* the previous metrics developed as aspects can be woven automatically to the auction system.

For readability reason we present in Table 2 only a part of the execution trace of the case study. This presented table allows to explaining the results presented in the Figs. 6 and 7.

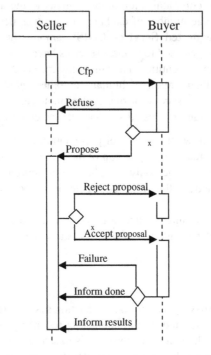

Fig. 5. Sequence diagram of the interaction between Seller and Buyer.

Table 2. A small part of the execution trace.

Time	Event
22	Creation of the agents (Seller, Buyer1, Buyer2 and Buyer3);
24	The *Seller* agent executed *step*() then it send *CFP* to the *Buyer* agents; The *Buyer2* agent executed respectively *step*() then *wwait*();
37	The agent *Buyer2*executed *step*();
38	The *Seller* agent executed *step*() followed by another *step*(); The *Buyer2* agent executed *step*(); followed by *wwait*();
39	The *Seller* agent executed *step*(); followed by *step*();
52	The *Buyer2* agent executed *step*(); The end of the execution.

Figure 6 shows the *Average of Requested Service (ARS)* metric of the seller agent. Known that this metric represent the number of requested services per executed behaviour, we can remark that this agent starts its first behaviour by sending **CFP** message in time 24 s. Hence, the result metric becomes 1. However, during its execution, this agent executed other behaviours (in times 38, 38, 39 and 39 s) without sending any request for service. Consequently, the result of the *Average of Requested Services* metric decreases progressively (respectively to 0.5, 0.33, 0.25 and finally 0.20).

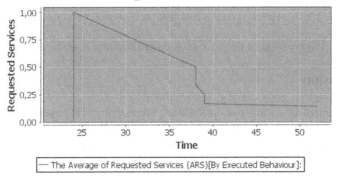

Fig. 6. The evolution of the *Average of Requested Service* metric of the *Seller* agent.

Known that the *Average of Broken Behaviours* (ABB) metric is calculated as the number of *wwait*() execution compared to the step() execution, we can explain the results of this metric applied on Buyer2 agent (Fig. 7). After its creation, the *Buyer2* agent executed in time 24 *step*() followed by *wwait*() in the same time. Consequently, the value of ABB metric became 1. In the time 37, the agent *Buyer2* executed *step*(), and its ABB metric became 0.5 = 1/2. Then, the agent Buyer2 executed *step*() followed by *wwait*() in time 38. Thus, the *Average of Broken Behaviours* metric became 0.33 = 1/3 followed by the value 0.66 = 2/3. Finally, the *Average of Broken Behaviours* metric became 0.5 = 2/4 because the execution of the *step*() by the agent *Buyer2* in time 52.

This case study clarifies and demonstrates the advantages of our approach. First, the reusability characteristic is obvious, because the aspects are not designed for this example. So, we can consider the use of these aspects in this example as a reusable attribute. We can reuse these aspects with other examples too. Second, the aspects are designed independent from each other. Hence, we can extend these metrics by other ones. Finally, once we identify the joint point and we develop the aspects, the approach became very simple because the weaver integrates the aspect automatically to the MAS.

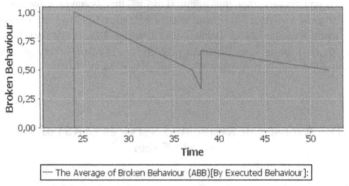

Fig. 7. The evolution of the *Average of Broken Behaviours* of the agent *Buyer2*.

5   Conclusion

The measurement is a vital task in software engineering. However, it is difficult to measure objectively the software attributes. This difficulty increases when we want to measure the dynamic attributes. We think that the measurement method must provide some characteristics like, the simplicity, the reusability, the extensibility. In this paper, we propose an approach to measure the dynamic metrics of multi-agent systems using the aspect-oriented programming. Our approach is applied to DIMA multi-agent platform thanks to a tool we developed.

The use of the aspect-oriented programming to measure the dynamic metrics of multi-agent systems provides several advantages. First of all, the metrics are developed independently to the system under analysis (as aspects) which allows reusing. Secondly, it is easy to extend the proposed metrics to measure more attributes because the metrics are independent between them on the one hand and independent to the application under analysis on the other hand. Moreover, it is simple to use the proposed approach because it is fully automatic. Finally, the proposed approach can be applied even if we have not the code of the application under analysis.

In order to ensure an objective evaluation of the system under analysis, we recommended the optimization of the aspects' code. We think that heavy code (with important execution time) can influence negatively on the normal execution of the system under analysis. Consequently, we propose as future works to study the impact of the application of our approach on the multi-agent execution. Moreover, we propose to extend our tool to support more multi-agent platforms.

References

1. Jones, C.: Applied Software Measurement - Global Analysis of Productivity and Quality. Third edn., The McGraw-Hill (2008)

2. Laird, L.M., Brennan, M.C.: Software Measurement and Estimation A Practical Approach. Wiley, New York (2006)
3. ISO: ISO/IEC 9126-1 Software Engineering – Product Quality – Part 1: Quality Model, International Organization for Standardization, Geneva, Switzerland (2001)
4. Chhabra, J.K., Gupta, V.: A survey of dynamic software metrics. J. Comput. Sci. Technol. 25(5), 1016–1029 (2010). doi:10.1007/s11390-010-1080-9
5. Dufour, B., Driesen, K., Hendren, L., Verbrugge, C.: Dynamic Metrics for Java. In: Proceedings of the 18th Annual ACM SIGPLAN Conference on Object-Oriented Programming, Systems, Languages, and Applications (OOPSLA 2003), pp. 149–168. ACM, New York (2003)
6. Tahir, A., Ahmad, R., Kasirun, K.M.: Maintainability dynamic metrics data collection based on aspect-oriented technology. Malays. J. Comput. Sci. 23(3), 177 (2010)
7. Chidamber, S.R., Kemerer, C.F.: A metrics suite for object oriented design. IEEE Trans. Softw. Eng. 20(6), 476–493 (1994)
8. Zakaria, A., Hosny, H.: Metrics for aspect-oriented software design. In: Workshop on Aspect-Oriented Modeling, Boston, (2003)
9. Sivakumar, N., Vivekanandan, K.: Measures for testing the reactivity property of a software agent. Int. J. Adv. Res. Artif. Intell. 1(9), 26–33 (2012)
10. Mahar, S., Bhatia, P.K.: Measuring the intelligence of software agent. Int. J. Innovative Sci. Eng. Technol. 1(6), 1–11 (2014)
11. Wooldridge, M.: An Introduction to Multi Agent Systems. Wiley, Chichester (2009)
12. Kiczales, G., Lamping, J., Mendhekar, A., Maeda, C., Lopes, C., Loingtier, J.M., Irwin, J.: Aspect-oriented programming. In: Akşit, E., Matsuoka, S. (eds.) ECOOP'97 — Object-Oriented Programming, pp. 220–242. Springer, Heidelberg (1997). doi:10.1007/BFb0053381
13. Guessoum, Z.: Modèles et Architectures d'Agents et de Systèmes Multi-Agents Adaptatifs, Dossier d'Habilitation à Diriger les Recherches, Université Pierre et Marie Curie (2003)
14. Lass, R.N., Sultanik, E.A., Regli, W.C.: Metrics for multiagent systems. In: Madhavan, R., Messina, E., Tunstel, E. (eds.) Performance Evaluation and Benchmarking of Intelligent Systems, pp. 1–19. Springer, Heidelberg (2009)
15. Basili, V., Caldiera, G., Rombach, H.: The goal question metric approach. Encycl. Softw. Eng. 1, 528–532 (1994)
16. Knuth, D.E.: An empirical study of FORTRAN programs. Softw. Pract. Experience 1(2), 105–133 (1971)
17. Doan Van Bien, D., Lillis, D., Collier, R.W.: Call graph profiling for multi agent systems. In: Dastani, M., El Fallah Segrouchni, A., Leite, J., Torroni, P. (eds.) LADS 2009. LNCS, vol. 6039, pp. 153–167. Springer, Heidelberg (2010)
18. Doan Van Bien, D., Lillis, D., Collier, R.W.: Space-time diagram generation for profiling multi agent systems. In: Braubach, L., Briot, J.P., Thangarajah, J. (eds.) ProMAS 2009. LNCS, vol. 5919, pp. 170–184. Springer, Heidelberg (2010)
19. Dimou, C., Symeonidis, A.L., Mitkas, P.A.: An integrated infrastructure for monitoring and evaluating agent-based systems. Expert Syst. Appl. 36(4), 7630–7643 (2009)
20. Bordini, R.H., Dastani, M., Dix, J., Seghrouchni, A.F. (eds.): Multi-Agent Programming Languages: Tools and Applications. Springer, New York (2005)
21. Laddad, R.: AspectJ in Action. Manning Publications, Greenwich (2003)
22. Garcia, A., Kulesza, U., Sant'Anna, C., Chavez, C., de Lucena, C.J.P.: Aspects in agent-oriented software engineering: lessons learned. In: Müller, J.P., Zambonelli, F. (eds.) AOSE 2005. LNCS, vol. 3950, pp. 231–247. Springer, Heidelberg (2006)

23. Garcia, A., Chavez, C., Choren, R.: An aspect-oriented modeling framework for multi-agent systems design. In: Padgham, L., Zambonelli, F. (eds.) AOSE VII / AOSE 2006. LNCS, vol. 4405, pp. 35–50. Springer, Heidelberg (2007)

24. T. Mehmood, N. Ashraf, K. Rasheed and S. Rehman.: Framework for modeling performance in multi-agent systems (MAS) using aspect oriented programming (AOP). In: The Sixth Australasian Workshop on Software and System Architectures (AWSA 2005), pp 40–45. Brisbane, Australia (2005)

25. The Official JADE site web. http://jade.tilab.com/

26. Faci, N., Guessoum, Z., Marin, O.: DimaX: a fault-tolerant multi-agent platform. In: Proceedings of the 2006 International Workshop on Software Engineering for Large-Scale Multi-Agent Systems, SELMAS 2006. ACM, New York (2006)

DeCoF: A Decentralized Coordination Framework for Various Multi-Agent Systems

Thomas Preisler[✉], Tim Dethlefs, and Wolfgang Renz

Multimedia Systems Laboratory, Faculty of Engineering and Computer Science,
Hamburg University of Applied Sciences, Berliner Tor 7, 20099 Hamburg, Germany
{thomas.preisler,tim.dethlefs,wolfgang.renz}@haw-hamburg.de

Abstract. A key requirement to realize modern distributed systems is the ability to adapt the system's behavior autonomously at runtime towards changing environmental conditions, in order to preserve their operation even in the presence of uncertain changes. The different parts of such a distributed self-organizing system have to be coordinated in order to achieve meaningful adaptations. To avoid single point of failures, decentralized coordination is a key element for the realization of robust and scalable self-adaptation. Due to their inherently decentralized system architecture Multi-Agent Systems (MAS) are well suited to realize such self-organizing systems relying on decentralized coordination. This paper proposes a decentralized coordination framework which focuses on equipping different types of MAS with self-organizing capabilities. Thereby, it shall support various types of MAS so that developers are not limited to a specific platform, while also supporting the coordination of applications consisting out of different, heterogeneous (Multi-Agent) technologies, e.g. required in the area of co-simulations.

Keywords: Decentralized coordination · Self-organizing systems · Multi-Agent Systems

1 Introduction

Current distributed software systems are characterized by an increasing size and complexity and have to be able to adapt their behavior to changing environmental conditions to preserve their operation. Thereby, they have to face uncertain changes like resource fluctuation, new user needs, intrusions, and faults, while also having to deal with the satisfaction of non-functional requirements like robustness, availability, and scalability. This challenges traditional software engineering and operation approaches substantially. Therefore, the management of this complexity has drawn attention towards systems that are able to maintain themselves automatically. Such systems have been described with terms as self-healing, self-protecting, self-optimizing, self-configuring etc. Collectively they are referred to as self-* properties [3]. According to [25] approaches dealing with these properties can be mapped to two different classes. Approaches using centralized control concepts, belong to the class of self-adaptive systems, while

© Springer International Publishing Switzerland 2016
M. Klusch et al. (Eds.): MATES 2016, LNAI 9872, pp. 73–88, 2016.
DOI: 10.1007/978-3-319-45889-2_6

approaches relying on decentralized control concepts, distributed feedback loops, and coordination mechanisms belong to the class of self-organizing systems. Due to their decentralized system architecture, they seem to be better suited to deal with the afore-mentioned non-functional requirements [30].

Due to their inherently decentralized system architecture Multi-Agent Systems (MAS) are well suited to realize self-organizing systems [8]. Thereby, the realization of decentralized coordination or control concepts is the core challenge when developing such systems [22]. According to [22], it requires a systematic development approach that copes with three inherent characteristics of these systems: (1) non-linear dynamics, (2) stochastic behavior and (3) emergent phenomena. The approach presented in this paper builds upon an already established approach for engineering and operating self-organizing MAS [27], that has been implemented for the *Jadex* agent platform [18], and extends it in order to realize a general decentralized coordination framework, that supports various types of MAS and even heterogeneous systems consisting out of multiple different agent frameworks respectively platforms.

An example for a subject with a combination of different MAS and even systems that do not rely on agent-technologies is *co-simulation*. Co-simulation is a prominent method to solve multi-physics problems. Such simulations combine well-established and specialized simulation tools for different fields [26]. Thereby, different subsystems forming a coupled problem are modeled and simulated in a distributed manner. As the modeling is done on the subsystem level without having the coupled problem in mind, the execution of these different subsystems has to be coordinated. Thereby, two different use cases requiring coordination arise. First, the coordination of different simulated entities within a co-simulation, e.g. different agent types running on different agent platforms, and second, the coordination of different sub-systems, e.g. two different MAS, of the co-simulation system. This can be summarized as coordination *within* MAS and the coordination *of* MAS. The decentralized coordination framework presented in this paper aims at offering a generalized solution that supports both use cases.

The remainder of this paper is structured as follows: Sect. 2 gives a short overview about related work. In Sect. 3 the architecture and design of the proposed coordination framework is described, before Sect. 4 presents two implementation examples for different agent platforms. Finally, Sect. 5 concludes the paper.

2   Related Work

There are several approaches which deal with the challenges of developing self-adaptive and self-organizing systems. Research areas like Autonomic [11] or Organic Computing [4] provide approaches to address the challenges in a systematic fashion. Both approaches rely on different types of feedback loops based on (usually) centralized control elements. According to [5] feedback loops are a key design element within a distributed system in order to be able to exhibit adaptivity. Feedback loops normally consist of three main components: (1) Sensors are in charge of observing the behavior and the (current) status of the component, resp. the environment it is situated in. (2) Actuators can change the configuration of the system, which can lead to changes in the component's behavior. (3) A computing entity serves as a connector between the system input (sensor) and the output (actuator). It can be very different with regards to its internal architecture and abilities (cf. [13]). The importance of decentralized control to achieve requirements like resilience, robustness and scalability in large distributed systems has been identified in [32]. The authors distinguish decentralized self-adaptive solutions from their centralized counterparts and also proof some of the key research challenges for the realization of decentralized self-adaptation. Overall decentralized coordination for adaptive applications is a wide spread area, with several applications and approaches on how to coordinate distributed systems. In the following, some of these approaches are presented and compared to the approach presented in this paper (cf. Table 1).

For instance, [15] presents a self-organizing infrastructure that offers coordination capabilities, inspired by chemical reactions utilizing the *TuCSoN* coordination space concept. It relies on a multiplicity of independent communication abstractions, called tuple centers. These can be spread over internet nodes and are used by agents to interact with each other. TuCSoN exploits tuple centers as its coordination media, where a tuple center enhances a tuple space with a behavior specification. Therefore, the tuple centers are a communication abstraction whose behavior can be defined to embed an overall law of coordination. This is similar to the approach presented in this paper which utilizes coordination media as communication abstractions. The approach also propagates a clean separation of concerns between application and coordination logic as introduced by [9]. The authors of [9] propagate a loose coupling between the core functionality of an application (computation) and the coordination. Thereby coordination is an orthogonal aspect w.r.t. to the computation when it comes to the realization of distributed systems. According to [9] this increases the generality when the coordination is swapped in a separate model. The authors of [7] picked up this idea and identified a separation between the core functionality and the coordination logic as desirable for the development of self-adaptive systems.

In [10] another tuple space oriented approach for decentralized coordination is presented. *DTuples* is a peer-to-peer tuple space middleware built on top of a distributed hash table (DHT). The approach aims at combining the advantages of peer-to-peer systems with the tuple space model firstly introduced in *Linda* [1]. Since a standard tuple space model like Linda is based on a central space for communication and coordination, it has to deal with problems like single point of failure and scalability issues. Peer-to-peer systems overcome these issues as they are based on a decentralized approach, but most of them lack coordination primitives like given in tuple spaces. Therefore, [10] combines the advantages from DHTs and tuple spaces.

A different approach is presented in [24]. According to the presented *Agents and Artifacts (A&A)* meta-model a MAS consists of agents and so called artifacts. These represent elements of the environment which can be used by the agents. For the purpose of coordination via artifacts, specific coordination artifacts can be devised. Such artifacts can include blackboards similar to the mentioned tuple spaces, maps or task schedulers. A&A expects the agents to explicitly use the artifacts for coordination. This implicates that coordination is not brought transparently to the agents. Therefore, coordination has to be part of the application's functional system. The work on the A&A metamodel has been extended in [23] where the notion of environment programming in MAS was introduced and a concrete computation and programming model based on the artifact abstraction was described with the *CArtAgO* framework.

Table 1. Comparison of on different decentralized coordination approaches.

Approach	Separation of concerns	Specific agent frameworks	Coordination description	Coordination model
TuCSoN	Yes	No	Programmatic	Tuple space
DTuples	Yes	No	Programmatic	Tuple space
CArtAgO (A&A)	No	No	Programmatic	Coordination artifacts
SCEL	No	No	Programmatic	Programming abstractions
DeCoMAS	Yes	Yes (Jadex [18])	Declarative	Coordination mechanisms
DeCoF	Yes	No	Declarative	Coordination mechanisms

A formal approach for the programming of autonomic systems is presented in [16] with the introduction of the *Software Component Ensemble Language* (SCEL). It proposes a set of programming abstractions to represent behaviors, knowledge and aggregations according to specific policies and supports programming context- and self-awareness as well as adaptation. Besides the set of linguistic abstractions, it also provides a Java implementation. Contrasting to the approach presented in this paper, the adaptive behavior is described in a programmatic way instead of using declarative terms. Also it does not encourage a separation of concerns between the application and coordination logic.

The approach presented in this paper is based on a tailored programming model for the software-technical utilization of coordination mechanisms as reusable design elements in MAS to realize self-organizing systems [29]. The programming model provides a systematic modeling and configuration language called *MASDynamics* to describe decentralized coordination mechanisms in a declarative way, as well as a reference architecture and implementation to enable the enactment of pre-described coordination models for the Jadex agent platform [18] called *DeCoMAS* [27]. This approach has been extended recently (cf. [20]) in order to provide a middleware for constructing decentralized control in self-organizing systems that are based on the concept of *Active Components* [17]. The approach presented in this paper picks up the concepts from [27] and extends them, so that distributed systems in general are supported rather than a specific agent-platform.

Table 1 lists and compares the related approaches presented in this section as well as the framework (*DeCoF*) presented in this paper. The approaches are compared w.r.t. the separation of concerns between application and coordination logic as introduced by [9] and whether or not their applicability is limited to a specific agent framework or if they support distributed systems in general. Also additional information is given about the type of the coordination description and the used coordination model.

3 Design and Architecture

The design of the Decentralized Coordination Framework (*DeCoF*) is based on the concept that the self-organizing dynamic that causes a system to adapt to external and internal influences is mapped by decentralized coordination processes. The processes describe the self-organizing behavior that continuously structures, adapts and regulates aspects of the application. Thereby, they instruct a set of decentralized coordination media and coordination endpoints. Coordination media deal with the interactions between the components (information propagation), while the coordination endpoints handle the adaptation of the components (local entity adaptation). Together, they control the microscopic activities of the components, that lead to the manifestation of the intended self-organization dynamic on a macroscopic level. The integration of coordination media and endpoints is described by declarative defined coordination processes that structure and instruct their operations. The connection between described self-organizing dynamic and the coordination processes is depict in Fig. 1.

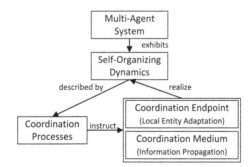

Fig. 1. Self-organizing dynamic of a MAS based on coordination processes following [28].

The DeCoF emerges from a tailored programming model for the software-technical utilization of coordination processes as reusable design elements in MAS. The DeCoMAS (Decentralized Coordination for Multi-Agent Systems) [27] architecture introduced concepts like coordination media for the propagation of coordination information and coordination endpoints for the observation and adaptation of the local entities. But while the DeCoMAS architecture was especially designed to equip BDI-agent systems with coordination processes and therefore, is limited to such, the DeCoF supports distributed systems in general. By that, different and heterogeneous software components in general as well as heterogeneous agent systems in particular are supported. Allowing to equip such systems with decentralized coordination processes in order to extend them with self-organizing capabilities.

Figure 2 shows the conceptual architecture of the proposed framework. Components resp. agents that should be equipped with coordination capabilities to realize self-organizing behavior based on the aforementioned concepts are labeled as *Coordinatable Components*. As the framework aims at supporting various types of MAS resp. distributed systems in general, there are no inherent characteristics that could be used to monitor or control the behavior of the agents resp. components, e.g. different types of MAS use different scheduling and life-cycle mechanisms, while component-based systems might lack them at all. Therefore, the concept of *Coordination Events* is introduced. These are events that are fired by a coordinatable component, whenever something relevant for the coordination happened inside the component. A coordination event (ce) is a tuple with the length 2 (double or 2-tuple) containing contextual data about the specific coordination event (cd) as well as a representation of the event's originator (eo). A coordination event is thus defined as: $ce = (cd, eo)$.

Following a separation of concerns between the application and the coordination logic as propagated by [9], the actual processing of the coordination events is handled by a related *Coordination Endpoint* (cf. Fig. 1). The coordination endpoints are loosely coupled to the coordinatable component via a so called *Coordination Event Bus*. An event bus[1] allows publish-subscribe-style communication between components without requiring the components to explicitly register with one another (and thus be aware of each others). The separation of concerns requirement is fulfilled by the loosely coupling between the coordinatable component and the coordination endpoint realized by the coordination event bus. Thus, the component is only responsible for realizing the application logic and do not need to have knowledge about (the present of) the coordination endpoint.

When a coordinatable component fires a coordination event, it is received by the related coordination endpoint via the coordination event bus. The endpoint then processes the event according to a prescribed coordination process definition. The process definitions defines how different coordination events have to handled by the endpoints. These descriptions contain instructions on *how* to distribute the coordination event to *which* other coordinatable components. The *how* is described by indicating what kind of *coordination medium* should be used

---

[1] See: https://www.github.com/google/guava/wiki/EventBusExplained (accessed April 11, 2016).

for the information dissemination. As described before, coordination media deal with the information propagation among the components (cf. Fig. 1). The *which* is realized with a role-concept. A coordination process definition specifies various roles that components might adopt. Thereby, a component can have multiple roles and a role may be carried out by various component types. So to process a coordination event the endpoint encapsulates it and enriches it with additional information about the originating coordination endpoint. The resulting *Coordination Information* (ci) is a 2-tuple containing the coordination event (ce) and information about the originating endpoint (oe), thus is defined as: $ci = (ce, oe)$. Besides prescribing which coordination event, originating from which coordinatable components should be published to which other components, a coordination process definition also prescribes which type of coordination event should be triggered in the receiving components. How the coordination information are actually propagated is part of the implementation of the actual coordination medium. This regards the technical realization of how the information should be distributed, as well as how the subset of receivers is selected. Therefore, simple coordination medium relying on a network-topology for the information dissemination as well as complex ones, where the dissemination of the information relies on, e.g. diffusion processes in an (virtual) environment are possible.

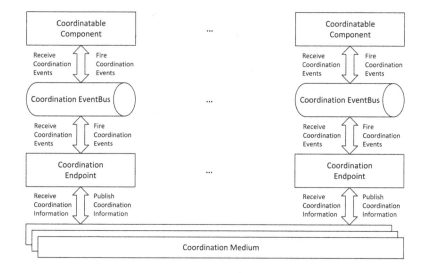

Fig. 2. Architecture of the decentralized coordination framework

The UML class diagram of the framework's relevant classes and interfaces is depicted in Fig. 3. A component resp. agent that should be equipped with coordination capabilities has to implement the `ICoordinatable` interface. It requires the component or agent to implement two methods. The `getId` function returns an unique string identifying the component. The `handleCoordinationEvent` method is called whenever a relevant coordination event has been received by its coordination endpoint. Here the component-specific coordination event handling, that specifies how the component behaves upon receiving a specific coordination event has to be implemented. Also, a coordination endpoint has to be created for each component. The framework provides a helper function that creates a coordination endpoint and connects it to the component via a coordination event bus. Additionally, the framework provides a ready-to-use implementation of the `CoordinationEndpoint` class as well as a generic implementation of the `CoordinationInformation` class. Abstract super classes exist for the `CoordinationMedium` and `CoordinationEvent` implementation. Thus, the methodology for equipping an application with self-organizing behavior based on decentralized coordination processes with DeCoF consists of the following steps:

1. Writing declarative coordination process description that instructs the coordination endpoints and media. The framework supports this step by providing an XML-based coordination language and an according mapping to Java-classes that are automatically processed by the ready-to-use implementation of the `CoordinationEndpoint`
2. Implementing the `ICoordinatable` interface for the components resp. agents that should be coordinated, by writing the `getId` and `handleCoordination Event` methods.
3. Identifying the relevant coordination events and implementing them using the abstract `CoordinationEvent` super class. The `CoordinationEndpoint` will automatically observe the component/agent and process the events when they occur.
4. Implementing the coordination logic for the information propagation by extending the abstract `CoordinationMedium` super class. Here the application dependent coordination logic is to be realized, e.g., based on a network-topology or diffusion processes in an virtual environment.

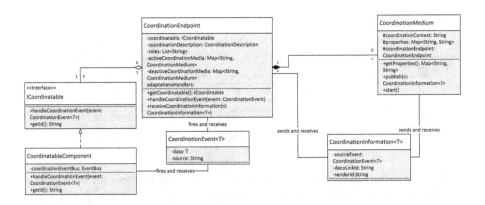

Fig. 3. UML class diagram of the decentralized coordination framework

4   Implementation Examples

The main reason for the development of the DeCoF was to provide a coordination framework for different types of MAS. Therefore, the framework was designed to be able to be used in conjunction with different agent platforms. This section provides two different examples on the technical integration and usage of the framework. The first one shows the usage in combination with the widely-spread *Java Agent DEvelopment Framework* (JADE) [2] and the second one shows the application for the agent-based logistics simulator *RinSim* [12].

4.1   Jade: Party

This example continues the *Jade Party*[2] scenario where a host sets a party to which a number of agents are invited. The sequence of the scenario is as follows: When the party starts, the host agent creates N guests agents, these guests report their arrival by sending an *hello* message to the host. The host selects one guest randomly, and tells it a *rumor*. Then the host selects randomly two other guests and *introduces* them to each other. The party proceeds as follows: Each guest that is introduced to someone asks the host to introduce them to another random guest. If a guest has someone introduce themselves, and the guests knows the rumor, they tell the other guest. When a guest hears the rumor for the first time, they notify the host. When all guests have heard the rumor, the party ends.

The original example implementation uses *FIPA*[3] messages to realize the agent interactions. In order to demonstrate the usage of the DeCoF in combination with Jade, the message-based interactions were replaced by three coordination processes. These coordination processes map the interactions between a guest and the host (1), between the host and a guest (2), and among two guests (3). As described in Sect. 3, the coordination process description is based on a role-concept, thus two different roles were introduced for the host and the guests. Furthermore, the ICoordinatable interface had to be implemented for both agent types and they had to be equipped with a coordination endpoint. Also the XML-based coordination process description for instructing the operations of the coordination endpoints had to be written. Figure 4 depicts a visual representation of the three coordination processes. When a guest agent wants to be introduced to another guest, arrives at the party, or hears the rumor for the first time it causes an according coordination event. The event is processed by the coordination endpoint and the coordination medium described in the coordination process description is used to distribute the coordination information. Accordingly, for the second coordination process, when the host agent introduces a guest to another guest, tells a rumor to a guest, or tells a guest to leave the party coordination events are caused by the host agent (cf. Fig. 4). The third coordination process maps the interactions among the guests: A guest greeting another

---

[2] See: http://jade.tilab.com/documentation/examples/party/ (accessed April 11, 2016.

[3] http://www.fipa.org/ (accessed April 11, 2016).

guest, or telling the rumor to another guest. In this example all three coordination processes use a coordination medium based on the *Apache ActiveMQ*[4] message broker. Thus, resulting in an infrastructure where a topic is created for each coordination endpoint and coordination information are distributed by publishing them to the receiver's topic. This example shows how different technologies (in this case the Jade agent platform and the Apache ActiveMQ message broker) can be combined using DeCoF to meet requirements that may arise from the realization of distributed, heterogeneous, and scalable applications. As described in Sect. 3, whenever a coordination endpoint receives a coordination information it unwraps the encapsulated coordination event and publishes it to the component respectively agent over the `handleCoordinationEvent` method of the `ICoordinatable` interface. How the agent processes the received coordination event is part of this method. When using an agent framework with specific life-cycle management and scheduling mechanism the processing has to be scheduled accordingly to the framework's standards. For the Jade example the processing of a receiving coordination event is carried out by adding a Jade-specific `OneShotBehaviour` to the agent, so that the Jade framework can schedule and execute it accordingly.

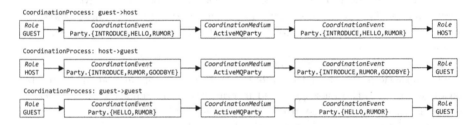

Fig. 4. Visual representation of the coordination processes for the Jade Party example

4.2   RinSim: Bike-Sharing Simulation

Recent challenges like climate changes, declining supplies of fossil fuels, noise emissions and congestion lead to discussions about individual means of transportation in urban areas. Especially bicycles (bikes in the following) have received an increased attention in city transportation, as they offer a healthy and environment-friendly way of transportation and allow to reach areas in cities that do not have direct access to public transportation. Combined with technical improvements of the underlying information systems, this results in a rapid extension of bike-sharing systems worldwide [31]. Information systems are very important for this increasing success, as they support the whole renting process (finding available bikes in the departure area as well as renting and returning them) [6]. Today, many cities aim at implementing bike-sharing systems in order

---

[4] http://activemq.apache.org/ (accessed April 11, 2016).

to improve inner-city air quality and to reduce congestion [14]. The main challenge for the operation of modern bike-sharing systems in big cities is to ensure the *availability* of bikes at the stations. In rush-hour situations, stations may run out of bikes while others become full, thus reducing the overall *reliability* of the systems. Therefore, the planning and operation of redistribution attempts is essential to ensure reliability and user satisfaction. A possible solution to improve the availability of bikes at the stations is described in [19]. There, an incentive scheme was explored that encourages the users of a bike-sharing system to approach nearby stations for renting or returning bikes in order to redistribute them in a self-organized fashion. The microscopic simulation of the actual bike-sharing system is based on data taken from Washington, D.C. (2014). From these data, stochastic parameters like the rush of users for a station given as a function over time were determined. The simulation is realized using *RinSim* [12], an agent-based logistics simulator.

The redistribution approach proposed in [19] is based on the concept that whenever a user tries to rent a bike at an empty station, an alternative rental station with a sufficient amount of bikes is suggested to the user. Analogous, whenever an user tries to return a bike at a full or critical occupied station, an alternative return station with a sufficient amount of free docks is suggested to the user. Thus, the distribution of bikes among the stations will be balanced in a self-organizing way, as users renting a bike are detoured from empty stations to preferably full or critical occupied ones or at least non-empty ones.

This concept has been taken up to realize a decentralized coordination approach using the DeCoF. A decentralized coordination process is used to calculate the alternative rent and return stations that are suggested to the users. Bike stations periodically send their current occupancy rate to all other bike stations within a certain circular communication range. Stations receiving such status updates from other stations collect them and use them to calculate alternative rent and return stations. Whenever such status updates are received, the receiving bike station determines the station with the lowest and the highest occupancy rate from the list of stations. The station with the lowest occupancy rate is selected as the alternative return station and the station with the highest occupancy rate is selected as the alternative rent station. The bike stations realized as RinSim agents, implement the `ICoordinatable` interface and are equipped with a coordination endpoint. Every minute of the simulated time they cause a bike station status update coordination event which contains their current occupancy rate. The according coordination endpoint publishes this as part of a coordination information over a `RoadBasedCoordinationMedium`. This medium extends the abstract `CoordinationMedium` super class with RinSim specific coordination logic. Therefore, it has a reference to the simulator's road model, so it has knowledge about the simulation environment and the position of all the bike stations. The circular communication range is a configurable coordination parameter of the medium. Based on the road model, the medium selects all bike stations within the communication range and publishes the coordination information to their according coordination endpoints. When receiving such coordination information the endpoints trigger a bikestation status update event in the coordinatable bike stations and thus, initialize the calculation of the alternative rental and return stations. The visual representation of this coordination process is depict in Fig. 5.

Fig. 5. Visual representation of the coordination process for the RinSim Bike-Sharing example

A typical Monday was examined in order to simulate Washington D.C.'s bike-sharing system and to evaluate the impact of the proposed coordination strategy. Therefore, the trip history data of all Mondays (except holidays) from 2014 provided by Capital Bikeshare (the system's operator) was analyzed. To do so, the day was divided into 24 time slices. For each of these 24 time slices the departure probabilities q and the dependent destination probabilities q for the bike-stations were calculated based on the ventured trips: The departure probability p_A for a station A is denoted by

$$p_A = \frac{n_A}{N},$$

with n_A as the number of all trips started at station A while N is the total number of trips. The dependent destination probability q_B is denoted by

$$q_B = \frac{d_B}{D_A}.$$

It is characterized by the fraction of numbers of departures to station B from station A denoted as d_B and the total number of departures from station A denoted as D_A. The simulated scenario starts at 12 a.m. In order to simulate the different rush at different times of the day, the mean total number of trips for each of the 24 h of the day was determined based on the trip history data. During the execution the simulator generates the number of cyclist agents specified by the rush equally distributed for the currently simulated time slice. As a simplification, all cyclists move with a constant speed along the graph-based road model. In order to find a route from the departure to the destination stations, they use a shortest path approach and traverse the edges of the graph road model, considering the edge weight as the distance to the next node. The simulation was configured to allow an overcrowding of bike stations, when no free docks are available. If a cyclist agent tries to rent a bike at and empty station, this incident is reported and the total number of rides that did not take place is returned as part of the simulation results for evaluation purposes. In order to map the road model of Washington, D.C., the corresponding area was extracted from OpenStreepMap[5]

---

[5] https://www.openstreetmap.org/ (accessed June 15, 2016).

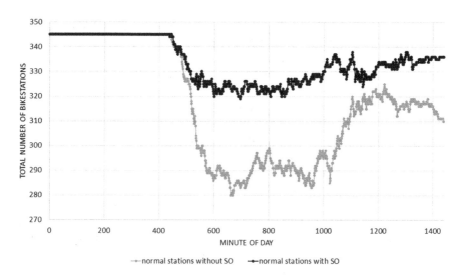

Fig. 6. Results of the bike-sharing simulation with and without self-organizing redistribution of bikes.

and transformed into the graph-based road model supported by RinSim. During the scenario the cyclists moved with a constant speed of 18 km/h and all bike stations had a maximum number 20 docks, whereof 10 were initially occupied.

Figure 6 shows and compares the results of a simulation scenario with no self-organizing redistribution of bikes with one where a communication range of 3 km was used as coordination parameter. In this example it was assumed that an user always follows a proposed detour when renting or return a bike (further studies on the impact of this cooperativeness rate were conducted in [19]). The figure depicts the number of stations that are in a normal state (neither full nor empty) for both scenarios. It is observable for both cases, how the number of normal stations declines with the morning rush-hour beginning at around 7 a.m. (minute 420). Over the day, these numbers fluctuate only a little. In the late afternoon (around minute 1000) the number of normal stations recovers a bit. This behavior can be explained by the rush-hour movements of commuters. The figure gives a first impression about how the self-organizing redistribution of bikes improves the number of normal stations over the whole day. It shows that a maximum deviation of 10,7 % can be achieved. This means that about 10 % more of the total amount of stations are in the normal state in comparison to the scenario with no self-organizing behavior. Additionally, this results in decreasing the number of stations that are empty or full/overflown by about 55 %. The self-organizing behavior in this study emerges from interaction between the decentralized coordination process and the cooperativeness of the users. Thereby, the coordination process is responsible for dissemination of the required coordination information (the occupancy rate of the bikestations). The coordination logic consists of the selection of the bikestations that are within the reach and in the algorithm used by the bikestations to determine the alternative rent and return stations. A relevant parameter for the coordination is the communication range which affects the number of possible detours. The coordination is brought transparently to the application, as the application logic does not necessary require the coordination efforts in order to function.

5   Conclusion and Future Work

In this paper we presented a decentralized coordination framework to equip various MAS with self-organizing capabilities. It is based on the concept that the self-organizing dynamic that causes the system to adapt to external and internal influences is mapped by decentralized coordination processes. These processes describe the self-organizing behavior that continuously structures, adapts and regulates aspects of the application. These processes instruct a set of decentralized coordination media (information propagation) and coordination endpoints (local entity adaptation). Thereby, the proposed framework aims at supporting not only specific agent-systems but distributed systems in general, allowing to realize systems that combine different agent-frameworks and technologies like, e.g. required for the realization of co-simulation systems. The usage of the framework was shown based on two examples. The first one showed the usage in combination with the wide spread *Jade* agent platform, utilizing an already existing example from the Jade library where the interactions of a host of a party and his guests were modeled as coordination processes. The second example was implemented for *RinSim* an agent-based logistics simulator. It picked up previous experiments on self-organizing redistribution strategies for bike-sharing systems. Thereby, a coordination process was realized allowing bike-stations to coordinate the movement of the users by proposing near-by alternative rent and return stations to them, in case the stations are empty or full. Thus, utilizing the users to redistribute the bikes in self-organizing fashion. A microscopic simulation of a idealized Monday based on trip history data taken from Washington D.C.'s bike-sharing system was conducted to measure the impact of the strategy.

Future work will deal with the utilization of the proposed framework in the *GEWISS* [21] project, where a co-simulation system will be realized to provide a geographical heat information and simulation system, that shall provide a planning and simulation tool for the interlinking of urban development and district heat network development to support the political decision making process in the City of Hamburg.

References

1. Ahuja, S., Carriero, N., Gelernter, D.: Linda and friends. Computer **19**(8), 26–34 (1986)
2. Bellifemine, F., Poggi, A., Rimassa, G.: Jade-a fipa-compliant agent framework. In: Proceedings of PAAM, London, vol. 99, p. 33 (1999)
3. Berns, A., Ghosh, S.: Dissecting self-* properties. In: Third IEEE International Conference on Self-Adaptive and Self-Organizing Systems, SASO 2009, pp. 10–19 (2009)

4. Branke, J., Mnif, M., Müller-Schloer, C., Prothmann, H., Richter, U., Rochner, F., Schmeck, H.: Organic computing - addressing complexity by controlled self-organization. In: Proceedings of the 2nd International Symposium on Leveraging Applications of Formal Methods, Verification and Validation, ISOLA 2006, pp. 185–191. IEEE Computer Society (2006)

5. Brun, Y., Di Marzo Serugendo, G., Gacek, C., Giese, H., Kienle, H., Litoiu, M., Müller, H., Pezzè, M., Shaw, M.: Engineering self-adaptive systems through feedback loops. In: Cheng, B.H.C., Lemos, R., Giese, H., Inverardi, P., Magee, J. (eds.) Software Engineering for Self-Adaptive Systems. LNCS, vol. 5525, pp. 48–70. Springer, Heidelberg (2009)

6. Bührmann, S.: Bicycles as public-individual transport - European developments. Technical report, Rupprecht Consult Forschung und Beratung GmbH, Cologne, Germany (2008)

7. Cheng, S.-W., Garlan, D., Schmerl, B.R.: Making self-adaptation an engineering reality. In: Babaoğlu, Ö., Jelasity, M., Montresor, A., Fetzer, C., Leonardi, S., van Moorsel, A., van Steen, M. (eds.) SELF-STAR 2004. LNCS, vol. 3460, pp. 158–173. Springer, Heidelberg (2005)

8. Di Marzo Serugendo, G., Gleizes, M.P., Karageorgos, A.: Self-organization in multi-agent systems. Knowl. Eng. Rev. **20**(2), 165–189 (2005). http://dx.doi.org/10.1017/S0269888905000494

9. Gelernter, D., Carriero, N.: Coordination languages and their significance. Commun. ACM **35**(2), 97–107 (1992). http://doi.acm.org/10.1145/129630.129635

10. Jiang, Y., Xue, G., Jia, Z., You, J.: Dtuples: a distributed hash table based tuple space service for distributed coordination. In: Proceedings of the Fifth International Conference on Grid and Cooperative Computing, GCC 2006, pp. 101–106 (2006). http://dx.doi.org/10.1109/GCC.2006.41

11. Kephart, J.O., Chess, D.M.: The vision of autonomic computing. Computer **36**(1), 41–50 (2003)

12. van Lon, R., Holvoet, T.: Rinsim: a simulator for collective adaptive systems in transportation and logistics. In: 2012 IEEE Sixth International Conference on Self-Adaptive and Self-Organizing Systems (SASO), pp. 231–232 (2012)

13. Mano, J.P., Bourjot, C., Lopardo, G.A., Glize, P.: Bio-inspired mechanisms for artificial self-organised systems. Informatica **30**(1), 55–62 (2006). (Slovenia)

14. Midgley, P.: The role of smart bike-sharing systems. In: Urban Mobility Journeys, vol. 2, 23–31 May 2009

15. Nardini, E., Viroli, M., Casadei, M., Omicini, A.: A self-organising infrastructure for chemical-semantic coordination: experiments in Tucson. In: Omicini, A., Viroli, M. (eds.) Proceedings of the 11th WOA 2010 Workshop, Dagli Oggetti Agli Agenti, Rimini, Italy, 5–7 September 2010. CEUR Workshop Proceedings, vol. 621. CEUR-WS.org (2010). http://ceur-ws.org/Vol-621/paper17.pdf

16. Nicola, R.D., Loreti, M., Pugliese, R., Tiezzi, F.: A formal approach to autonomic systems programming: the scel language. ACM Trans. Auton. Adapt. Syst. **9**(2), 7:1–7:29 (2014)

17. Pokahr, A., Braubach, L.: The active components approach for distributed systems development. Int. J. Parallel Emergent Distrib. Syst. **28**(4), 321–369 (2013). http://dx.doi.org/10.1080/17445760.2013.785546

18. Pokahr, A., Braubach, L., Jander, K.: The Jadex project: programming model. In: Multiagent Systems and Applications: Volume 1: Practice and Experience, pp. 21–53. Springer, Heidelberg (2013). http://dx.doi.org/10.1007/978-3-642-33323-1_2

19. Preisler, T., Dethlefs, T., Renz, W.: Data-adaptive simulation: Cooperativeness of users in bike-sharing systems. In: Kersten, W., Blecker, T., Ringle, C.M. (eds.) Proceedings of the Hamburg International Conference of Logistics, vol. 20. epubli GmbH (2015)
20. Preisler, T., Dethlefs, T., Renz, W.: Middleware for constructing decentralized control in self-organizing systems. In: 2015 IEEE International Conference on Autonomic Computing, Grenoble, France, 7–10 July 2015, pp. 325–330. IEEE (2015). http://dx.doi.org/10.1109/ICAC.2015.56
21. Preisler, T., Dethlefs, T., Renz, W.: Simulation as a service: a design approach for large-scale energy network simulations. In: Ganzha, M., Maciaszek, L.A., Paprzycki, M. (eds.) 2015 Federated Conference on Computer Science and Information Systems, FedCSIS 2015, Lódz, Poland, 13–16 September 2015, pp. 1765–1772. IEEE (2015). http://dx.doi.org/10.15439/2015F116
22. Renz, W., Sudeikat, J.: Modeling feedback within MAS: a systemic approach to organizational dynamics. In: Vouros, G., Artikis, A., Stathis, K., Pitt, J. (eds.) OAMAS 2008. LNCS, vol. 5368, pp. 72–89. Springer, Heidelberg (2009)
23. Ricci, A., Piunti, M., Viroli, M.: Environment programming in multi-agent systems: an artifact-based perspective. Auton. Agents Multi-Agent Syst. **23**(2), 158–192 (2010). http://dx.doi.org/10.1007/s10458-010-9140-7
24. Ricci, A., Viroli, M., Omicini, A.: The A&A programming model and technology for developing agent environments in MAS. In: Dastani, M., El Fallah Seghrouchni, A., Ricci, A., Winikoff, M. (eds.) Programming Multi-Agent Systems. LNCS, vol. 4908, pp. 89–106. Springer, Heidelberg (2008). http://dx.doi.org/10.1007/978-3-540-79043-3_6
25. Salehie, M., Tahvildari, L.: Self-adaptive software: landscape and research challenges. ACM Trans. Auton. Adapt. Syst. **4**(2), 1–42 (2009). http://doi.acm.org/10.1145/1516533.1516538
26. Sicklinger, S., Belsky, V., Engelmann, B., Elmqvist, H., Olsson, H., Wüchner, R., Bletzinger, K.U.: Interface jacobian-based co-simulation. Int. J. Numer. Methods Eng. **98**(6), 418–444 (2014). http://dx.doi.org/10.1002/nme.4637
27. Sudeikat, J., Renz, W.: Decomas: an architecture for supplementing mas with systemic models of decentralized agent coordination. In: IEEE/WIC/ACM International Joint Conferences on Web Intelligence and Intelligent Agent Technologies, WI-IAT 2009, vol. 2, pp. 104–107 (2009)
28. Sudeikat, J.: Engineering self-organizing dynamics in distributed systems: a systemic approach. Ph.D. thesis, Universität Hamburg, Fachbereich Informatik, Verteilte Systeme und Informationssysteme (2010)
29. Sudeikat, J., Renz, W.: MASDynamics: toward systemic modeling of decentralized agent coordination. In: Kommunikation in Verteilten Systemen (KiVS), pp. 79–90. Springer, Heidelberg (2009)
30. Sudeikat, J., Renz, W.: Building complex adaptive systems: on engineering self-organizing multi-agent systems (reprint). In: Hunter, M.G. (ed.) Strategic Information Systems: Concepts, Methodologies, Tools, and Applications, pp. 767–787. IGI Publishing Hershley, Hershley (2010)
31. Vogel, P., Mattfeld, D.: Modeling of repositioning activities in bike-sharing systems. In: Proceedings of the World Conference on Transport Research (WCTR), Lisbon, Portugal (2010)
32. Weyns, D., Malek, S., Andersson, J.: On decentralized self-adaptation: lessons from the trenches and challenges for the future. In: Proceedings of the 2010 ICSE Workshop on Software Engineering for Adaptive and Self-Managing Systems, SEAMS 2010, pp. 84–93 (2010). http://doi.acm.org/10.1145/1808984.1808994

Spatiotemporal Pattern Matching in RoboCup

Tom Warnke$^{(\boxtimes)}$ and Adelinde M. Uhrmacher

Institute of Computer Science, University of Rostock,
Albert-Einstein-Straße 22, 18059 Rostock, Germany
{tom.warnke,adelinde.uhrmacher}@uni-rostock.de
https://mosi.informatik.uni-rostock.de

Abstract. Whereas agent-based models are built on the micro-level, the interesting model output is often observed on the macro-level. In models with agents moving in space this leads to complex movement patterns. We propose a method to describe the simultaneous movement of agents by graphs that encode qualitative spatial relations between object pairs and the change of these relations over time. Movement patterns can then be expressed as graph patterns. We present two approaches to find occurrences of such graph patterns, using a graph database query and using a customized graph algorithm. Based on the example of the RoboCup soccer simulation, we demonstrate the use of our approach to define and find movement patterns in spatial multi-agent systems.

1 Introduction

A characteristic property of multi-agent systems is the emergence of phenomena through the interaction of single agents [30]. For example, agents in a trading model might interact by buying and selling goods [23], giving rise to price developments; a demographic model might represent individuals with family ties as linked agents to predict the cost for social care [24]. An agent-based model is designed by defining the behavior of single agents. However, the interesting output often appears when observing the model as a whole.

Many multi-agent models include some spatial behavior of agents, leading to spatiotemporal macro-level output during simulations. Consequently, approaches that describe *spatiotemporal patterns* in the model output, i.e., patterns that involve time and space, have been developed in several domains: for mobile agents [7], mobile processes [9], agents migrating between populations [5], spatial patterns of bacteria [25], and distributed artificial intelligence [14]. Most of these approaches extend temporal logics by spatial operators to obtain spatiotemporal logics.

In this work, we propose a novel method to describe spatiotemporal patterns in the simultaneous movement of agents in continuous space and discrete time. Our approach uses graphs instead of logics to formally describe spatiotemporal patterns. We also present two methods to find occurrences of such patterns in recorded simulation output (*pattern matching*). Based on the RoboCup 2D Soccer Simulation as an application example, we show how analysis of team sports tactics can be supported by movement pattern description and matching.

© Springer International Publishing Switzerland 2016
M. Klusch et al. (Eds.): MATES 2016, LNAI 9872, pp. 89–104, 2016.
DOI: 10.1007/978-3-319-45889-2_7

2   Application Scenario - RoboCup

The RoboCup 2D Soccer Simulation League [1] is a simulation of a football match with realistic rules and game play. In this multi-agent model, two teams of 11 autonomous player agents play a ten-minute football match against each other. In turns of 100 ms, each player agent evaluates his perception of the match, communicates with his teammates and sends his next move to a central server. Binaries of the soccer server, a visualization tool and several teams are freely accessible on-line, which facilitates running and observing simulations. Regarding the properties of this application domain, we can see that

– agents are point objects rather than region objects,
– the space the agents live in is two-dimensional, continuous, and bounded, and
– the time scale consists of equidistant time points.

A concrete application for spatiotemporal pattern matching in football matches is the analysis of tactics. Tactics of teams can be extracted from movement patterns of the players and the ball. For example, a common defensive strategy is the back-four, where four defenders line up as the last defensive line in front of their own goal. The properties of this line can already give clues about the strategy of the team: How far away from the goal is it positioned? How far are the defenders away from each other? Do the defenders actively mark opponents or do they try to keep their formation? If occurrences of a pattern that describes a disassembled back-four are found, the corresponding time points can be presented to an analyst. He may use this information to visually investigate the sequences, or compare it with time points where goals were conceded.

Such techniques can not only be applied to simulated football, but also to real-life matches. Many tactical patterns, such as the back-four, can be described by relative positioning of players and the ball, possibly involving development of this relative positioning over time. Empirical sources such as the tactics blog *Zonal Marking*[1] exemplify how tactical analysis makes use of spatiotemporal observations. But also the scientific analysis of football tactics (cf. [6]) has recently gained some interest, and several approaches have been developed by computer scientists during the last years.

Sakr and Güting propose a method that is based on a moving object databases [26,27]. A language for spatiotemporal pattern queries is proposed that allows statements about the temporal ordering of spatial predicates and thus spatiotemporal patterns. However, only operators for simple patterns are available yet. Operators for more complex behaviors are mentioned as future work in the latest publication [27]. These would be crucial to specify more complex spatiotemporal patterns as common for football tactics.

Laube et al. propose a matrix-based description of movement patterns involving multiple objects [21]. The "relative motion analysis concept" uses a two-dimensional representation of movement data. One movement feature, such as movement direction or speed, is encoded in a matrix. Based on the matrix, some

---

[1] http://www.zonalmarking.net/.

spatiotemporal patterns can be expressed with respect to the chosen movement feature. However, this method is restricted to simple patterns; for example, spatial proximity of objects can not be included.

A third approach to handle spatiotemporal patterns as well as football analysis are algorithms that are tailored for specific problems. Gudmundsson and Wolle present a set of tools to conduct analysis of football matches [18]. In another work, Gudmundsson et al. define some general spatiotemporal patterns and propose tailored algorithms to find these patterns [17]. Although these solutions for specific problems can be designed to be highly efficient, they do neither provide support for describing patterns in general nor finding them.

Other approaches that deal with spatiotemporal patterns or football analysis can be classified as pattern recognition rather than pattern matching, most notably the work of Memmert and Perl [16]. Instead of searching for occurrences of a pattern that has been described beforehand, frequent movement patterns in a football match record are recognized and clustered. Such approaches tackle a different challenge than defined in this work, and do not support the description of patterns.

The examples above show that a suitable representation of movement data is the key for the development of a pattern description method. The actual description method is then a logical consequence of this *data model*. Thus, as a next step we investigate how movement data, e.g., produced by a RoboCup simulation, can be structured to allow for an easy definition and finding of movement patterns.

3   Modeling Movement Data

When we think about modeling the movement data that we extract from a RoboCup simulation, we are looking for a way to formally represent knowledge about the movement of the agents. Thus, we can employ methods from the field of knowledge representation and reasoning [29]. A plethora of concepts have been developed in this field. Generally, two different approaches for reasoning can be distinguished [11].

Quantitative reasoning operates directly on values of the application domain. For example, "An answer was received *12.3* s after the request was sent" would be a quantitative temporal statement. Conversely, *qualitative reasoning* abstracts from values of the application domain and uses symbolic representations instead. The above example could be expressed qualitatively as "An answer was received *soon* after the request was sent." A characteristic of qualitative reasoning is apparent here: the symbolic representation ("soon") is chosen specifically for the application. In another application context, 12.3 s might correspond to "much later" rather than "soon". Thus, by using domain-specific interpretations of terms, qualitative reasoning offers a vocabulary tailored to a specific application.

Another criterion by which reasoning methods can be distinguished is their target dimension. For example, approaches have been proposed for reasoning about space and for reasoning about time. To represent spatiotemporal knowledge, some spatiotemporal reasoning methods have been developed as well. Many spatiotemporal reasoning methods combine existing spatial and temporal reasoning approaches [8]. In our application domain of football movement patterns we expect the spatial aspects of patterns to be more complex than the temporal aspects. Thus, we continue by investigating spatial reasoning methods, and will integrate the temporal aspects afterward.

3.1   Spatial Reasoning

For now, we want to ignore change over time and employ a spatial reasoning method to describe the state of the model at one instant. Spatial reasoning typically considers at least two dimensions, and considers points or regions in these dimensions [2]. As we model the players and the ball in the RoboCup simulation as points, we are interested in a point-based reasoning method.

An approach for qualitative reasoning about points in space was introduced by Frank [12]. It uses the relative direction between points to obtain binary relations. Frank distinguishes between two general approaches to define direction between a reference object and a target object: First, the angle between the locations of the objects can be the defining property of the relation. Thus, all objects that have the same relation to the reference object lie in a cone that extends infinitely away from the reference object (Fig. 1a). Corresponding to the compass directions, typically four or eight relations are defined this way. Second, the plane around the reference object can be divided into two half-planes by a line that runs through the reference object. Doing this twice with two orthogonal lines results in four regions around the reference object (Fig. 1b). Frank continues to extend both approaches by a neutral zone, representing the immediate surrounding of the reference object where a distinguation of relative direction is less meaningful. This increases the precision of the abstraction.

Frank extends this work by additionally taking the distance between objects into account [13]. A qualitative distance measure is acquired by discretizing the continuous geometrical distance between objects into a finite number of ordered abstract distance symbols, e.g., *close* and *far*. The combination of direction and distance abstractions has to take into account that the underlying discrete values are not independent from each other. Consequently, not all combinations of direction and distance symbols are meaningful, especially if a neutral zone for direction is considered. Specifically, it may not be sensible to combine a neutral direction with a distance other than the smallest one. Conversely, when the distance is known to be very small, it may not make sense to assign a non-neutral direction. Comparing both direction abstractions and their interaction with distance reasoning, Frank finds that inference with the projection-based direction model produces more exact results. However, for knowledge representation both direction definitions are equally appropriate.

Frank's method gives us a way to discretize the continuous coordinates of the moving players and the ball, and obtain a set of qualitative relations. The relations describe the relative positioning of two objects in a model state. Thus,

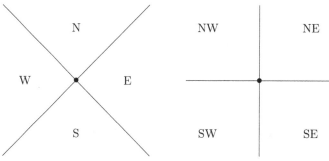

(a) Cone-shaped directions: Directions are defined based on the angle from the reference object, here resulting in four regions.

(b) Projection-based directions. The surroundings of a reference object are divided by two lines into two regions each, resulting in four regions.

Fig. 1. Definitions of direction after Frank [12]

we can describe a complete model state with the pairwise relations between all objects. Assuming we choose an appropriate discretization, this description of the state contains all necessary information about interesting spatial patterns in that state.

3.2   Knowledge Representation

As shown in the previous section, the position of one object referring to a reference object can be mapped to one relation in a relation set. Such relation sets have two important properties: First, all relations are binary. Second, the set of defined relations forms a jointly exhaustive and pairwise disjoint (JEPD) [10] partition of all possible relative placements of two entities in space. Thus, a specific state can be encoded with a number of such binary relations between the involved entities. It is also possible to represent a state with several entities and their relations as a *relation graph*, where the entities are mapped to nodes. The relation between two entities is then mapped to a directed labeled edge between the corresponding nodes. An example is shown in Fig. 2.

To obtain a relation graph for a single observed model state, we abstract the observed state into a number of meaningful spatial relations. We focus on direction and distance between points objects pairs. Using Franks approach, we define a partition of the space surrounding an object into regions (Fig. 3). We distinguish three distances, where very close and very far objects are not distinguished further. For objects in a middle distance we additionally determine their relative direction as one of eight canonical directions. We chose this kind of space partition in order to obtain relations that, in our understanding, contribute to tactical patterns in football. The relation between two objects is given by the region the second object falls into when the space around the first object is

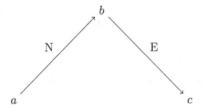

Fig. 2. A relation graph encoding that a is north (N) of b and b is east (E) of c.

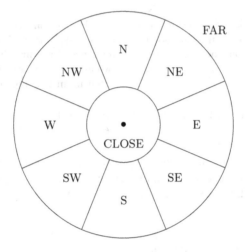

Fig. 3. Our chosen partition of the space surrounding an object.

partitioned. Thus, for every ordered pair of objects exactly one relation can be determined. The relations between all object pairs at one time point is encoded as a relation graph. For each time point, we obtain a complete directed graph with a node for each object, where each edge is labeled with a relation.

The graphs for single time points must now be related to include information about their order in time. To this end, we add a node for each time point. Each time point node is connected to its successor by a directed edge. Furthermore, each time point node has an edge to every node representing a location at that time point. To also relate location nodes that represent the same object at different time points to each other, nodes for all objects are added. Again, all location nodes are connected to the corresponding object node. The edges between time point nodes, between time point and location nodes as well as between object and location nodes are labeled accordingly. A graph exemplifying the resulting structure is shown in Fig. 4.

This *data graph* now contains complete qualitative information about an observed simulation run of a multi-agent model. It is able to handle agents entering and leaving the model or time points with missing observations for one or several agents by omitting the corresponding nodes. Assuming suitable

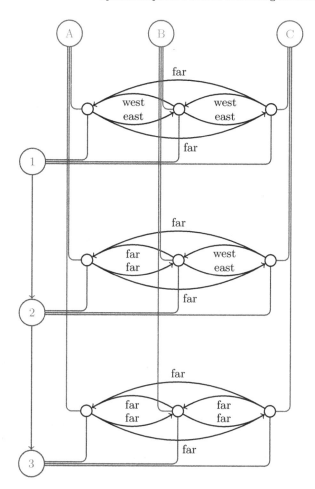

Fig. 4. A data graph containing the movement data of three objects at three consecutive time points. We omitted some labels and replaced them with colors. Object nodes and the corresponding edges are red, time points and edges connecting time points to their successor as well as time points to location nodes are blue. We also omitted the direction of some edges for simplicity. (Color figure online)

qualitative relations were chosen, spatiotemporal patterns are now encoded in this graph as subgraphs. Thus, the definition of a spatiotemporal pattern is reduced to the definition of a subgraph pattern. The question whether a spatiotemporal pattern has occurred during a simulation run is equivalent to the question whether a defined *pattern graph* is a subgraph of the data graph (Fig. 5). As shown by Gallagher [15], a plethora of variants of this graph pattern matching problem exist. If the subgraph pattern is a plain graph, it is known as the *subgraph isomorphism* problem, which is NP-hard. We will see that feasible approaches for this problem exist, however, and focus on this kind of patterns

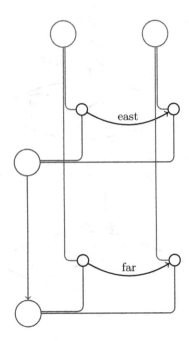

Fig. 5. A pattern graph representing an object that moves away from another object. In on time step, the relation between them changes from "east" to "far". This pattern occurs twice in the data graph in Fig. 4.

in this paper. Our patterns also include semantic information (labels on nodes or edges). More complex patterns, such as only partially specified ones (e.g., a path with a maximal length), can also be applied when necessary. Next, we will look into practical approaches to describe patterns and algorithmically find their occurrences.

4   Implementation

We implemented a Java tool to configure, start and observe RoboCup simulation matches and convert the observations to a data graph. Our simulation setup is based on the RoboCup Soccer Server sserver[2]. The length of a simulation step in the RoboCup 2D Soccer Simulation League protocol is fixed to 100 ms. Our implementation uses this time window between observations to compute the spatial relations and add the corresponding nodes and edges to the data graph on-the-fly. How the data graph is constructed technically is tightly connected with the kind of patterns that can be defined and the method to find their occurrences. In the following we present two different approaches. The complete source code of the implementation described in this paper is available at git.informatik.uni-rostock.de/mosi/RobocupAnalysis.

---

[2] Source code available at http://sourceforge.net/projects/sserver/.

4.1 Graph Database

Graph databases offer a natural way to represent graphs and query them. Neo4j[3] is a widely used, actively developed, well-performing graph database system [20]. It offers the query language Cypher, which is often praised for its expressiveness and intuitiveness [19].

We implemented the construction of the data graph in a Neo4j database (version 3.0.1). This database is then queried with Cypher expressions. Cypher expressions can be used to describe simple pattern graphs, including node and edge labels. The pattern graph in Fig. 5 can be expressed with the following Cypher query by listing nodes and edges with labels and variables:

```
MATCH
  (l1:Location)-[:EAST]->(l2:Location),
  (l1)<--(one:Object), (l2)<--(two:Object),
  (l3:Location)-[:FAR]->(l4:Location),
  (l3)<--(one:Object), (l4)<--(two:Object),
  (l1)<--(t1:TimePoint), (l2)<--(t1),
  (l3)<--(t2:Timepoint), (l4)<--(t2),
  (t1)-[:NEXT_TIMEPOINT]->(t2)
RETURN one.id, two.id, t1.id
```

If the database is queried with this query, all subgraph matches of the pattern graph are found and the IDs of the matching objects and the first time point of the match are returned. Besides this enumerative, verbose definition of a subgraph to match in a data graph, Cypher allows for complex queries. Through wildcards and cardinality operators or nesting and pipelining queries, descriptions of large patterns can be formulated succinctly. Efficient query processing can also be supported this way. However, currently Neo4j can store graph data only on the hard drive. This potentially slows down the reading of data and processing of queries

4.2 Ullmann's Algorithm

To remedy the disadvantages of the hard drive storage of the data graph, we developed a representation of the data graph in Java. The graph consists of Java objects that are stored on the heap, i.e., in memory. This speeds up the access to the graph. However, this also means that a pattern matching algorithm has to be provided. We implemented Ullmann's algorithm [28], as it easily allows for exploiting the structure of the graph. Our implementation matches one pattern graph node after another. The general approach is depicted in Algorithm 1.

The process of matching a pattern graph on a data graph corresponds to a depth-first search in a tree. The nodes of the tree represent matchings, with the root being the empty matching. Every other tree node extends the matching of its parent by one pattern graph node. Our implementation of Ullmann's algorithm exploits the known structure of the pattern and data graphs in several ways to

---
[3] neo4j.org.

input   : $P = (V_P, E_P)$ - The pattern graph
          $D = (V_D, E_D)$ - The data graph
output   : $R = \{M_1, M_2, \ldots\}$ - All valid matchings
variables: $M \subseteq V_P \times V_D$ - The current matching
          $O = (v_1, v_2, \ldots)$ - The matching order with $\{v_1, v_2, \ldots\} = V_P$
          $n \in V_P$ - The pattern node to match
          $C \subseteq V_D$ - The matching candidates
          $c \in V_D$ - The current matching candidate

main(P, D)
 | $R \longleftarrow \emptyset$
 | $M \longleftarrow \emptyset$
 | $O \longleftarrow$ determineMatchingOrder(P)
 | match(P, D, M, R, O)
 | **return** R

match(P, D, M, R, O)
 | **if** $|M| = |V_P|$ **then**
 | | $R \longleftarrow R \cup \{M\}$
 | **else**
 | | $n \longleftarrow O[|M|]$
 | | $C \longleftarrow$ determineCandidates(n, P, D, M)
 | | **for** $c \in C$ **do**
 | | | $M' \longleftarrow M \cup \{(n, c)\}$
 | | | match(P, D, M', R, O)
 | | **end**
 | **end**
 | **return**

Algorithm 1. The matching algorithm after Ullmann [28]. The function match recursively extends a matching M of pattern graph nodes on data graph nodes. Once all pattern graph nodes are matched, the matching is added to the set of valid matchings R. The algorithm initially determines an optimal matching order of the pattern graph nodes. From this sequence the next pattern node to match n is chosen, which helps to discard uncompletable matchings early. Once the pattern node to match is chosen, all matching nodes in the data graph, the candidates, are determined. When the algorithm terminates, R contains all valid matchings.

speed up the tree search. Most importantly, the order in which the pattern graph nodes are matched is optimized heuristically. We determine an optimal matching order of the nodes in the pattern graph by looking at labels and directions of the edges in the pattern graph. In each step, the algorithm selects the next node to match according to the determined matching order. The optimal matching order leads to early failure of tree branches that do not end in a complete matching, saving computation time.

To match a pattern graph node, all matching nodes in the data graph, the candidates, are determined. Determining the candidate set is the second crucial aspect of the algorithm. It takes node and edge labels into account and is heavily influenced by the existing matchings. If nodes are connected in the pattern graph with an edge of a certain type, their matches in the data graph must be connected with such an edge as well ("Forward Checking", cf. [15]). Consider for example the pattern graph in Fig. 5: If the object nodes (red) and time point nodes (blue) are already matched to nodes of the data graph, for each pattern location node only one data node is a candidate. This emphasizes how important the right choice of node matching order is. Assume that in the same example the two time point nodes and the location nodes for the upper time point are already matched. If now one of the location nodes for the lower time point would be matched next, all candidates but one would lead to matchings that can not be completed. If however the red object nodes are matched next, only one data node has to be considered as candidate for each. For each of the location nodes for the lower time point, the lone candidate can also be directly determined in the next steps.

Thus, the branching of the search tree can be minimized by smartly choosing the next pattern node to match and generating candidate sets. This optimization relies heavily on knowledge about the structure of the graph.

5 Application Example

We generated movement data by running matches of two instances of the team WrightEagle[4] [31]. From these movement data, we constructed data graphs for both the Neo4j implementation and our implementation of Ullmann's algorithm. We then queried the data graphs with different patterns that were expressed as Cypher query for Neo4j or as pattern graph for Ullmann's algorithm. To evaluate both methods, we measured the computation time to answer the queries on a standard notebook and assessed the returned results.

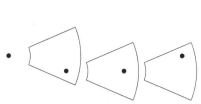 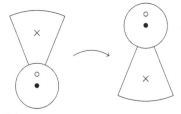

(a) Illustration of the back-four. Each player ● except the first one is located in the east region of the previous player. The east regions for the first three players are shown.

(b) Illustration of attacker ● getting past defender ×. ○ represents the ball. The defender's goal line is located to the top.

5.1 Back-Four

The first pattern is the back-four that we described in Sect. 2. We defined it as four players of the same team with the relationship "east" between neighboring

---

[4] Source code available at http://ai.ustc.edu.cn/2d/.

players for five consecutive time points. To find this pattern in Neo4j efficiently, we constructed a query that first looked for all single time points with a back-four and then, by using a path query, extracted instances of five consecutive time points with the same players in a back-four:

```
MATCH (l1 :LOCATION) −[:EAST]−>(l2 :LOCATION) −[:EAST]−>
  (l3 :LOCATION) −[:EAST]−>(l4 :LOCATION) ,
  (l1)−−(one :OBJECT) , (l2)−−(two :OBJECT) ,
  (l3)−−(three :OBJECT) , (l4)−−(four :OBJECT) ,
  (l1)−−(t :TIME_POINT)
WHERE one.team = two.team AND two.team = three.team AND three.team =
    four.team
WITH one , two , three , four , collect(t) AS times
MATCH path=(start :TIME_POINT) −[:NEXT_TIME_POINT*5]−>(end :TIME_POINT)
WHERE ALL (t in nodes(path) WHERE t in times)
RETURN one.id , two.id , three.id , four.id , start.time
```

The pattern graph for Ullmann's algorithm was created programmatically. Both methods yielded the same results. As expected, the two defensive lines of each team constituted the majority of back-four occurrences (about 30 % each). Neo4j answered the query after 2 min, our implementation of Ullmann's algorithm took 8 min. When we required that the back-four holds for ten time consecutive time units (roughly doubling the nodes to match), the computation time increased to 3 and 12 min. To check whether players belong to the same team with Neo4j, we could use a WHERE clause in Cypher. For Ullmann's algorithm, however, we needed to insert additional edges in the data and pattern graph to represent membership in the same team.

5.2   Getting Past a Defender

The second pattern we used for evaluation represents an attacking move. First, a player is close to the ball, but his way towards the opponent's goal is blocked by a defender. Shortly afterwards, the attacking player is still close to the ball, but the defender is now behind him. The second state must occur during 100 time steps (10 s) after the first state. This pattern models an important step in an attack play, and can, for example, result from a one-two pass.

To formulate this query, we had to adapt the canonical directions that are used for reasoning to take into account that both teams play in opposite directions. Therefore, we replaced the compass directions with directions such as front or left, where front is the direction towards the reference player's opponents' goal line. Neo4j answered the query after less than one minute. The results of the query showed that one player in each team is much more often involved in the pattern than its teammates. As both teams were instances of the same team binary, it was not surprising that it was actually the same player, a central forward, in both teams. However, we were not able to reproduce these results with our implementation of Ullmann's algorithm. The pattern as we defined it includes a path of time point nodes between the two described states. The length of this path is constrained to be at most 100. As a pattern graph for our implementation of Ullmann's algorithm only contains plain nodes and edges (and no paths), this constraint could not be mapped to this method.

6   Discussion

We developed a concept to specify movement patterns in multi-agent systems and to find occurrences of these patterns algorithmically by using graphs. Thus, our contribution is the translation of the initial problem in the domain of multi-agent systems to a different problem in the domain of graph pattern matching. We now reflect what we have gained with this translation.

As a first aspect, we want to emphasize the inherent declarativity of a graph approach. The modeling of movement data as a graph allows for a declarative description of movement patterns as graph patterns. In contrast to operational, imperative pattern descriptions, declarativity facilitates a separation of concerns: Pattern descriptions are independent of the algorithms to find the pattern occurrences. This is comparable to temporal logics, where declarative expressions can be algorithmically handled in different ways [22].

Few approaches for the description of relative movement patterns exist. Using our graph-based concept, we were able to flexibly define spatiotemporal patterns that are relevant for tactics in football. The same approach should be feasible for other domains where concepts like formations and choreographed movement

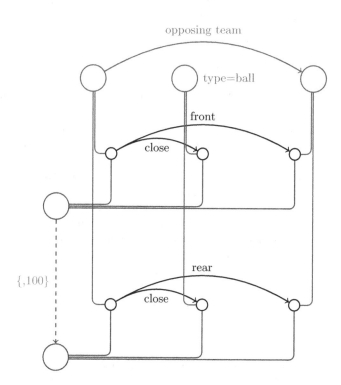

Fig. 6. Pattern graph for "Getting past a defender" employing a regular expression. The cardinality expression states that at most 100 blue edges have to connect the depicted blue time point nodes. (Color figure online)

of agents play a role. Patterns in other team sports, such as American Football, or military tactics should be expressible. We are not aware of methods that offer a similar expressiveness for such applications.

The idea to use graph patterns to describe interesting phenomena in data represented as a graph has been applied successfully in different domains. Angles and Gutierrez review examples of graph data modeling [3]. The success of graph pattern matching methods in various application domains is a strong hint for the general usefulness of this approach. The plethora of applications also gave rise to the development of diverse methods for applied graph pattern matching. By shifting our problem to this domain, these methods constitute a toolbox for different extensions of the concept proposed here.

In this paper we already made use of two existing methods to find occurrences of a pattern in data: Neo4j is a well-established database system that offers the powerful query language Cypher and efficient algorithms to process queries. Ullmann's algorithm is a very general graph pattern matching algorithm that we tweaked to exploit the known structure of the graphs at hand. Comparing our application of both approaches, Neo4j takes the lead in terms of pattern definition and efficient query processing. Whereas we had to programmatically build a pattern graph to apply Ullmann's algorithm, Cypher allowed for succinct description of patterns, also including complex concepts such as variable path lengths. It was faster than our implementation of Ullmann's algorithm in all non-trivial cases. However, the efficiency of Neo4j's pattern matching depends on how the query is formulated. For more complex queries, advanced Cypher techniques such as query nesting or pipelining are necessary to enable efficient processing. Thus, the higher efficiency and expressiveness is bought with a loss in declaritivity.

To make declarative graph patterns similarly expressive as Neo4j queries, advanced graph concepts must be integrated into the definition of pattern graphs. Different uses of existing graph-based methods are imaginable to tackle different tasks in the specification and matching of movement patterns. For example, incomplete graph descriptions that incorporate paths with a constrained length instead of edges have been proposed, e.g., by using regular expressions [4]. Such an extension enables the representation of complex movement patterns as graph patterns, such as our second example pattern "Getting past a defender" (Fig. 6).

Independently of the technology used, we hope to have shown the potential of representing movement data and movement patterns as graphs for analyzing spatial multi-agent systems. Our approach may offer a new perspective on research questions about the coordination and cooperation of autonomous agents in space.

Acknowledgments. We would like to thank Roland Ewald, Stefan Leye, and Arne Bittig for their valuable input on the concepts developed in this paper. This research is partly supported by the German Research Foundation (DFG) via the research grant MoSiLLDe (UH-66/15-1).

References

1. Soccer Simulation League - RoboCup Federation Wiki. http://wiki.robocup.org/wiki/Soccer_Simulation_League
2. Aiello, M., Pratt-Hartmann, I., van Benthem, J. (eds.): Handbook of Spatial Logics. Springer, Heidelberg (2007)
3. Angles, R., Gutierrez, C.: Survey of graph database models. ACM Comput. Surv. **40**(1), 1:1–1:39 (2008)
4. Barceló, P., Libkin, L., Reutter, J.L.: Querying graph patterns. In: Proceedings of the 13th ACM SIGMOD-SIGACT-SIGART Symposium on Principles of Database Systems, pp. 199–210. ACM (2011)
5. Bortolussi, L., Nenzi, L.: Specifying and monitoring properties of stochastic spatio-temporal systems in signal temporal logic. In: Proceedings of the 8th International Conference on Performance Evaluation Methodologies and Tools, pp. 66–73. ICST (2014)
6. Braun, H.J.: Soccer tactics as science? On 'Scotch Professors', a Ukrainian soccer Buddha, and a Catalonian who tries to learn German. J. Int. Comm. Hist. Technol. **19**, 216–243 (2013)
7. Cheng, J.D.: Qualitative spatio-temporal reasoning about movement of mobile agents/objects. In: Proceedings of the 7th International Conference on Machine Learning and Cybernetics, pp. 3341–3346 (2008)
8. Cohn, A.G., Renz, J.: Qualitative spatial representation and reasoning. In: van Harmelen, F., Lifschitz, V., Porter, B. (eds.) Foundations of Artificial Intelligence, Handbook of Knowledge Representation, vol. 3, pp. 551–596. Elsevier (2008)
9. De Nicola, R., Katoen, J.P., Latella, D., Loreti, M., Massink, M.: Model checking mobile stochastic logic. Theor. Comput. Sci. **382**(1), 42–70 (2007)
10. Düntsch, I.: Relation algebras and their application in temporal and spatial reasoning. Artif. Intell. Rev. **23**(4), 315–357 (2005)
11. Forbus, K.D.: Qualitative modeling. In: van Harmelen, F., Lifschitz, V., Porter, B. (eds.) Foundations of Artificial Intelligence, Handbook of Knowledge Representation, vol. 3, pp. 361–393. Elsevier (2008)
12. Frank, A.U.: Qualitative spatial reasoning with cardinal directions. In: Kaindl, H. (ed.) 7. Österreichische Artificial-Intelligence-Tagung/Seventh Austrian Conference on Artificial Intelligence. Informatik-Fachberichte, vol. 287, pp. 157–167. Springer, Heidelberg (1991)
13. Frank, A.U.: Qualitative spatial reasoning about distances and directions in geographic space. J. Vis. Lang. Comput. **3**(4), 343–371 (1992)
14. Gagné, D., Pang, W., Trudel, A.: A spatio-temporal logic for 2D multi-agent problem domains. Expert Syst. Appl. **12**(1), 141–145 (1997)
15. Gallagher, B.: Matching structure and semantics: a survey on graph-based pattern matching. In: Papers from the 2006 AAAI Fall Symposium, vol. 6, pp. 45–53 (2006)
16. Grunz, A., Memmert, D., Perl, J.: Tactical pattern recognition in soccer games by means of special self-organizing maps. Hum. Mov. Sci. **31**(2), 334–343 (2012)
17. Gudmundsson, J., van Kreveld, M., Speckmann, B.: Efficient detection of motion patterns in spatio-temporal data sets. In: Proceedings of the 12th Annual ACM International Workshop on Geographic Information Systems, pp. 250–257. ACM (2004)
18. Gudmundsson, J., Wolle, T.: Football analysis using spatio-temporal tools. Comput. Environ. Urban Syst. **47**, 16–27 (2014)

19. Holzschuher, F., Peinl, R.: Querying a graph database – language selection and performance considerations. J. Comput. Syst. Sci. **82**(1), 45–68 (2016)
20. Jouili, S., Vansteenberghe, V.: An empirical comparison of graph databases. In: Proceedings of the 2013 International Conference on Social Computing, pp. 708–715. IEEE Computer Society (2013)
21. Laube, P., Imfeld, S., Weibel, R.: Discovering relative motion patterns in groups of moving point objects. Int. J. Geog. Inf. Sci. **19**(6), 639–668 (2005)
22. Legay, A., Delahaye, B., Bensalem, S.: Statistical model checking: an overview. In: Barringer, H., et al. (eds.) RV 2010. LNCS, vol. 6418, pp. 122–135. Springer, Heidelberg (2010)
23. Lux, T., Marchesi, M.: Scaling and criticality in a stochastic multi-agent model of a financial market. Nature **397**(6719), 498–500 (1999)
24. Noble, J., Silverman, E., Bijak, J., Rossiter, S., Evandrou, M., Bullock, S., Vlachantoni, A., Falkingham, J.: Linked lives: the utility of an agent-based approach to modeling partnership and household formation in the context of social care. In: Proceedings of the Winter Simulation Conference, pp. 93:1–93:12. WSC (2012)
25. Pârvu, O., Gilbert, D., Heiner, M., Liu, F., Saunders, N., Shaw, S.: Spatial-Temporal modelling and analysis of bacterial colonies with phase variable genes. ACM Trans. Model. Comput. Simul. **25**(2), 13:1–13:25 (2015)
26. Sakr, M.A., Güting, R.H.: Spatiotemporal pattern queries. GeoInformatica **15**(3), 497–540 (2011)
27. Sakr, M.A., Güting, R.H.: Group spatiotemporal pattern queries. GeoInformatica **18**(4), 699–746 (2014)
28. Ullmann, J.R.: An algorithm for subgraph isomorphism. J. ACM **23**(1), 31–42 (1976)
29. van Harmelen, F., Lifschitz, V., Porter, B.: Handbook of Knowledge Representation. Elsevier Science, San Diego (2007)
30. Wilensky, U.: Modeling natures emergent patterns with multi-agent languages. In: Proceedings of EuroLogo, pp. 1–6. Citeseer (2001)
31. Zhang, H., Jiang, M., Dai, H., Bai, A., Chen, X.: WrightEagle 2D soccer simulation team description 2014. In: RoboCup (2014)

Joint Human-Agent Activities: Challenges and Definition

Sebastian Ahrndt[(✉)] and Sahin Albayrak

Faculty of Electrical Engineering and Computer Science, DAI-Laboratory,
Technische Universität Berlin, Ernst-Reuter-Platz 7, Berlin 10587, Germany
sebastian.ahrndt@dai-labor.de

Abstract. When the situation involves artificial and natural agents
in the same environment that work together to achieve joint goals we
talk about cooperative activities, human-agent teamwork, joint activities, or joint human-agent activities. Although, teamwork has become a
widely accepted metaphor for multi-robot/multi-agent cooperation there
are several challenges towards making agents "teammates" – some of
them are present independently from the teams mixture, whereas others
are particularly challenging for the development of human-agent teams.
This work presents an overview about the challenges and brings together
knowledge from the different involved research areas, further, we provide
an attempt to define the term joint human-agent activity in order to
motivate a discussion about the necessary elements.

1 Introduction

A joint-activity is a set of behaviours that is executed by at least two people that work together towards an achievement—coordinating their individual
behaviours [4,8]. This coordination process possesses different characteristics
including the commitment to a joint-goal, the commitment to mutually support
each other, and the commitment to act mutual responsive [4]. In joint human-
agent activities the agreement to work together is accomplished between humans
and agents; building a human-agent team. The humans and agents involved,
coordinate with each other to reach a goal that cannot be reached by a single individual [18]. In consequence, they form a symbiotic relationship in which
agents fulfil tasks for humans, humans in return help agents to perform tasks,
and agents and humans work together in order to accomplish tasks jointly [21].

The term itself evolved from two sides: The first one being agent-based teamwork settings and the second one observation of human-human teams that work
together. Thus, synonyms and similarities for these activities can be found when
reading about teamwork settings and cooperative activities in both areas, either
examining human-human, human-agent, or agent-agent teams. For instance,
comparing the works of *M.E. Bratman* [4] on shared cooperative activities and
the work of *Klein et al.* and their co-authors [17,18] on joint human-agent activities reveals that they identified the same basic properties, which are some-
time renamed. In order to build a better understanding of the nature of such

© Springer International Publishing Switzerland 2016
M. Klusch et al. (Eds.): MATES 2016, LNAI 9872, pp. 105–112, 2016.
DOI: 10.1007/978-3-319-45889-2_8

coordinative interactions this work introduces and discusses existing challenges (*cf.* Sect. 2). Although these challenges prevail for either teamwork setting, we highlight which parts are particularly challenging when approaching the human-agent case. After introducing the challenge, we introduce an attempt to define the term joint human-agent activity (*cf.* Sect. 3). The objective is to provide an overview about this area by bringing together the different terms used by different groups and pointing to related material.

2   Challenges

There are many challenges and requirements associated with the task of developing artificial agents that act as "team members". Work that summarises or investigates these challenges has been presented by multiple authors that frequently use different terms for the same characteristics (*cf.* [3,11,13,15,17,18,22,23]). Furthermore, the different groups sometimes distinguish ten challenges [18], sometimes six [17], or even less defining most of the requirements within the terms directability and observability [6]. As this makes it difficult to capture the entire field, we provide an overview about the elements necessary for effective teams, summarising the different explanations with respect to the ten challenges presented by *Klein et al.* [18], next. Afterwards, we will show that the different authors agree on the same set of requirements while using different names and descriptions.

2.1   Elements of Joint Activities

Challenge 1 – Basic Compact addresses the requirement that all participants must enter into an agreement to work together. This agreement is called Basic Compact. It is often tacit and a commitment of the participants to a mutual goal. Hence, '[t]o be a team player, an intelligent agent must fulfil the requirements of a Basic Compact to engage in common-grounding activities' [18, p. 92]. In the context of cooperative activities this is also named joint-goal. These joint goals are an inherent part of cooperation and present a primitive concept that can not be analysed by only taking into account the individual goals of each agent [12]. However, the challenge also claims that there has to be a common ground, meaning, that the individuals have some kind of shared knowledge about possible actions, existing rules and norms, communication capabilities and so forth. Since coordination is a continuous process, the basic compact and the common ground are not seen as a discrete state. Rather, both are subject to an everlasting communication process including negotiating, testing, updating, adapting, and repairing the mutual understanding of the joint goal and the joint knowledge [5]. This process is also named *grounding* and can be found as premise/characteristic in several fields, e.g. study of conversations and negotiations, human-computer interaction, or even service matching.

Challenge 2 – Adequate Models addresses the requirement to adequately model the other participants' intentions and actions. Furthermore, it includes the ability to reason about these models to infer knowledge about the participants. One example for a required model is the basic compact itself, which has to be represented somehow. Other examples are related to the common ground that has to be established, e.g. sharing the same vocabulary, or preferences and skills of the other participants. This challenge must be addressed by different fields including knowledge representation, learning, reasoning and planning. In fact, another adjacent research field—opponent modelling—presents several techniques for building such models and inferring knowledge (a recent, comprehensive survey is presented by *Baarslag et al.* [2]).

Challenge 3 – Predictability (sometimes Interpredictability or Mutual Predicability) addresses the requirement of building knowledge about other participants' attitudes, capabilities and course of action. Furthermore, as the participants agreed to work together it is assumed that the participants act in a way that enables the others to predict their behaviour [17]. This is part of what some authors have named observability (*cf.* [6,16]). In [1], we provide a more detailed analysis of this challenge.

Challenge 4 – Directability addresses the requirement of adapting the own degree of autonomy if necessary—sometimes named sliding, flexible, adaptable, and adjustable autonomy; or levels of autonomy/degrees of automation [14]. Directability is related to the possible hierarchical structure of teams, where one team member can delegate actions, task, or sub-goals to others [6,18]. Indeed, the earlier work on agent-based systems presented two types of agents: fully-autonomous agents or teleoperated agents, which are agents that require guidance in each step [20]. Soon, it was recognised that in teamwork settings—such as mixed initiative approaches—it is required to not only delegate tasks but also to accept guidance during the decision-making process.

Challenge 5 – Revealing Status and Intention addresses the communication capabilities of agents; particularly focusing on the capability to inform other team members about the current status and intentions including information about objectives, capacities, resources to be used, errors, and planned course of action. Although, the spreading of this information is important it comes with the trade-off of overwhelming others' – in particular humans – with information. Thus, its not only a technical issue but also a cognitive and organisational one, e.g. including the judgement if a partner is currently interruptible; or which modality should be used to forward information [17].

Challenge 6 – Interpreting Signals addresses the fact that agents have to be able to receive signals and to process these signals in terms of building knowledge, e.g. models of the teammates. It includes the possibility to interpret/reason about different types of information reaching from facts that are directly related to joint actions (like a partner has finished a task) over information about the state of the joint activity (like the fulfilment of a sub-goal) to information about teammates (like humans are getting tired). Thus, this challenge is directly related to communication capabilities of agents and their capabilities to infer knowledge from observations (indirect communication) and speech-acts (direct communication) – both being long-term research areas in agent-based systems.

In human-agent activities it adds the requirement to interpret the humans' cognitive states, e.g. learning about affective phenomena and coping strategies.

Challenge 7 – Goal Negotiation addresses the active involvement of agents into the bargaining process about goals and sub-goals of a joint activity. Agreeing to a basic compact includes a step of negotiating about this compact and the intended role of the team member. This includes the capability of arguing and reasoning about potential goals. Goal negotiation is also related to directability; as part of the negotiation process might be the agreement on using specific resources or applying specific set of norms. Both restrict the team members in their individual level of autonomy. Work on agent-based (automated) negotiation can be found in several research areas. *Lin et al.* [19] present a review on human-agent negotiation and point out different characteristics that are notably challenging. They are related to the fact that agents have to handle incomplete information (e.g., not known social preferences) and negotiate with an opponent that is bounded in rationality.

Challenge 8 – Collaboration addresses collaborative approaches for the decision-making process; bringing together the above mentioned concepts by assuming that collaborations are a forever tentative process. One example is the interdependence of the actions of the individuals. It implies that one partner has to consider the intentions, states, and course of action of others during its own planning process. An early approach is the SharedPlan model introduced by *Grosz et al.* [10]. It is a theoretical vehicle for collaborative planning, that defines collaborative plans not only as a sum of individual plans but as a 'refinement process' [10, p. 1] of partial plans of the individuals. In fact, agents also need the ability to replan, e.g. when one team member failed to reach an important sub-goal. Thus, an agent should continuously monitor the overall situation, should be able to inform and negotiate about changes, to plan in collaboration with other team members, and so forth. Although, classical AI planning do not account for these requirements, the research area of Human-Aware Planning (*cf.* [7]) presents techniques for the human-agent case.

Challenge 9 – Attention Management addresses the necessity of spreading information in the right form, using the right interaction modality at the right moment. For example, one team member should inform another team member about a resource that is running short that is required to fulfil the joint goal – leading the attention of the other team member towards this issue. This can be done by repeatedly sending status signals, resulting in a vast amount of information that may overwhelm the partner. Hence, there exists a trade-off between not overwhelming teammates with too much information and not informing them too late. *Klein et al.* [17] discuss several examples that show how bad attention management can lead to what is called 'Fundamental Common Ground Breakdown' and conclude that this challenge is an important issue for human-computer interaction research.

Challenge 10 – Cost Control addresses the fact that the benefits cooperative activities can provide do not come for free. Rather, the advantages that are offered by joint activities can be abrogated if the coordination itself is too costly. An example is given by *Klein et al.* [17, p. 31]: *'One typical arrangement for a relay race is to use four runners to cover 400 meters. It would be inefficient to have 24 runners stationed around a 400-meter track. The coordination costs would outweigh advantages of the freshness and energy of each new runner.'*. Even in this example the coordinative actions include different of the above mentioned facts, e.g. one runner has to provide signals, the partners have to predict each others behaviour, have to monitor the status of each other, to name only a few. Thus coordinating joint activities is a continuous process and part of an effective teamwork is to handle what can be named the coordination economy.

2.2 Discussion

In the following, we elaborate the essential challenges that have been identified by the majority of the authors. However, explicitly classifying the challenges is not an easy task, as they depend on each other. For instance, predictability includes building adequate models, which includes reasoning about information, which requires that other team member reveal their status and intention. Yet, comparing the available works shows that the authors agree on three basic categories of properties necessary to make agents team player (thus can be found in work on human-human teamwork as well [4]). These are:

– **Grounding** (esp. Challenges 1 and 2): The grounding-process of the joint-activity that includes the (tacit) agreement to a basic compact and the continuous process of building and maintaining a common ground.
– **Mutual Engagement** (esp. Challenges 2, 3, 7 and 8): The mutual predictability and mutual responsibility of each team member in the joint activity. This includes building models of other team members and acting cooperative in terms of action planning, execution, communication, and goal management.
– **Acceptance** (esp. Challenges 4, 5 and 6): The directability and observability of a team members' behaviour, which addresses among others the capability to dynamically adjust the own level of autonomy, the necessity to not act capricious, and the requirement of managing the attention of others.

In a comprehensive work, *Sycara* and *Sukthankar* [22] discuss these categories by highlighting the importance of information exchange, fruitful communication, supporting behaviour, and team initiative. The authors state that the key factors for enabling human-agent teamwork are related to mutual predictability, to building a shared understanding, which is here named team knowledge, and the ability of the teammates to redirect and adapt to each other.

3 Definition

We started to approach the concept of joint human-agent activities by discussing challenges and requirements for making artificial agents team members. One conclusion we can draw is that there are several keywords used when talking about joint human-agent activities—reaching from teamwork, human-agent teamwork, human-automation teamwork to joint activities, cooperative activities, cooperation, shared activities, to name but a few. One common aspect one can find within these terms is the concept of an action as atomic building block of each activity. Furthermore, it is frequently talked about the coordination of actions in this setting—leading to the concept of joint actions as atomic building block of joint activities. *H.H. Clark* defines joint actions with respect to the usage of language in communication as follows: *'A joint action is one that is carried out by an ensemble of people acting in coordination with each other.'* [8, p. 3].

Joint Actions: The first clarification we are receiving is that joint actions/-coordination takes place between two or more individuals. In fact, coordination is the inherent part of each joint action. That is to say, that during a joint activity the individuals perform actions and that the coordination of these actions between each other is named joint action – note that the joint action includes the coordinated actions as well [8]. This coordination process includes the mutual characteristics that have been introduced; adding a context to the joint action. This context also provides the actions' goal. That means, that (joint)-actions are always performed with an intention. Writing about agent teamwork, *Cohen et al.* claims that this intention is an essential concept for the overall teamwork as well: *'A team is a set of agents having a shared objective and a shared mental state – without either, there is no unified activity and hence no team'* [9, p. 94].

Joint Goals: In this description the intention is named shared objective. Earlier, we have talked about it describing the concepts of a joint goal and a basic compact. Introducing the shared goal enables us to exclude independent cooperation. Indeed, the notion of a shared goal differs from the notion of a common goal in that a common goal can be established by individuals independent of each other, whereas a shared goal requires an active coordination process [9].[1] The shared mental state is the second important concept in the statement of *Cohen et al.* We have referred to this concept as the challenge to build a common ground and to build adequate models about the teammates. This allows us to infer that teams perform joint activities during the teamwork. Furthermore, we again see that coordination is a major part of the joint activity, not only at the actual action level, but also at the goal level. This is because the coordinated actions might affect the goal-directed activities of the partners, making it necessary to coordinate the individual goals [17]. We have learned about this requirement introducing the challenges goal negotiation and collaboration. An attempt to define the term joint activity is provided by *Klein et al.* and reads as follows: *'We define joint activity as an extended set of actions that are carried out by an ensemble of people who are coordinating with each other.'* [18, p. 91].

Extended Set of Behaviours: Writing about an extended set of actions this statement emphasises that joint activities are more than actions that are coordinated. Unfortunately the authors miss to describe what is represented by this set. However, we would like to highlight that the definition is limited when talking about actions only:

---

[1] Thus, the shared goal is a synonym to the prior introduced joint goal.

– *M.E. Bratman* [4] argues that each cooperative activity involves appropriated behaviour by its participants. This includes, among the actions, characteristics such as mutual responsiveness and mutual support.
– *Johnson et al.* [16] support this while writing about required interdependence relationships (capabilities/actions/set of actions) and opportunistic interdependence relationships (behaviours making joint work more effective).
– *Joe et al.* [13] argue that not the automation of tasks is the challenge any longer, but providing 'soft' skills that lead to an effective behaviour during the teamwork.

These comments reveal that we should talk about behaviours and not actions. Interestingly, *Klein et al.* defined joint activity in a succeeding work as follows: '*A joint activity is an extended set of behaviors that are carried out by an ensemble of people who are coordinating with each other.*' [17, p. 8]. While arguing that a joint activity consists of behaviours that must be coordinated, the nature of the extended set remains undefined. For this work, we follow the argumentation of *Johnson et al.* [16] and refer to interdependence relationships as what defines the extended set of behaviours. Thus the extended set of behaviours refers to all characteristics necessary for a fluent teamwork.

Taking these clarifications and the explanations of the different authors together eventually enables us to define the term joint human-agent activity:

A joint human-agent activity is an extended set of behaviours that is executed by an ensemble of natural and artificial agents who are coordinating with each other working in relative continuous interaction to achieve a joint goal.

The definition builds on the idea that we should explicitly distinguish between natural and artificial agents. This idea is grounded on the observation that we are far away from achieving the fluid action-meshing found in human-human teams [13]. Thus highlighting that there is, by nature, a difference in the capabilities, e.g. cognitive and locomotoric skills, of the individuals. Additionally, we have made explicit the continuous interaction. It is necessary to enable the team partners to build a common ground and adequate models. Thus excluding settings, where participants negotiate a joint goal and coordinate actions once and work towards the joint goal without further interaction.

References

1. Ahrndt, S., Fähndrich, J., Albayrak, S.: Human-agent teamwork: what is predictability, why is it important? In: SAC 2016, pp. 284–286. ACM Press (2016)
2. Baarslag, T., Hendrikx, M.J., Hindriks, K.V., Jonker, C.M.: Learning about the opponent in automated bilateral negotiation: a comprehensive survey of opponent modeling techniques. Auton. Agent Multi Agent Syst. pp. 1–50 (2015)
3. Bradshaw, J.M., Feltovich, P., Johnson, M., Breedy, M., Bunch, L., Eskridge, T., Jung, H., Lott, J., Uszok, A., van Diggelen, J.: From tools to teammates: joint activity in human-agent-robot teams. In: Kurosu, M. (ed.) HCD 2009. LNCS, vol. 5619, pp. 935–944. Springer, Heidelberg (2009)

4. Bratman, M.E.: Shared cooperative activity. Philos. Rev. **101**(2), 327–341 (1992)
5. Brennan, S.E.: The grounding problem in conversations with and through computers. In: Fussell, S., Kreuz, R. (eds.) Social and Cognitive Psychological Approaches to Interpersonal Communicaton, pp. 201–225. Lawrence Erlbaum Associates, Hillsdale (1998)
6. Christoffersen, K., Woods, D.D.: How to make automated systems team players. Adv. Hum. Perform. Cogn. Eng. Res. **2**, 1–12 (2002)
7. Cirillo, M., Karlsson, L., Saffiotti, A.: Human-aware planning for robots embedded in ambient ecologies. Pervasive Mob. Comput. **8**, 542–561 (2012)
8. Clark, H.H.: Using Language. Cambridge Univ. Press, Cambridge (1996)
9. Cohen, P.R., Levesque, H.J., Smith, I.: On team formation. In: Holmstrom-Hintikka, G., Tuomela, R. (eds.) Contemporary Action Theory, Synthese, vol. 2, pp. 87–114. Social Action (1997)
10. Grosz, B.J., Kraus, S.: Collaborative plans for complex group actions. Artif. Intell. **86**(2), 269–357 (1996)
11. Hoffman, G., Breazeal, C.: Effects of anticipatory action on human-robot teamwork – efficiency, fluency, and perception of team. In: HRI 2007, pp. 1–8. ACM Press (2007)
12. Jennings, N.R.: Commitments and conventions: the foundation of coordination in multi-agent systems. Knowl. Eng. Rev. **8**(3), 223–250 (1993)
13. Joe, J.C., O'Hara, J., Medema, H.D., Oxstrand, J.H.: Identifying requirements for effective human-automation teamwork. In: PSAM 12 (2014)
14. Johnson, M., Bradshaw, J.M., Feltovich, P.J., Jonker, C.M., van Riemsdijk, B., Sierhuis, M.: The fundamental principle of coactive design: interdependence must shape autonomy. In: Vos, M., Fornara, N., Pitt, J.V., Vouros, G. (eds.) COIN 2010. LNCS, vol. 6541, pp. 172–191. Springer, Heidelberg (2011)
15. Johnson, M., Bradshaw, J.M., Feltovich, P.J., Jonker, C.M., van Riemsdijk, B., Sierhuis, M.: Autonomy and interdependence in human-agent-robot teams. IEEE Intell. Syst. **27**(2), 43–51 (2012)
16. Johnson, M., Bradshaw, J.M., Feltovich, P.J., Jonker, C.M., van Riemsdijk, M.B., Sierhuis, M.: Coactive design: designing support for interdependence in joint activity. J. Hum. Rob. Interact. **3**(1), 43–69 (2014)
17. Klein, G., Feltovich, P.J., Bradshaw, J.M., Woods, D.D.: Common ground and coordination in joint activitiy. In: Rouse, W.B., Boff, K.R. (eds.) Organizational Simmulation, Chap. 6, pp. 139–184 (2005)
18. Klein, G., Woods, D.D., Bradshaw, J.M., Hoffmann, R.R., Feltovich, P.J.: Ten challenges for making automation a "team player" in joint human-agent activity. Hum. Centered Comput. **19**(6), 91–95 (2004)
19. Lin, R., Kraus, S.: Can automated agents proficiently negotiate with humans? Commun. ACM **53**(1), 78–88 (2010)
20. Myers, K.L., Morley, D.N.: Human directability of agents. In: K-CAP 2001, pp. 108–115. ACM Press (2001)
21. Rosenthal, S., Biswas, J., Veloso, M.: An effective personal mobile robot agent through symbiotic human-robot interaction. In: AAMAS 2010, pp. 915–922 (2010)
22. Sycara, K., Sukthankar, G.: Literature review of teamwork models. Technical report CMU-RI-TR-06-50, Robotics Institute, Pittsburgh, PA (2006)
23. Sycara, K.P., Lewis, M.: Integrating intelligent agents into human teams. In: Salas, E., Fiore, S. (eds.) Team Cognition: Understanding the Factors that Drive Process and Performance, pp. 1–36. American Psychological Association, March 2004

Innovative and Emerging
Applications of MAS

S²CMAS: An Agent-Based System for Planning and Control in Semiconductor Supply Chains

Raphael Herding and Lars Mönch[✉]

Chair of Enterprise-Wide Software Systems, University of Hagen,
Universitätsstraße 1, 58097 Hagen, Germany
{Raphael.Herding,Lars.Moench}@fernuni-hagen.de

Abstract. In this paper, we describe the design and the implementation of an agent-based system that supports planning and control activities in semiconductor supply chains. The proposed system extends the FABMAS prototype for production control of single wafer fabs by additional enterprise-wide planning-related decision-making agents and staff agents. Web services are used to implement parts of the new planning functionality. Results of simulation experiments with the proposed multi-agent system prototype are presented that indicate that the proposed approach is feasible.

Keywords: Semiconductor supply chains · Agent-based decision support · Design of multi-agent systems · Web services · Simulation-based performance assessment

1 Introduction

Semiconductor manufacturing is characterized by a set of complex manufacturing processes to produce integrated circuits, i.e. chips. The manufacturing process starts with thin silicon discs, so called wafers. Several hundred chips can be produced on each single wafer by fabricating the chips layer by layer in a wafer fab. Then electrical tests identify the dies that are likely to fail when packaged in a probe/sort facility. Probed wafers are sent to assembly facilities where dies that fulfill the requirements are put into a package. In a last step, the assembled dies are sent to a test facility where they are tested to ensure that only high-quality products are delivered to customers. Wafer fab and sort operations are subsumed under frontend operations, whereas assembly and test operations are combined into backend operations. The manufacturing process in the semiconductor industry is very complex because of reentrant process flows on extremely expensive machines, long cycle times, and multiple sources of uncertainty. Capacity expansions are time-consuming and very expensive. The related decisions are based on forecasts that are rarely accurate since the demand is highly volatile [1, 18].

Supply chain management (SCM) issues have become more and more important in the last decade for the semiconductor domain. This is because of the fact that front-end operations are often performed by highly industrialized countries, while backend operations are typically carried out in countries where the labor rates are cheaper.

© Springer International Publishing Switzerland 2016
M. Klusch et al. (Eds.): MATES 2016, LNAI 9872, pp. 115–130, 2016.
DOI: 10.1007/978-3-319-45889-2_9

Semiconductor supply chains are an extreme field for SCM solutions from an algorithmic and also from a software point of view [1]. At the same time, the decision support for semiconductor supply chains is often based on packaged Advanced Planning and Scheduling (APS) software [11, 14, 21] that is not tailored to the specific needs of semiconductor supply chains.

While some multi-agent systems (MAS) are proposed for operational decisions in single wafer fabs [15, 16, 29] to the best of our knowledge, this is not the case for semiconductor supply chains. In the present paper, we present design and implementation details for the S^2CMAS prototype, a MAS that is hybridized with web services to provide planning and control functionality for semiconductor supply chains.

The paper is organized as follows. In the next section, we describe the problem. Therefore, we identify requirements for an agent-based decision support in enterprise-wide semiconductor supply chains. In addition, related literature is discussed. The design of the S^2CMAS prototype is specified in Subsect. 3. The results of simulation experiments with the prototype are presented in Subsect. 4. Conclusions and future research directions are provided in Sect. 5.

2 Problem Setting

2.1 Requirements for Agent-Based Planning and Control

The planning functionality and control functionality for semiconductor supply chains include demand and inventory planning, network design, long and mid-term capacity planning, master planning, order release planning, i.e. operational production planning, and various production control activities such as scheduling and dispatching. Demand and inventory planning, network design, capacity planning and master planning are performed on the network level, while order release planning and scheduling and dispatching is often carried out for single frontend and backend facilities. A distributed hierarchical decision making process (cf. [24] for details) is implemented in semiconductor supply chains [18] where two entities are in a hierarchical relationship if they exhibit some asymmetric relationship with respect to their decision rights, their information status, or simply the point of time where decisions are made [24].

It is well-known that monolithic packaged software systems for planning and control purposes have some limitations in semiconductor supply chains (cf. [14, 21, 23]) since it is challenging to deal with the demand uncertainty, the long cycle times, and the reentrant flows. Therefore, companies tend to offer more specialized functionality by extending commercial software packages or using fully home-grown solutions. In this situation, the packaged software systems often provide the data for the tailored systems. However, since supply chains are distributed and contain by nature decision-makers with a certain level of autonomy, it seems that planning and control functionality offered by software agents provides some advantage in this situation.

Next, we summarize requirements that have to be fulfilled by a planning and control system for semiconductor supply chains:

1. The total functionality of the system must span the entire range of planning and control functions required to manage a semiconductor supply chain ranging from

long-term demand and inventory planning for the entire network to short-term detailed scheduling for single wafer fabs. Therefore, the distributed hierarchical structure of semiconductor supply chains has to be taken into account by the system architecture. This means that a decentralized decision-making has to be allowed by the planning and control system. This includes especially iterative feedforward and feedback cycles to implement communication or even negotiation processes among the different decision-making entities.

2. The system has to be able to communicate with other application systems and human decision makers in the semiconductor supply chain to foster an information exchange. Existing communication standards have to be respected if appropriate.

3. It is required that the planning and control system is scalable, i.e., increasing the size of the base system and the base process does not lead to a loss in performance of the provided planning and control algorithms.

4. The frequent changes in the base system and process of semiconductor supply chains have to be reflected by the system architecture, i.e., it is desirable that certain functionality of the overall planning and control system can be replaced during run time of the system. Therefore, a clear separation between the planning and control algorithms and the planning and control system is required.

5. The planning and control system has to allow for a situation-dependent parameterization of the provided planning and control algorithms.

6. Since the system must be able to support planning decisions, it is required that appropriate what-if analysis functionality is provided. That means especially that the system is able to derive meaningful variants of given base scenarios to analyze and understand the consequences of future decisions.

7. The system must be capable to support assessing the performance of the planning and control algorithms using simulation. Simulation can also be used as a tool that supports decisions or can be used as an important ingredient of a what-if analysis.

8. The system must be able to integrate functionality that is provided by other application systems in the semiconductor supply chain since it cannot be expected that the proposed system provides the entire production planning and control functionality.

9. There is often more than one service candidate to provide a specific functionality. In this situation, an appropriate selection of service candidates has to be supported by the proposed system.

10. The system architecture must be open to adopt new trends in manufacturing such as cloud computing [8] or in-memory computing [7].

According to Schneeweiss [24] it is possible to implement distributed hierarchical decision-making systems by means of MAS if the corresponding software agents are equipped with optimization and advanced coordination capabilities. At the same time, agents allow for a meaningful, rich communication. Since MAS are distributed systems, the scalability of the system is ensured. Therefore, we are interested in providing agent-based decision support for semiconductor supply chains to fulfill the requirements 1–4.

The concept of decision-making and staff agents is provided by the Product Resource Order Staff Architecture (PROSA) reference architecture [27] in holonic manufacturing. Staff agents support decision-making agents in course of solving their decision problems. They encapsulate algorithms for decision-making. PROSA is extended towards generic application domains by differentiating between resources, tasks, and task types in [26]. We argue that a separation between decision-making and staff agents is useful to fulfill the requirements 5–7. A separation of planning and control algorithms from the planning and control system is ensured by differentiating between decision-making and staff agents. Staff agents are able to provide situation-dependent parameter settings in the various planning and control algorithms, i.e. requirement 5 is supported. Scenario agents as specific staff agents fulfill requirement 6. Discrete-event simulation can be embedded into staff agents to meet the requirement of simulation-based support of performance assessment and decision-making capabilities.

The remaining three requirements are supported by hybridizing the MAS with web services. Planning and control functionality provided by legacy systems can be encapsulated into web services. The operations of these web services can be used by the software agents, i.e., the web services can be discovered and engaged by software agents. Therefore, this allows us to meet requirement 8. Techniques for web service selection can be incorporated into staff agents. This results in supporting requirement 9. Finally, requirement 10 is supported by web services since web services are considered as one of the key enabling technologies for cloud manufacturing [7]. Moreover, web services support to a certain extent requirement 2 since they are based on human readable and machine readable, i.e., XML-based communication protocols.

2.2 Related Work

We discuss related work with respect to MAS in SCM, methods to hybridize service-oriented architecture (SOA) approaches with MAS and known MAS applications in semiconductor manufacturing. Agent-based approaches for SCM are discussed quite often in the literature. Requirements for agent-based systems to provide SCM functionality are discussed in [5]. We refer to [13] for a related survey.

There are several attempts described in the literature to equip MAS with SOA techniques and vice versa. Huhns [9, 10] argues that agents, on the one hand, have to applied in SOA-based information systems to support service composition and selection, to contribute the rich communication abilities, and to allow for a proactive behavior of the resulting hybrid systems. On the other hand, SOA solutions offer operability in a standardized way, and they are widely accepted in the industry. A similar discussion is presented in [28].

The ALIVE architecture described in [3] differentiates between a coordination layer that is based on software agents and a service layer that is formed by web services. The web services are invoked by the software agents of the coordination layer. The differentiation between agents and services in ALIVE is somewhat similar to the differentiation of decision-making and staff agents in the PROSA architecture, i.e., the staff agents from PROSA are replaced by web services. Decision support systems based on software agents that invoke services to build and run decision models are proposed in [4]. The proposed architecture is applied to solve a collaborative planning, forecasting and replenishment problem in supply chains. In a certain sense, this proposal is similar to replacing certain services provided by a staff agent in PROSA by web services.

An agent-based approach for supply chain collaboration is discussed in [12]. Web services are enriched by coordinating software agents to ensure autonomy and proactiveness of the decision-making entities in the supply chain. Combining agents with web services for decision-making in supply chains is also proposed in [22]. However, rather simple supply chains compared to semiconductor supply chains are considered in these two papers. The Supply Chain Optimization and Protocol Environment (SCOPE) [19] allows for a rapid prototyping of supply chains. The nodes of a supply chain are represented by simple agents that are able to make production planning decisions based on linear programming models.

It is expected that industrial agent-based systems for automation will incorporate SOA concepts since web services can be implemented directly on devises [2]. The agents can be integrated with the devises or act as a service orchestrator. A framework for developing service-oriented agent-based manufacturing systems is proposed in [6]. It equips the ANEMONA approach for developing holonic manufacturing systems with service-based features that are required to apply ANEMONA for the SCM domain. However, in contrast to [6], we believe that the decision problems should be the starting point to design MAS applications for complex supply chains.

MAS approaches applied to the semiconductor manufacturing domain are rarely discussed in the literature. We are only aware of the FABMAS system prototype [15, 16] and a MAS for scheduling with hard real-time restrictions in wafer fabs described in [29]. FABMAS is a hierarchically organized MAS that provides scheduling support for single wafer fabs. The FABMAS design is based on PROSA. The system is implemented using the ManufAg framework [17]. SCOPE is applied in [20] to model fairly simple semiconductor supply chains. Simulation models based on system dynamics are used to study the dynamic behavior of the supply chain. However, the strengths of agent-based approaches such as rich communication capabilities or distributed computing abilities are not fully used in this paper. Overall, to the best of our knowledge, agent-based systems for semiconductor supply chains are not described in the literature so far. Based on the discussion in this subsection, it seems reasonable to develop hybrid systems that involve software agents and web services at the same time.

3   Design and Implementation of the S²CMAS Prototype

3.1   Identifying Appropriate Agents

We start by identifying appropriate software agents. This step should be based on the analysis of the decision problems to be solved. Because of requirement 1, it makes sense to extend the FABMAS system towards the new functionality needed to carry out planning and control tasks in semiconductor supply chains. This means especially that the agents provided by FABMAS will be included in S²CMAS too. The most important decision-making and staff agent types summarized in Table 1 are considered in the S²CMAS prototype. The abbreviation DM refers to decision-making agents while S indicates that a staff agent is used.

Table 1. Main functionality of the members of the FABMAS agency

Agent	Type	Description
Lot agent	DM	Represents a single lot
Product agent	DM	Encapsulates the product knowledge
		Decision-making for selecting alternative machines in the case of machine breakdowns
Fab agent	DM	Coordinates the lot planning agent
		Coordinates the work area agents
		Decision-making for lot-based decomposition approaches
Lot planning agent	S	Prepares to run a specific lot planning algorithm
		Runs the algorithm
		Provides lot plans
Work area agent	DM	Coordinates the work of the corresponding work area scheduling agent
		Decision-making in form of choosing appropriate shifting bottleneck heuristic ingredients
Work area scheduling agent	S	Prepares to run the shifting bottleneck heuristic
		Runs the heuristic
		Provides scheduling information
Work center agent	DM	Implements the work area schedules
		Serves as mediator for contract net-based allocation algo-Rythms

The agents in Table 1 exploit the fact that lots, a collection of wafers, are the moving entities in wafer fabs, and that a single wafer fab can be decomposed into several work areas. Each work area consists of different work centers. A single work center is formed by machines that provide the same functionality. The fab agent is responsible for decomposing the overall scheduling problem for a single wafer fab into a series of scheduling problems for work areas. Start and completion dates for the different work areas are assigned to each single lot using lot planning algorithms. The scheduling problem for a single work area is solved by the shifting bottleneck heuristic. Iterative exchange processes to compute modified start and completion dates based on the work area schedules are performed (cf. [16] for details of the algorithms).

Based on the additional production planning and control functionality described in Subsect. 2.1, new decision-making agent types are identified for the S^2CMAS system to support planning and control activities in the supply chain. We take into account the distributed hierarchical structure of semiconductor supply chains when identifying the agents. This approach again supports the fulfillment of requirement 1. The identified decision-making agent types are summarized in Table 2.

Note that several refinements and extensions of the agency in Table 2 are possible. For instance, a decision-making agent for inventory management might be added. We see from Table 2 that most of the identified agents are responsible for network-wide tasks whereas the agents in Table 1 only provide functionality to control a single wafer fab.

Table 2. Main functionality of the additional DM agents of the S²CMAS agency

Agent	Description
Demand planning agent	Coordinates the forecasting agent
	Coordinates the capacity planning agent
Capacity planning agent	Coordinates the long-term network-wide planning agent
	Coordinates the master planning agent
	Interacts with scenario agents
Master planning agent	Coordinates the different order release agents
	Coordinates the mid-term network-wide planning agents
	Interacts with scenario agents
Order release agent	Coordinates the fab planning agent
	Coordinates with the fab agent
Available to Promise (ATP) agent	Coordinates the ATP planning agent
	Interacts with the master planning agent
Order agent	Represents a single order (based on a customer request or on forecast)

Next, we summarize various staff agents in Table 3 that support the agents from Table 2 in the course of their decision-making. Staff agents encapsulate decision rules and support the decision-making agents to perform actions. We see from Table 3 that several staff agents exist that provide planning functionality. Moreover, the scenario agents and the simulation agents might provide support for several decision-making agents that have to provide planning functionality. The simulation agent offers discrete-event simulation functionality. Services encapsulate a concrete functionality that is stateless. They might offer a concrete planning or simulation functionality.

Table 3. Main functionality of the additional staff agents of the S²CMAS agency

Agent	Description
Forecasting agent	Prepares to run a specific forecast algorithm
	Runs the algorithm
	Aggregates/disaggregates the forecasts
	Provides forecast information
Long-term network-wide planning agent	Prepares to run a specific planning algorithm
	Runs the algorithm
	Provides plans for the network
Mid-term network-wide planning agents	Prepares to run the planning algorithm
	Runs the planning algorithm
	Provides master plans
Fab planning agent	Prepares to run a specific production planning algorithm
	Runs the algorithm for a single wafer fab or a set of wafer fabs
	Runs the algorithm
	Provides release plans for single wafer fabs

(Continued)

Table 3. (*Continued*)

Agent	Description
Scenario agent	Generates planning scenarios for various planning-related DM agents based on forecast evolution and capacity pattern
	Provides the scenarios
Simulation agent	Simulates plans to determine expected values of the performance measures
	Supports what-if functionality
ATP planning agent	Prepares algorithms for order acceptance/selection, due date assignment, and order scheduling
	Runs the algorithm
	Proves ATP-related information to master planning and order management
Order management agent	Provides order processing functionality
	Provides order status-related information

3.2 Providing Planning Functionality by Web Services

The different staff agent types identified in Subsect. 3.1 offer the following generic functionality:

1. Select an appropriate service that provides the requested functionality.
2. Prepare to use the specific functionality by collecting the required data.
3. Based on the data from Step 1, a situation-dependent parameterization of the requested functionality, for instance a specific planning algorithm, is performed.
4. Use the functionality, for instance, run the planning algorithms. This might include terminating the functionality based on specific events, for example, by reaching a given maximum computing time.
5. Inform the corresponding decision-making agents about the results of the previous steps.

Since it is unlikely that the entire planning and control functionality will be developed from scratch, decision-making and staff agents might use planning and control functionality from legacy systems. Therefore, it is desirable that the functionality is offered by web services since many packaged software systems are equipped with web services. Composite services can be used by orchestrating existing services. Step1 of the generic functionality ensures that an appropriate service candidate is chosen for each task of a service composition. This requires the solution of appropriate optimization problems.

We differentiate three different ways how services can be used by agents in the S^2CMAS prototype. The first approach is based on the idea that a web service is directly invoked by a decision-making agent. Such a setting is reasonable if only a single service candidate exists and if most of the generic functionality for staff agents is not required. This means especially that a situation-specific parameterization of the functionality does not offer much value. The second option uses a staff agent between

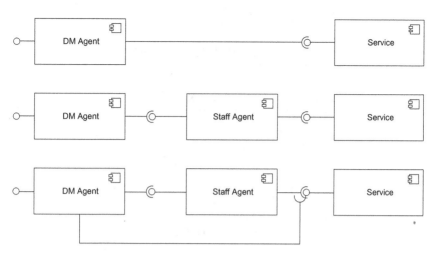

Fig. 1. Usage of services by agents in the S²CMAS prototype

the web service and the decision-making agent. This option is favorable if the full staff agent functionality is required. In a certain sense, staff agents serve as orchestrators. The third option, however, hybridizes the first and the second option. Here, services can be invoked by decision-making agents and by staff agents depending on the problem to be solved. The three principle approaches are shown in Fig. 1.

3.3 Implementation Issues

The S²CMAS prototype is implemented in the C# programming language by extending the FABMAS system [15, 16] that is based on the ManufAg framework [17]. ManufAG allows for implementing distributed hierarchically organized MAS. The web services are stateless. They are coded in the C# programming language. The communication between the agents of the MAS and the web services is based on the HTTP protocol.

The simulation agents are based on simulation services provided by the commercial simulation framework AutoSched AP 9.3 that is coded in the C ++ programming language. The simulation agents build and parameterize AutoSched AP simulation models in a problem- and situation-specific manner. Moreover, a preliminary analysis of the simulation results is performed by these agents. Appropriate demand signals are generated by a demand generator that is implemented in the C# programming language.

Discrete-event simulation is used to assess the S²CMAS prototype. The center point of the proposed architecture is a blackboard-type data layer coded in the C ++ programming language in the memory of the simulation computer that is between the S²CMAS prototype and a simulation model of the base system of the semiconductor supply chain. It contains all the relevant business objects such as lots, machines, and products with corresponding routes. These objects are updated whenever status changes occur in the simulation using the notification mechanism of the simulation engine AutoSched AP. The overall architecture is shown in Fig. 2.

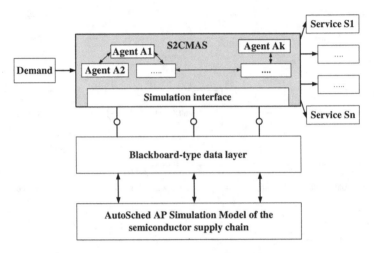

Fig. 2. Performance assessment architecture

4 Simulation Experiments with the S²CMAS Prototype

4.1 Provided Planning Functionality

A finite planning horizon of length T divided into discrete periods of equal length is given. Deterministic demand information is available for the planning horizon. The objective is to determine the amount of each product to release into the wafer fabs in each period so as to minimize the costs caused by these releases. Therefore, we use backward termination to determine the release quantities based on demand D_{gt} for product g in period t. For the sake of simplicity, we assume that D_{gt} is measured in number of lots. We set the release period r_j for each lot j that belongs to D_{gt} by

$$r_j := \left\lfloor \max\left(t - FF \sum_{k=1}^{n_j} p_{jk}, 0\right) \right\rfloor, \tag{1}$$

where p_{jk} is the processing time of process step k of lot j and n_j is the number of process steps for lot j. The quantity $FF \geq 1$ is the flow factor, i.e. the ratio of the amount of time a lot spends in a wafer fab and the raw processing time $\sum_{k=1}^{n_j} p_{jk}$. Of course, we assume that an amount of $(FF - 1)p_{jk}$ is associated with the waiting time for process step k of lot j. All lots to be released in the current period t are distributed uniformly over this period. The resulting detailed release date for lot j is s_j. The obtained release schedule is implemented until the next backward termination is computed along the timeline in a rolling horizon setting.

The quantity FF has to be chosen in Eq. (1). Since the cycle times of the lots increase in a nonlinear manner with increasing resource utilization that is a result of the release plan, we propose to use discrete-event simulation to find appropriate FF values. We consider the future demand to come up with a FF value for this situation.

The demand leads to a certain bottleneck utilization that can be used to determine a FF value FF_1. In addition, realized FF values from already executed release plans are taken into account to compute a second FF value FF_2. Several FF values from an equidistant grid of the interval $[\min(FF_1, FF_2), \max(FF_1, FF_2)]$ are used to determine release plans. These plans are then simulated using FIFO dispatching of the lots. The FF values associated with the release plane are calculated. The FF value $FF^* \in [\min(FF_1, FF_2), \max(FF_1, FF_2)]$ leading to the smallest absolute difference between the measured FF value and the FF value used for the backward termination is selected. Next, the lots to be released in the current period are assigned to individual wafer fabs by applying simple load balancing techniques.

The release plans are used to compute start and completion dates for the lots with respect to each single work area. This information is necessary to determine detailed schedules based on the distributed shifting bottleneck heuristic (DSBH).

The order release planning functionality is implemented in the S²CMAS prototype by adding an order release agent. This decision-making agent interacts with a single Fab planning agent. This agent is responsible to run the backward termination algorithm that is implemented by means of a web service. In order to parameterize the backward termination algorithm correctly, several simulation runs are necessary that are provided by a simulation agent. Therefore, the second option for invoking services by agents is used in this planning scenario. The final release plan is submitted to the fab agent of a single wafer fab that is responsible to determine lot plans that are a necessary ingredient to compute detailed schedules for the lots in each single wafer fab using the DSBH approach. The described situation is shown in the UML sequence diagram in Fig. 3.

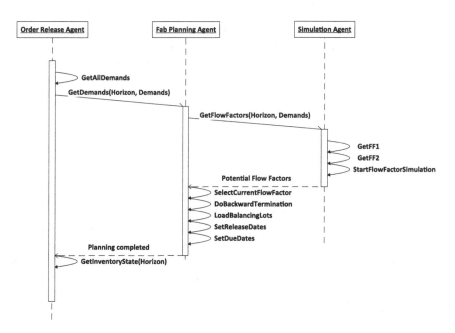

Fig. 3. Interaction of the different agents in the order release planning scenario

4.2   Simulation Environment and Design of Experiments

A small-sized enterprise-wide semiconductor supply chain that consists of two identical wafer fabs is used within the simulation experiments for applying the order release functionality and detailed scheduling in a rolling horizon manner. Each of them contains three work areas. A single work area consists of three work centers, among them one with batch processing machines, i.e., several lots are processed at the same time in a batch on a single machine, and another one with sequence-dependent setup times. The first work area of each wafer fab is visited two times. Each wafer fab has 15 machines and two products with 24 process steps.

We expect that the performance of the order release mechanism depends on the demand setting. Therefore, we generate normally distributed demand that leads to 70 % and 96 % planned bottleneck utilization in the two wafer fabs. In addition, a coefficient of variation of 0.1 and 0.25 is considered to generate the demand. The first setting refers to low variability demand (VL) and the latter to demand with high variability (VH). In addition, we consider two simple approaches to assign release quantities to a specific wafer fab. The first approach is load-based, i.e., the wafer fab with the smallest work in progress (WIP) is assigned to release the lots associated with a certain product and period. The second approach randomly assigns with equal probability one of the two fabs to the lots. The products and the periods are taken into account in a given sequence for both approaches.

Simulation runs are performed for 200 days. The length of a single period is two days. The release plan is revised after a single period, i.e., only the first period is implemented. A planning horizon of $T = 6$ periods is considered. The DSBH is used every two hours with a scheduling horizon of three hours. The scheduling subproblems that are a result of the SBH approach are solved using list scheduling based on the Apparent Tardiness Cost dispatching rule. The lot planning algorithm offered by the lot planning agent is applied twice per shift. Here, a fairly simple forward termination algorithm is used to determine the start and completion dates for the lots with respect to each single work area. A due date d_j is assigned to each released lot based on

$$d_j := s_j + z_j \cdot FF^* \sum_{k=1}^{n_j} p_{jk}, \tag{2}$$

where $z_j = 0.45$ if lot j belongs to the first product and $z_j = 2.35$ if j is a lot of the second product. We use this due date setting scheme to mimic the situation that the processing of lots of the first product is urgent whereas lots of the second product have a large slack. The lot weights are selected as $w_j = 10$ for the first product, whereas the setting $w_j = 1$ is used for the second product. We are interested in assessing the profit obtained over the simulation horizon. The profit is the difference of revenue and WIP, backlog, and inventory holding costs. The revenue value per lot is 180, while the unit backlog, WIP, and inventory costs per period are 50, 35, and 15, respectively. The computational experiments are carried out on a PC with 32 GB of RAM and an Intel Xenon E5-2620 CPU with 24 virtual cores where each core has a CPU frequency of 2.0 GHz.

4.3 Results of Computational Experiments

The simulation results are shown in Table 4. Here, we denote by BN the planned bottleneck utilization, whereas LB is used to indicate the load balancing approach used in the experiments. The results are presented as follows. Instead of comparing all simulation cases individually, the cases were grouped according to factor level values. For example, the results for *VL* and *BN* = 70 % are averaged over all runs where demand is generated with *CV* = 0.1 that leads to a bottleneck utilization of 70 % while all the other factors have been varied at their different levels. We show in each column first the value obtained by FIFO dispatching, while the corresponding value obtained by the DSBH scheme is in the cell below. For instance, for *VL* and *BN* = 70 % we have a profit value of 343540 for FIFO and a profit value of 358500 for DSBH. Superior profit values are marked in bold.

We see from Table 4 that using the order release planning approach together with the DSBH-based scheduling approach is beneficial, i.e., the scheduling approach leads to larger profit values compared to FIFO-based dispatching. The positive effects are larger in case of low variability demand and a highly utilized planned bottleneck. The two load balancing schemes do not lead to significantly different profit values. This

Table 4. Simulation results

	Revenue	WIP	Backlog	Inventory	Profit
	FIFO/SBH	FIFO/SBH	FIFO/SBH	FIFO/SBH	FIFO/SBH
VL					
BN					
70 %	474040	103985	11500	15015	343540
	484040	104055	9500	11985	**358500**
97 %	820380	212310	50400	20820	536850
	852020	217210	46150	16145	**572515**
LB					
L	631440	159145	31300	17595	423400
	667940	161805	28350	13720	**464065**
R	631980	157150	30600	18240	425990
	668120	159460	27300	14410	**466950**
VH					
BN					
70 %	461340	102970	11350	14745	332275
	466556	103215	8750	10544	**344047**
97 %	794520	208740	47200	20370	518210
	826160	214340	46900	18680	**546240**
LB					
L	627480	156135	28850	17310	425185
	646088	158690	27000	14402	**445996**
R	628380	155575	29700	17805	425300
	646628	158865	28650	14822	**444291**

result is expected since the lots are randomly released into one of the two wafer fabs with equal probability and the two fabs are identical.

5   Conclusions and Future Research

In this paper, we discussed an agent-based system prototype that supports planning and control activities in semiconductor supply chains. Appropriate agents are identified. We designed the interaction of the various agents with web services that implement the planning and control functionality. The results of experiments with the S^2CMAS prototype using a simulation model of a scaled-down semiconductor supply chain were presented and discussed.

There are several directions for future research. First of all, the functionality of the S^2CMAS prototype has to be extended. We are interested in adding functionality related to master planning, to the order management process and related to ATP. More simulation experiments with larger simulation models of semiconductor supply chains have to be performed. Standardized communication is an important ingredient for an agent-based decision support. Therefore, we are interested in designing an appropriate ontology based on the ISA 95 standard (cf. Scholten [25]).

Acknowledgement.   The authors would like to thank the attendees of the Dagstuhl Seminar 16062 "Modeling and Analysis of Semiconductor Supply Chains", especially Irvan M. Ovacik, Intel, and Kenneth Fordyce, Arkieva, for interesting discussions about modeling issues and planning software for semiconductor supply chains.

References

1. Chien, C.-F., Dauzère-Pérès, S., Ehm, H., Fowler, J.W., Jiang, Z., Krishnaswamy, S., Mönch, L., Uzsoy, R.: Modeling and analysis of semiconductor manufacturing in a shrinking world: challenges and successes. Eur. J. Ind. Eng. **5**(3), 254–271 (2011)
2. Colombo, A.W., Karnouskos, S., Mendes, J.M., Leitão, P.: Industrial agents in the era of service-oriented architectures and cloud-based industrial infrastructures. In: Leitão, P., Karnouskos, S. (eds.) Industrial Agents: Emerging Applications of Software Agents in Industry, Chap. 4, pp. 67–87. Elsevier, Amsterdam (2015)
3. Dignum, F., Dignum, V., Padget, J.A., Vázquez-Salceda, J.: Organizing web services to develop dynamic, flexible, distributed systems. In: Proceedings of the Eleventh International Conference on Information Integration and Web-based Applications and Services (iiWAS 2009), pp. 225–234 (2009)
4. Dong, C.-S.J., Srinivasan, A.: Agent-enabled service-oriented decision support systems. Decis. Support Syst. **55**, 364–373 (2013)
5. Fox, M.S., Barbuceanu, M., Teigen, R.: Agent-oriented supply-chain management. Int. J. Flex. Manuf. Syst. **12**, 165–188 (2000)
6. Giret, A., Botti, V.: ANEMONA-S + Thomas: a framework for developing service-oriented intelligent manufacturing systems. In: Borangiu, T., Thomas, A., Trentesaux, D. (eds.) Service Orientation in Holonic and Multi-agent Manufacturing, pp. 61–70. Springer, Heidelberg (2015)

7. Hahn, G.J., Packowski, J.: A perspective on applications of in-memory analytics in supply chain management. Decis. Support Syst. **76**, 45–52 (2015)
8. He, W., Xu, L.: A state-of-the-art survey of cloud manufacturing. Int. J. Comput. Integr. Manuf. **28**(3), 239–250 (2015)
9. Huhns, M.N.: Software agents: the future of web services. In: Kowalczyk, R., Müller, J.P., Tianfield, H., Unland, R. (eds.) NODe-WS 2002. LNCS (LNAI), vol. 2592, pp. 1–18. Springer, Heidelberg (2003)
10. Huhns, M.N.: Services must become more agent-like. Wirtschaftsinformatik **50**, 74–75 (2008)
11. Kallrath, J., Maindl, T.I.: Planning in semiconductor manufacturing. In: Kallrath, J., Maindl, T.I. (eds.) Real Optimization with SAP APO, Chap. 5, pp. 105–117. Springer, Heidelberg (2006)
12. Kwon, O., Im, G.P., Lee, K.C.: An agent-based web service approach for supply chain collaboration. Scientia Iranica1 Trans. E Ind. Eng. **18**(6), 1545–1552 (2011)
13. Lee, J.-H., Kim, C.-O.: Multi-agent systems applications in manufacturing systems and supply chain management: a review paper. Int. J. Prod. Res. **46**(1), 233–265 (2008)
14. Lin, C.-H., Hwang, S.-L., Wang, M.-Y. E.: The mythical advanced planning systems in complex manufacturing environment. In: Proceedings of the 12th IFAC Conference on Information Control Problems in Manufacturing, pp. 691–696 (2006)
15. Mönch, L., Stehli, M., Zimmermann, J.: FABMAS: an agent-based system for production control of semiconductor manufacturing processes. In: Mařík, V., McFarlane, D.C., Valckenaers, P. (eds.) HoloMAS 2003. LNCS (LNAI), vol. 2744, pp. 258–267. Springer, Heidelberg (2003)
16. Mönch, L., Stehli, M., Zimmermann, J., Habenicht, I.: The FABMAS multi-agent-system prototype for production control of waferfabs: design, implementation, and performance assessment. Prod. Plan. Control **17**(7), 701–716 (2006)
17. Mönch, L., Stehli, M.: ManufAg: a multi-agent-system framework for production control of complex manufacturing systems. Inf. Syst. e-Bus. Manag. **4**, 159–185 (2006)
18. Mönch, L., Fowler, J.W., Mason, S.J.: Production Planning and Control for Semiconductor Wafer Fabrication Facilities: Modeling, Analysis, and Systems. Springer, New York (2013)
19. Orcun, S., Asmundsson, J.M., Uzsoy, R., Clement, J.P., Pekny, J.F., Rardin, R.L.: Supply Chain Optimization and Protocol Environment (SCOPE) for rapid prototyping of supply chains. Prod. Plan. Control **18**(5), 388–406 (2007)
20. Orcun, S., Uzsoy, R.: The effect of production planning on the dynamic behavior of a simple supply chain: an experimental study. In: Kempf, K.G., Keskinocak, P., Uzsoy, R. (eds.) Planning Production and Inventories in the Extended Enterprise: A State of the Art Handbook, Chap. 3, vol. 2, pp. 43–80. Springer, New York (2011)
21. Ovacik, I.M.: Advanced planning and scheduling systems: the quest to leverage ERP for better planning. In: Kempf, K., Keskinocak, P., Uzsoy, R. (eds.) Planning Production and Inventories in the Extended Enterprise: A State of the Art Handbook, Chap. 3, vol. 1, pp. 33–43. Springer, New York (2011)
22. Pal, K., Karakostas, B.: A multi agent-based service framework for supply chain management. Procedia Comput. Sci. **32**, 53–60 (2014)
23. Roundy, R.: Report on practices related to demand forecasting for semiconductor products. Technical report. School of Operations Research and Industrial Engineering Cornell University (2001)
24. Schneeweiss, C.: Distributed Decision Making, 2nd edn. Springer, Berlin (2003)
25. Scholten, B.: The Road to Integration: A Guide to Applying the ISA-95 Standard in Manufacturing. ISA, Research Triangle Park, Durham (2007)

26. Van Belle, J., Philips, J., Ali, O., Germain, B.S., Van Brussel, H., Valckenaers, P.: A service-oriented approach for holonic manufacturing control and beyond. In: Borangiu, T., Thomas, A., Trentesaux, D. (eds.) Service Orientation in Holonic and Multi-Agent Manufacturing Control. SCI, vol. 402, pp. 1–20. Springer, Heidelberg (2012)
27. Van Brussel, H., Wyns, J., Valckenaers, P., Bongaerts, L., Peeters, P.: Reference architecture for holonic manufacturing systems: PROSA. Comput. Ind. 37(3), 225–276 (1998)
28. Wobcke, W., Desai, N., Dignum, F., Ghose, A., Padmanabhuni, S., Srivastava, B.: What can agent-based computing offer service-oriented architectures, and vice versa? In: Desai, N., Liu, A., Winikoff, M. (eds.) PRIMA 2010. LNCS, vol. 7057, pp. 1–10. Springer, Heidelberg (2012)
29. Yoon, H.J., Shen, W.: A multiagent-based decision-making system for semiconductor wafer fabrication with hard temporal constraints. IEEE Trans. Semicond. Manufact. 21(1), 83–92 (2008)

Hybrid Teams: Flexible Collaboration Between Humans, Robots and Virtual Agents

Tim Schwartz[1(✉)], Ingo Zinnikus[1], Hans-Ulrich Krieger[1], Christian Bürckert[1], Joachim Folz[1], Bernd Kiefer[1], Peter Hevesi[1], Christoph Lüth[1], Gerald Pirkl[1], Torsten Spieldenner[1,2], Norbert Schmitz[1], Malte Wirkus[1], and Sirko Straube[1]

[1] German Research Center for Artificial Intelligence, DFKI GmbH,
Trippstadter Strasse 122, 67663 Kaiserslautern, Germany
`tim.schwartz@dfki.de`
[2] Saarbrücken Graduate School of Computer Science, Saarbücken, Germany

Abstract. With the increasing capabilities of agents using Artificial Intelligence, an opportunity opens up to form team like collaboration between humans and artificial agents. This paper describes the setting-up of a Hybrid Team consisting of humans, robots, virtual characters and softbots. The team is situated in a flexible industrial production. The work presented here focuses on the central architecture and the characteristics of the team members and components. To achieve the overall team goals, several challenges have to be met to find a balance between autonomous behaviors of individual agents and coordinated teamwork.

1 Introduction

In our everyday life, the role of robots and other agents using Artificial Intelligence (AI) changes rapidly: from purely automated machines and programs up to companions that make suggestions, advises or assist in physical tasks, e.g. carrying heavy weight loads. This process is most obvious in factories where robots become lightweight and work in close vicinity or even in direct collaboration with human workers. At the same time, the industrial production methods and requirements are also changing, demanding more flexible production lines. One concept to accomplish both – using these new possibilities of AI and meeting the requirements of Industrie 4.0 [18] of complex and flexible production – is to establish a new kind of collaboration of humans, robots and virtual agents as Hybrid Teams. As in all teams, the idea here is to benefit from the different characteristics of the individual team members and at the same time make use of the fact, that team members can substitute each other temporarily in completing tasks when resources are running low. For purely human teams, this is completely natural behavior: if a team member drops out, the team tries to compensate this. However, industrial robots are still highly specialized in their task, so that a new level of flexibility and universality is required to make a robot capable to temporarily substitute a human or robotic team member. With this

© Springer International Publishing Switzerland 2016
M. Klusch et al. (Eds.): MATES 2016, LNAI 9872, pp. 131–146, 2016.
DOI: 10.1007/978-3-319-45889-2_10

new robotic skill, the goal of the team can be achieved with higher robustness and flexibility at the same time. The work presented in this article is based on first results of the project *Hybrid Social Teams for Long-Term Collaboration in Cyber-physical Environments* (HySociaTea) [35,40] that targets the setting-up of a Hybrid Team. The rationale of the presented work is to develop a general framework in which Hybrid Teams can be practically realized. The actual team organization within the respective setting is therefore not the focus here, but will be subject to future work. In the following, we describe the setup, types of team members and components of this Hybrid Team, and focus on the central communication architecture that defines how the team interacts, how tasks are assigned to team members, and which levels of autonomous actions are possible within the team. The presented communication architecture is in line with the principles of 'Coactive Design' by Johnson et al. (see also Sect. 2), although not all of its aspects are currently implemented in our overall system.

2 Related Work

Agent-based approaches have already been used for some time in distributed manufacturing scenarios (for an overview see [23]). Team members in those scenarios have diverse capabilities, which need to be represented accordingly in order to be leveraged. [43] use autonomous agents to represent physical entities, processes and operations. For coordinating the activities among the agents, communication among team members is required which in general can be done using centralized or decentralized approaches. Agent-oriented approaches use negotiation protocols for resource allocation, e.g. the Contract Net Protocol or its modified versions, but also distributed market-based paradigms, auction-based models and cooperative auctions to coordinate agent and, in particular, robot actions. E.g. [27] propose a market-based multi-robot task allocation algorithm that produces optimal assignments. An influential line of research has been initiated by the concept of *joint actions* [25], leading to shared plans, where planning and execution in teams need to be interleaved in order to react to unforeseen circumstances [6,30]. In the STEAM framework [41], group activities are structured by team-oriented plans which are decomposed into specific sub-activities that individual robots can perform. Following that strand of research, [37] focuses on the impact that noisy perception of actors has on the coordination process and use cooperative perception techniques to address this problem. While many approaches consider inter-robot coordination, the problem of Hybrid Teams, where members have a certain autonomy has received much less attention so far. A prototype for human-robot teams for specific domains such as urban disaster management has been proposed and developed by [34]. Nevertheless, the investigation of the challenges and requirements involved in flexible human-robot teams and their coordination is still an open topic. In our approach, we focus on how to include human actions and human communication capabilities into the otherwise purely technical infrastructure for the artificial agents. Instead of using a rigid, machine planning-module, which controls the actions of each team member, we rely on the human's planning capabilities and thus keep him in the center and in control of the production process. Substantial work in the context of human-agent teamwork has been done by Johnson et al. [11,12]. Several of the aspects that the authors highlight as important in joint activities have been considered in our work, such as the balance between autonomy and interdependence, the importance of task-oriented coordination between team members including humans, e.g. using dialogs for mixed-initiative interaction (referred to as "soft interdependence" by [12]) and directing the execution of robot tasks. New tasks can be assigned based on capabilities and availability, while the final decision and commitment to take over a task is left to the agents. The status of task fulfillment is monitored and visible to other agents, which in turn can decide to assist in completing an open task if e.g. an agent is not successful. A core role for the usage of location detection, eye tracking and object recognition is the possibility to provide a 'common ground' for all participants which allows them to refer to the same objects in the scenario.

3 Setting and Agents

Hybrid Teams can have many goals depending on the field of application and the concrete mission at hand. In our vision, the team should organize itself according to the individual skills of each team member. Principally, the team members are one of three possible types of agents: Humans play the central role in the team, since they have the highest overall intelligence (the sum of cognitive, social, practical, creative etc. intelligence) and can thus react extremely flexible to new situations. If necessary, humans should be able to even reorganize the team by command (e.g. if the whole mission is in danger). Robots typically take over tedious or physically demanding tasks or go to hazardous (or even hostile to life) areas, and the virtual characters (VCs) have the role of assistants providing a straightforward interface to digitally available information. A typical setting is a production scenario [35]: The Hybrid Team handles jobs with batch size one, has to reorganize itself and even handle multiple tasks in parallel. While the actions of each worker in a standard manufacturing scenario are often predetermined, i.e. each team member follows a more or less rigorous plan, new production settings for highly customized products will demand a flexible behavior of the whole team. Tasks and responsibilities cannot easily be predetermined and the creativity of the team, especially by the human worker, plays an important role. In the following the different agents, their characteristics and role in our realized Hybrid Team are described in short. Examples are provided in the context of a production scenario. An overview of the team is given in Fig. 1.

3.1 Augmented Humans

Unlike robots and VCs, which are technological companions, humans need specialized devices, wearables and interfaces to communicate intuitively with the other members of a Hybrid Team and to feed the whole system with information. For humans, speech is the most natural way of transmitting information,

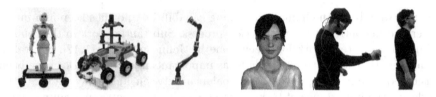

Fig. 1. Members of the Hybrid Team (from left to right): Aila (humanoid service robot), Artemis (logistics robot), Compi ("helping hand"), Gloria (virtual character), and two instrumented workers.

so information-input and -output via speech should be possible on all levels. In particular, the architecture connecting the team should contain an entity that decomposes speech acts, feeding planning- or task monitoring components (see Sect. 4) with information, so that, e.g., humans can ask for a specific item or action. In addition, the other team members need an elaborated speech recognition and speech generation system as well to interact with the human in a natural way. Human team members can interact with the system either using parts of the instrumented environment or via various wearables. Of course, interaction via more traditional devices like keyboards, mice or tablets is also possible, but for a truly natural interaction it would be preferable to have interfaces, which do not require workers to learn how to interact with them. The information of all human related sensors is ideally combined in a fusion module that is thus capable to produce data about the human that is similar to what the robotic team members can provide about themselves. Robots can then use this information for their own planning of movements or other actions. E.g., if a human is looking at a specific position, saying "I need this item", a combined information from speech, direction of gaze and location of objects in the environment will result in an understanding of the human intention. In the following we describe the subsystems that we currently obtain information about the human team members.

Localization. The position of the human can be an essential information for understanding the current context and tracking activity. To interpret for example a simple voice command like "Bring me a box" the system has to locate – amongst other things – the worker, in order to determine the delivery position of the box. Due to the demanding environment involving both human and robotic agents, a robust localization is necessary: For rough position estimation (error below 80 cm) of humans, we used a localization system based on oscillating magnetic fields (c.f. [32]) in the team. The system is relying on stationary anchor points, which are sequentially generating magnetic fields, and wearable receiver units, which measure the amplitude of the induced voltage signals at the human's position (Fig. 2). Each anchor point has a 4 m radius range. A magnetic field model can then determine a receiver's position based on the measured voltages and the known layout of the anchor points. Tasks requiring higher accuracies are supported by our mBeacon system (cf. [31]). The region of interest is tagged

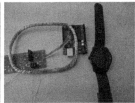

Fig. 2. Left: Hardware for the indoor localization system; Middle: mBeacon proximity detector; Right: Use-case for mBeacon in the scenario

by magnetic field coils encoding a region ID in a quasi-static magnetic field, by applying a PWM signal to the coil. Using typical magnetic field sensors, which are included in most of the smartwatches or smartphones, we can detect an ID up to a distance of 30–40 cm. Such a system can be used, e.g., to detect if the worker is interacting with specific tools or containers.

Eye Tracking and Object Recognition. Using eye-tracking glasses makes it much easier to determine what part of the scene an augmented human is looking at. Compared to a few years ago, technological advances have resulted in comfortable, much less intrusive, and lightweight devices, which makes wearing these glasses for extended periods of time much more realistic. Along with gaze data, such as focused point and pupil radius, eye tracking glasses usually feature a world camera which captures the point of view of the wearer. We stream all provided data along with compressed video to a fusion module (see Sect. 3.1) for processing. One of the unique applications of combining video with gaze is gaze-targeted object recognition. Since humans are more likely to attend objects rather than background [9,16,45], using gaze information provided by eye tracking glasses helps to alleviate confusion caused by clutter by only analyzing a much smaller part of the image. Furthermore, the gaze information explicitly hints at the currently most important object in the scene. Our object recognition system is based on the DeepSentiBank [3] deep convolutional neural network. It is implemented using the Caffe framework [10], which delivers real-time performance via GPU acceleration. To quickly adapt the network to the scenario, its $fc7$-layer output is fed to a linear support vector machine for classification. Initial tests were done on a small data set of 16 household objects with just 3 training images per class, that are bootstrapped to a total of 18000 samples by random rotation, cropping, noise, and brightness transformations. Test precision for this system is 61.7 %, which is already close to the best real-time capable method ORB [33] at 55.3 %. Slower methods like SURF [2] (63.8 %) and SIFT/SURF [28] (80.8 %) can perform significantly better.

Sensory Jacket. A sensory jacket [29] allows to sense the orientation of the upper torso and head, as well as the motion and position of the upper and lower arms. In HySociaTea, the worker is equipped with such a sensory jacket, which includes six motion sensors as depicted in Fig. 3a. All motion sensors are 9-axis inertial motion sensors providing acceleration, gyroscope and magnetic field data from the trunk, the head and both arms (upper and lower arm separated). Each motion sensor data is streamed to an Extended Kalman Filter implemented closely related to Harada et al. [7,17]. The state of the filter consists of a quaternion representing the orientation of each segment in relation to an earth-centered north aligned global coordinate frame. In contrast to Harada et al. the measurement models are not implemented according to the proposed reliability detection but an adaptive measurement noise is applied to the updates corresponding to the deviations from static acceleration and static magnetic field measurements. This modeling technique avoids false reliability detections. Each orientation estimator provides the global orientation of one of the segments. All segments together define the human skeleton model consisting of the six mentioned components as depicted in Fig. 3b. The update rate of the filters are 100 Hz and the achievable orientation accuracy under moderate magnetic field disturbances is in the range of $10°$.

Fusion Module. Though each of the sensors described previously can deliver useful information on its own, they only provide their full potential through sensor fusion where all generated data needs to be combined at one central hub. Also, wearable sensors need to be small, lightweight, and at low power: Complex processing should thus take place on an external machine. We realize this through a fusion module to which all worn sensors can connect through our communication middleware (see Sect. 4). From an architectural and semantical point of view, the fusion module feeds data about the human into the system that are similar to that of robots (which usually also contain such a module that combines e.g. the states of motors into information about the current pose of the robot). There are several benefits from this: First, we reduce the amount of data that has to be streamed though the team network. The unprocessed data streams generated by these sensors would not be useful to other agents in the Hybrid Team and would unnecessarily take away bandwidth. For instance, the world camera of the eye tracking glasses generates $\sim$84 MB/s (1280×960 pixels, 24 Hz) of uncompressed frame data. Later models feature cameras with even higher frame rates and resolutions. We also reduced transmission delays by connecting directly to the fusion module. Second, as more efficient algorithms are used and

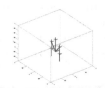

Fig. 3. (a) Sensor jacket with visualization in the background (b) Stick figure model of the upper body motion tracking with six segments (c) Dual Reality Visualization (Color figure online)

technology advances, later iterations of the Hybrid Team may apply the module closer to these sensors, so it will ultimately be a wearable component as well. At its core the fusion module performs the following steps: (i) Preprocessing: convert to common data representation, filtering; (ii) Synchronization: compensate for different sampling rates, system times, and delays of sensors; (iii) Fusion: select best-fitting samples from each stream and perform sensor fusion; (iv) Interfacing: convert to compatible types of the team network and publish to outside world. A simple example for fusion operation is the combination of location, orientation, and gaze direction to disambiguate the region of interest that the augmented human is currently attending. This can be used to enhance speech interactions. E.g., "Can you bring a box over there?", where other agents are able to resolve "over there" to the attended area (workbench, shelf, etc.). Further, combining this approach with object recognition allows determining which agent was addressed by checking recently attended agents.

3.2   Robots

The robots of Hybrid Teams are not classical industrial robots. Instead, these are autonomous agents, which are typically mobile and capable of performing certain manipulation tasks. In the future, these robots will gain higher levels of autonomy and solve sub-problems or tasks on their own. Because they share their work space with humans, safety is an important issue which is nowadays typically addressed by using lightweight systems with low forces. Robots can substitute or share tasks with virtual characters and humans to a certain degree. In the Hybrid Team presented here, three robots are integrated (see Fig. 1) The robot *COMPI* [1] is the only stationary robot in the team. COMPI can switch between various stages of flexibility or stiffness and acts as a "helping hand" for a human, e.g. holding objects. *AILA* [24] is a humanoid, mobile dual-arm robot, which was originally developed to investigate aspects of mobile manipulation. A robot like AILA is an ideal candidate for a real world communication partner for humans. *ARTEMIS* [36] is a rover equipped with a manipulator. In the Hybrid Team, rovers like ARTEMIS can act as logistics robots, transporting tools, building-material or objects from and to different locations.

Robot Control. The robots applied here are developed using BES-LANG [44], a set of domain-specific languages and tools for describing control systems, robot abilities and high-level missions for robotic mobile manipulation, based on ROCK [15], Syskit [13] and Roby [14]. For the mobile robots AILA and ARTEMIS, we have developed the abilities to generate geometrical and travers-ability maps from the data perceived from their laser scanners. The robots can localize themselves on the map and navigate on it. We provide contextual information on the map by defining distinct regions (e.g. "left shelf") using map coordinates. Navigation trajectories can be planned using the Anytime D-Star planning algorithm from the SBPL library [26]. A trajectory controller generates 2D motion commands from the planned trajectories, which are mapped to actual wheel actuation commands by the robot's motion controller module. For grasping objects, we use visual servoing controllers that receive their visual feedback using the ArUco marker detector [4]. Currently, we use those labels for both, the objects and the storage locations. Additionally, there are basic abilities to follow joint or Cartesian way-points or relative movements. By sequencing these abilities more complex tasks are realized. An example is a *bring task* composed of a navigation-ability to the location where the desired item is located, followed by a grasp-ability and then again followed by a navigation- and a hand-over-ability. For each robot, we map a set of high level tasks that is implemented in the robot and prioritize these tasks to reflect the robot's role within the team. To ensure determined robot behavior, only one such task can be executed at once per robot. During task execution feedback is reported to a Blackboard (see Sect. 4) indicating the progress of the task. To provide feedback about the state of the robots to other team members, we created a bridge that is similar to the fusion module for the human-centric sensors.

Collision Detection. In a Hybrid Team with (multiple) mobile robots, collision should be avoided with other robots, with objects, and–most importantly–with the humans. These concerns have actually been one of the main obstacles for the wider adaption of human-robot cooperation; current standards and practices make it nearly impossible to have the two cooperating in the same space, so it is of paramount importance to address this problem in HySociaTea. Collision avoidance works in many ways: on the planning level, we can attempt to make sure that the robot plans his trajectory free of collisions. This breaks down when obstacles appear unexpectedly, and moreover to base a safety argument on it, one would have to verify the planning algorithm. Thus, we supplement high-level collision avoidance with a low-level *collision detection*. This is a module which supervises all movements of the robot, and checks whether the current movement will lead to a collision. Before this is the case, an emergency brake is initiated. The key concept of our collision detection is a *safety zone*. This is the area of space which is covered by the robots manipulators at their current trajectories until breaking to a standstill. Calculating the safety zones efficiently in three dimensions is a hard problem which has been solved by the KCCD library [42]; it models the trajectories as sphere swept convex hulls (SSCH), which can be manipulated efficiently. The library needs reliable sensor input to detect obstacles, which is provided by laser scanners mounted on the robots. This required an extension to the KCCD library to check collisions (intersections) of the SSCH with the point clouds returned from the laser scanners. The collision detection is integrated into the ROCK framework, and runs locally on each robot.

3.3 Virtual Character

Virtual Characters (VCs) take over a special role in Hybrid Teams, because they are not physically present in the real world and so they cannot take-over physical tasks. Instead, VCs represent purely software-based components and serve as a more natural interface for humans than pure text output (written text or spoken text) without such a graphical impression of a human. In addition, they can also transmit emotions via gestures and facial expressions. Our VC Gloria (Fig. 1) is realized using a commercial SDK called CharActor, provided by Charamel (http://www.charamel.com). The CharActor SDK already includes the complete rendering engine, a text-to-speech (TTS) engine including lip-synchronization, and a large library of facial expressions and motions.

3.4 SoftBots

In contrast to VCs, SoftBots are purely software based modules without physical or graphical embodiment. These SoftBots typically aggregate data produced by other team members (e.g. raw sensor data, speech acts) and in turn update databases or provide meaningful, refined data. There are several SoftBots in our current system, e.g. to keep track of the location of objects, tools and materials, or to convert numeric position-coordinates into semantic descriptions. As an example for a more complex SoftBot, we implemented a module that collects information about the worker's requests for building-material, and that automatically learns, which materials are often used together. The VC uses the information provided by this SoftBot, to pro-actively ask if the additional material is also needed. This behavior is an example of what [11] describe as 'soft interdependence'.

4   General Architecture and Communication

A central question when setting up a Hybrid Team is the realization of suitable interfaces. Humans usually use speech, gestures and facial expressions to transfer information. Artificial agents however can use direct data streams to communicate with the system and other artificial team members. In our vision, the team is centered around the human worker. He is the one who uses his creativity, skills and knowledge to determine which tasks have to be fulfilled in order to reach the main goal. An example for a main goal is the already mentioned building of a sturdy packaging for a hand-built–and thus unique–vase. While taking measurements of the vase, the worker could for example dictate the needed materials into the system. The team, which is then informed about the needs of the worker, should then autonomously fulfill these needs, if possible. To deal with these different levels and requirements, we designed and implemented four core modules to realize the communication within a Hybrid Team: a communication middleware, a blackboard for task management, a dialog engine, and a dual reality module. The overall architecture with these core modules and the team members is shown in Fig. 4. The central idea is this: the worker issues commands or his needs using the dialog engine. The dialog engine creates tasks (e.g. bring(item, toLocation)) and puts them on the blackboard. Other team members access the blackboard to identify open tasks, and vouch to execute them, if they are able to fulfill them. In a nutshell: the blackboard exposes current tasks to the team, the middleware distributes the information within the team and the dialog planner enables a human-friendly translation (and access) to the middleware. The dual reality contains a representation of the scene on-site based on the information that is distributed via the central middleware. In the following, we describe each of these modules in more depth.

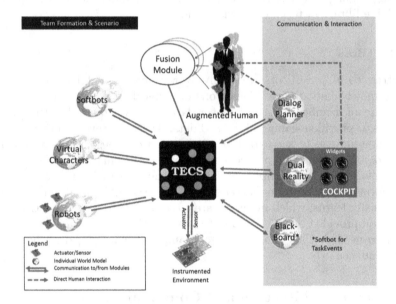

Fig. 4. Architecture of HySociaTea: communication is established via our TECS middleware. Each agent has an individual world model.

Event-Based Middleware: TECS. Communication between all team members as well as between all sub-modules and potential sensors and actuators of the instrumented environment is established via an event-based middleware that has been developed in the project. TECS is short for Thrift Event-based Communication System. As the name already implies, it is based on Apache's cross-language services-framework Thrift (https://thrift.apache.org). TECS uses the Thrift IDL (Interface Definition Language) to describe data-structures, which can then be translated into data objects of various programming languages (e.g. Java, C#, C++, Python etc.) using the Thrift compiler. These objects can then be transmitted via the TECS server as event-based messages. All clients can be addressed via a publish-subscribe mechanism. For bound connections between clients, TECS also provides remote-procedure-calls and message-passing mechanisms. Communication partners find each other using a UDP multicast discovery strategy, which has also been integrated into TECS. In contrast to other systems that advertise services regularly, the TECS discovery strategy uses a client-side multicast request, which is answered by the service provider directly with a unicast description response. Services are always encoded into URIs, which are combined with service-type-descriptors and UUIDs to identify appropriate communication partners. For instance, each TECS server responses with `tecs-ps://<ip>:<port>` to a client-side request with service-type-descriptor `TECS-SERVER`. Since a TECS server can have multiple IPs and ports in the same scenario, depending on the hardware interfaces, each unique instance is identified by a 128-bit UUID. Remote-procedure-calls and message-passing providers can use the same strategy to find appropriate communication partners. The independence from a particular programming language as well as a unified discovery strategy are very important features for Hybrid Teams, as the multiple subsystems –that are typically present in real production scenarios– are usually implemented in various programming languages, and clients can join and leave the environment regularly, which makes hard-wired connections at least impractical. We have published TECS under Creative Commons (CC BY-NC 4.0, https://creativecommons.org/licenses/by-nc/4.0/) License and it can be downloaded via our website (http://tecs.dfki.de).

Task Management: Blackboard. As mentioned above, the blackboard is a viable component of the presented architecture of the Hybrid Team. It stores all subtasks that have to be fulfilled in order to accomplish the main goal. In a strict sense, the blackboard is a (rather single minded) SoftBot with a very restricted world model: it only cares about unfinished working tasks. All team members have access to the information on the blackboard. Artificial agents do this via TECS, as the blackboard broadcasts all tasks it receives. Humans have access to the blackboard through a graphical representation. Each team member can decide if they are capable to fulfill the task and can then commit themselves to it. This is done with a first-come- first-serve policy, i.e. the fastest team member gets the job. As of now, humans can commit to a task using speech commands (e.g. "I will do task number eight"), through a GUI on a tablet or via swipe gestures on Google Glass. In a more elaborated system this should be done by plan- or action-recognition, i.e. humans can just start fulfilling a task and the system will automatically assign the appropriate task to them.

Dialog Planner. The dialog planner processes speech input of the users and plans dialog acts for the artificial team members. In the Hybrid Team of the project HySociaTea the robots and the VC are capable of producing speech output via a Text-To-Speech (TTS) module. The components for natural language generation and interpretation themselves are located within the respective artificial team members. The dialog manager follows the *information state/update* approach [22], albeit in a modified form. The implementation of the information state for the manager is based on RDF and description logics, which is uniformly used for specification as well as storage of dialog memory, belief states and user models. The extended functionality of the description logic reasoner *HFC* (see below) makes it possible to equip the collected data with time information, which allows us to use the whole history of dialogs, user and other data for decision making. The management engine itself consists of complex reactive rules which are triggered by incoming data, be it from automatic speech recognition (ASR) or other external sensors or information sources, and additionally have access to the complete data and interaction history. An external probabilistic process helps to resolve alternative proposals for the next dialog moves, and, together with the uniform data representation, opens the door for machine learning approaches to improve the decision making. Although hierarchical state-machines are somehow the "standard" for dialogue management (aside from pure machine learning approaches à la Gasic and Young [5]) previous experiences have shown that they badly generalize to new situations, and are cumbersome when it comes to modularization and reuse, which is why we have decided to go for a rule-based formalism.

Ontologies. In HySociaTea we have developed an ontology that consists of three sub-ontologies which are brought together via a set of interface axioms, encoded in OWL [8]. The first ontology is a minimal and stripped-down upper ontology. Most notable for HySociaTea is a representation which distinguishes between atomic Situations and decomposable Events. The second ontology represents knowledge about the HySociaTea domain, basically distinguishing between Actors and Objects. The domain ontology also defines further XSD datatypes, such as point or weight. The ontology is used by the dialogue planner and also employed to encode time-varying data (e.g., *positional* information about tools or packaging material). Through the transitivity of spatial properties such as contains, natural language communication involving spatial reference then becomes more natural: instead of saying "Give me the tape from the *box* in the *upper shelf*", we might simply say "Give me the tape from the *rack*". The temporal representation extends the RDF triple model by two further arguments to implement a special form of *transaction time* [38] in *HFC* [21]. The ontologies are available as OWL-XML and N-triple files through the Open Ontology pages (http://www.dfki.de/lt/onto/hysociatea/). The ontology together with instance data (e.g., information from the dialogue) is hosted by the semantic repository and inference engine *HFC* [20].

Dual Reality. A dual reality component can be useful as a management or remote monitoring tool. It is visualizing information that is sent by the team via the central middleware. The dual reality also serves as an intuitive introspection in the system, visualizing what information is available. Therefore, a coordinator (even when not being on-site) can see what is going on and eventually influence the scene. Furthermore, new team members have a direct access to the current and previous states. The dual reality applied here is based on FiVES (Flexible Virtual Environment Server, http://catalogue.fiware.org/enablers/synchronization-fives) as server component, and a Web-browser based interactive 3D visualization, implemented as HTML5/JavaScript application, using XML3D [39] as rendering framework. The respective client is shown in

Fig. 3(c): Robots and humans are represented as 3D models. Their position, orientation and posture of the actors, as well as the gaze direction of the worker (green cone), are visualized as they currently appear at the real world counterpart. XML3D provides convenient mechanisms to express a 3D scene in terms of a assembly of configurable *Assets* [19], which fits very well to a scenario of independent actors in a shared work space. In this case, each actor is represented as individual Asset, with the data transferred via TECS being the input parameters for the individual asset configurations (e.g. individual joint values for different robot actors). FiVES is a Virtual Environment server that provides real-time communication to heterogeneous clients. It stores the current world state in a generic Entity-Component-Attribute format and allows heterogeneous clients to receive updates to the world states in real-time in a publish- subscribe manner. We used the plug-in mechanism provided by FiVES to extend the existing server implementation with a C# TECS client, so we can directly apply events that are broadcast in the TECS network, in particular, position updates of human worker and robots, as well as events that describe changes in joint angles of robots or the worker. Incoming TECS events are continuously applied to the local scene representation, so that the virtual counterpart is always consistent to the actual work site. The benefit of introducing a server module over attaching the dual reality client directly to TECS is twofold: First, the data stored in FiVES is always reflecting the actual state of the work site. This means for actors that join the dual reality later after numerous changes to the scene happened already, they still find the correct World state in FiVES, while the individual events are unaware of their effect on the overall world state. Second, having the data transmitted by the events converted to the unified Entity-Component-Attribute representation as used by FiVES allows for simple serialization of the world data into a JSON (Java Script Object Notation) format which allows immediate application of the server data to our browser-based 3D visualization.

5   Conclusions

Setting up Hybrid Teams of humans, robots, virtual agents and several softbots is a powerful strategy to explore new application fields and deal with increasing demands for flexibility in manufacturing. However, the realization of these teams still bears a lot of challenges for artificial agents and their collaboration with humans, since suitable and intuitive interfaces have to be implemented to connect physical and digital information, and autonomous and flexible robots have to be perceived as adequate partners in the team. With the presented work we have established a structural and architectural basis for Hybrid Teams for Industrie 4.0 applications. Still, recent techniques in AI contain many more options how the performance of such a team can be improved, so that this can only be seen as a starting point to create teamwork within the team. Besides research on the technical feasibility of setting-up a Hybrid Team, another key aspect is the development of (robotic) team-competencies as well as intelligent multiagent behavior, both of which are also important aspects in purely human teams.

The work of Johnson, Bradshaw, Feltovich, Jonker, van Riemsdijk and Sierhuis on Coactive Design and Joint Activity describe guidelines on how to realize such hybrid teamwork. The incorporation of these ideas into HySociaTea will be our next steps. However, we have to keep in mind that the technical systems developed in HySociaTea are mainly meant to be used as assistance systems for humans working in production plants; the robots should therefore be perceived as partners in the overall working process, which puts an emphasis on the emotional acceptance of such systems. A demonstration video showing our hybrid team in action can be seen and downloaded from http://hysociatea.dfki.de/?p=441.

Acknowledgment. The research described in this paper has been funded by the German Federal Ministry of Education and Research (BMBF) through the projects HySociaTea and MADMACS (grant no. 01IW14001 and 01IW14003). The authors would like to thank the reviewers for their really valuable input.

References

1. Bargsten, V., de Gea Fernández, J.: COMPI: development of a 6-DOF compliant robot arm for human-robot cooperation. In: Proceedings of the International Workshop on Human-Friendly Robotics. Technische Universität München (TUM) (2015)
2. Bay, H., Tuytelaars, T., Van Gool, L.: SURF: Speeded Up Robust Features. In: Leonardis, A., Bischof, H., Pinz, A. (eds.) ECCV 2006, Part I. LNCS, vol. 3951, pp. 404–417. Springer, Heidelberg (2006)
3. Chen, T., Borth, D., Darrell, T., Chang, S.F.: DeepSentiBank: visual sentiment concept classification with deep convolutional neural networks. arXiv preprint (2014). arXiv:1410.8586
4. Garrido-Jurado, S., Muñoz-Salinas, R., Madrid-Cuevas, F.J., Marin-Jimenez, M.J.: Automatic generation and detection of highly reliable fiducial markers under occlusion. Pattern Recogn. **47**(6), 2280–2292 (2014)
5. Gasic, M., Young, S.J.: Gaussian processes for POMDP-based dialogue manager optimization. IEEE/ACM Trans. Audio Speech Lang. Process. **22**(1), 28–40 (2014)
6. Grosz, B.J., Hunsberger, L., Kraus, S.: Planning and acting together. AI Mag. **20**(4), 23–34 (1999)
7. Harada, T., Mori, T., Sato, T.: Development of a tiny orientation estimation device to operate under motion and magnetic disturbance. Int. J. Robot. Res. **26**, 547–559 (2007)
8. Hitzler, P., Krötzsch, M., Parsia, B., Patel-Schneider, P.F., Rudolph, S.: OWL 2 web ontology language primer, 2nd edn. Technical report, W3C (2012)
9. Itti, L., Koch, C., Niebur, E.: A model of saliency-based visual attention for rapid scene analysis. IEEE Trans. Pattern Anal. Mach. Intell. **20**(11), 1254–1259 (1998)
10. Jia, Y., Shelhamer, E., Donahue, J., Karayev, S., Long, J., Girshick, R., Guadarrama, S., Darrell, T.: Caffe: convolutional architecture for fast feature embedding. In: Proceedings of the International Conference on Multimedia, pp. 675–678. ACM (2014)
11. Johnson, M., Bradshaw, J.M., Feltovich, P.J., Jonker, C.M., van Riemsdijk, B., Sierhuis, M.: The fundamental principle of coactive design: interdependence must shape autonomy. In: De Vos, M., Fornara, N., Pitt, J.V., Vouros, G. (eds.) COIN 2010. LNCS, vol. 6541, pp. 172–191. Springer, Heidelberg (2011)

12. Johnson, M., Bradshaw, J.M., Feltovich, P.J., Jonker, C.M., van Riemsdijk, M.B., Sierhuis, M.: Coactive design: designing support for interdependence in joint activity. J. Hum.-Rob. Interact. **3**(1), 43–69 (2014)

13. Joyeux, S., Albiez, J.: Robot development: from components to systems. In: Proceedings of National Conference on Control Architectures of Robots (2011)

14. Joyeux, S., Kirchner, F., Lacroix, S.: Managing plans: integrating deliberation and reactive execution schemes. Robot. Auton. Syst. **58**(9), 1057–1066 (2010)

15. Joyeux, S., Schwendner, J., Roehr, T.M.: Modular software for an autonomous space rover. In: Proceedings of the International Symposium on AI, Robotics and Automation in Space. i-SAIRAS, p. 8 (2014)

16. Judd, T., Ehinger, K., Durand, F., Torralba, A.: Learning to predict where humans look. In: Proceedings of the International Conference on Computer Vision, pp. 2106–2113. IEEE (2009)

17. Jung, Y., Kang, D., Kim, J.: Upper body motion tracking with inertial sensors. In: Proceedings of the International Conference on Robotics and Biomimetics, pp. 1746–1751. IEEE (2010)

18. Kagermann, H., Helbig, J., Hellinger, A., Wahlster, W.: Recommendations for implementing the strategic initiative INDUSTRIE 4.0: securing the future of German manufacturing industry; final report of the industrie 4.0 working group. Acatech - National Acadamy of Science and Engineering (2013)

19. Klein, F., Spieldenner, T., Sons, K., Slusallek, P.: Configurable instances of 3D models for declarative 3D in the web. In: Proceedings of the International Conference on 3D Web Technologies, pp. 71–79. ACM (2014)

20. Krieger, H.U.: An efficient implementation of equivalence relations in OWL via rule and query rewriting. In: Proceedings of the International Conference on Semantic Computing (ICSC 2013), pp. 260–263. IEEE (2013)

21. Krieger, H.U.: Integrating graded knowledge and temporal change in a modal fragment of OWL. In: van den Herik, J., Filipe, J. (eds.) Agents and Artificial Intelligence. Springer, Berlin (2016, in press)

22. Larsson, S., Traum, D.R.: Information state and dialogue management in the TRINDI dialogue move engine toolkit. Nat. Lang. Eng. **6**(3&4), 323–340 (2000)

23. Leitão, P.: Agent-based distributed manufacturing control: a state-of-the-art survey. Eng. Appl. Artif. Intell. **22**(7), 979–991 (2009)

24. Lemburg, J., Mronga, D., Aggarwal, A., de Gea Fernández, J., Ronthaler, M., Kirchner, F.: A robotic platform for building and exploiting digital product memories. In: Wahlster, W. (ed.) SemProM - Foundations of Semantic Product Memories for the Internet of Things. Cognitive Technologies, pp. 91–106. Springer, Berlin (2013)

25. Levesque, H.J., Cohen, P.R., Nunes, J.H.T.: On acting together. In: Proceedings of the International Conference on AI, vol. 1, pp. 94–99. AAAI Press, Boston (1990)

26. Likhachev, M., Ferguson, D., Gordon, G., Stentz, A., Thrun, S.: Anytime search in dynamic graphs. Artif. Intell. **172**(14), 1613–1643 (2008)

27. Liu, L., Shell, D.A.: Optimal market-based multi-robot task allocation via strategic pricing. In: Robotics: Science and Systems IX (2013)

28. Lowe, D.G.: Distinctive image features from scale-invariant keypoints. Int. J. Comput. Vis. **60**(2), 91–110 (2004)

29. Mourkani, S.S., Bleser, G., Schmitz, N., Stricker, D.: A low-cost and light-weight motion tracking suit. In: Proceedings of the International Conference on Ubiquitous Intelligence and Computing, pp. 474–479. IEEE (2013)

30. Nguyen, M.H., Wobcke, W.: A flexible framework for sharedplans. In: Sattar, A., Kang, B.-H. (eds.) AI 2006. LNCS (LNAI), vol. 4304, pp. 393–402. Springer, Heidelberg (2006)

31. Pirkl, G., Hevesi, P., Cheng, J., Lukowicz, P.: mBeacon: accurate, robust proximity detection with smart phones and smart watches using low frequency modulated magnetic fields. In: Proceedings of the EAI International Conference on Body Area Networks, pp. 186–191. ICST (2015)

32. Pirkl, G., Lukowicz, P.: Robust, low cost indoor positioning using magnetic resonant coupling. In: Proceedings of the International Conference on Ubiquitous Computing, pp. 431–440. ACM (2012)

33. Rublee, E., Rabaud, V., Konolige, K., Bradski, G.: ORB: an efficient alternative to sift or surf. In: Proceedings of the International Conference on Computer Vision (ICCV 2011), pp. 2564–2571. IEEE (2011)

34. Scerri, P., Pynadath, D., Johnson, L., Rosenbloom, P., Si, M., Schurr, N., Tambe, M.: A prototype infrastructure for distributed robot-agent-person teams. In: Proceedings of the International Joint Conference on Autonomous Agents and Multi-agent Systems, AAMAS 2003, pp. 433–440. ACM (2003)

35. Schwartz, T., Feld, M., Bürckert, C., Dimitrov, S., Folz, J., Hutter, D., Hevesi, P., Kiefer, B., Krieger, H.U., Lüth, C., Mronga, D., Pirkl, G., Röfer, T., Spieldenner, T., Wirkus, M., Zinnikus, I., Straube, S.: Hybrid teams of humans, robots and virtual agents in a production setting. In: International Conference Intelligent Environments (IE) (2016, accepted)

36. Schwendner, J., Roehr, T.M., Haase, S., Wirkus, M., Manz, M., Arnold, S., Machowinski, J.: The Artemis rover as an example for model based engineering in space robotics. In: Workshop Proceedings of the International Conference on Robotics and Automation (ICRA-2014), p. 7. IEEE (2014)

37. Settembre, G.P., Scerri, P., Farinelli, A., Sycara, K., Nardi, D.: A decentralized approach to cooperative situation assessment in multi-robot systems. In: Proceedings of the International Conference on Autonomous Agents and Multiagent Systems, AAMAS 2008, vol. 1, pp. 31–38. International Foundation for Autonomous Agents and Multiagent Systems (2008)

38. Snodgrass, R.T.: Developing time-oriented database applications in SQL. Morgan Kaufmann, San Francisco (2000)

39. Sons, K., Klein, F., Rubinstein, D., Byelozyorov, S., Slusallek, P.: XML3D: interactive 3D graphics for the web. In: Proceedings of the International Conference on Web 3D Technology, Web3D 2010, pp. 175–184. ACM (2010)

40. Straube, S., Schwartz, T.: Hybrid teams in the digital network of the future - application, architecture and communication. Industrie 4.0 Manag. 2, 41–45 (2016)

41. Tambe, M.: Towards flexible teamwork. J. Artif. Int. Res. 7(1), 83–124 (1997)

42. Täubig, H., Frese, U.: A new library for real-time continuous collision detection. In: Proceedings of the German Conference on Robotics, pp. 108–112. VDE (2012)

43. Van Dyke Parunak, H., Baker, A.D., Clark, S.J.: The AARIA agent architecture: an example of requirements-driven agent-based system design. In: Proceedings of the International Conference on Autonomous Agents, AGENTS 1997, pp. 482–483. ACM (1997)

44. Wirkus, M.: Towards robot-independent manipulation behavior description. In: Proceedings of the International Workshop on Domain-Specific Languages and Models for Robotic Systems (2014). arXiv:1412.3247

45. Zhang, J., Sclaroff, S.: Exploiting surroundedness for saliency detection: a boolean map approach. IEEE Trans. Pattern Anal. Mach. Intell. 38(5), 889–902 (2016)

Analysing the Cost-Efficiency of the Multi-agent Flood Algorithm in Search and Rescue Scenarios

Florian Blatt[(✉)], Matthias Becker, and Helena Szczerbicka

Simulation and Modelling Group,
Faculty of Electrical Engineering and Computer Science,
Leibniz University Hannover, Hanover, Germany
{blatt,xmb,hsz}@sim.uni-hannover.de

Abstract. A Multi-Agent algorithm works by using at least two agents to create a synergistic effect, resulting in an emergence of new possibilities which are not programmed implicitly into the various agents. To achieve this synergistic effect the algorithm has to provide the possibility to communicate and consecutively allow cooperation between the agents. Considering the use of multi-agent algorithms in search and rescue scenarios the targeted effect of the emergence is on one hand a more effective search and rescue process or on the other hand only an optimized rescue process. This paper examines the number of agents that is needed for the Multi-Agent Flood algorithm to yield the most beneficial ratio between the used number of agents and time it takes to complete the search process. Our studies show that adding more robots may not be cost efficient for the search and rescue process. This in turn allows for a better planning and coordination of robotic search teams, as the number of needed agents can be anticipated and the possible transport logistics of robots can be optimized.

1 Introduction

More and more approaches propose the use of multiple robotic agents for search and rescue processes [9,15]. Current state of the art shows that single robots directly controlled by a human controller may not be the most efficient way to search for victims after a disaster struck. This raises the question on how many robots are necessary for a successful search in the disaster area. And in turn this also leads to the economical and the logistical component of the search and rescue process. How much does a single robot cost and how many can be realistically transported in time to the disaster area? Is it feasible to have a team of about one hundred agents on stand by and transport them in timely manner to the accident? Right after a disaster happened the clock starts running down for the victims, the longer it takes to find a victim the lower the chances are to find the wounded still alive. Usually the chances of the rescue process to find victims alive in urban search and rescue scenarios after about 48 to 72 h are rather low [11]. This means that every second is important and an effective process should not only optimize the time needed to do the search but also the time that may be needed to start the search in the first place.

© Springer International Publishing Switzerland 2016
M. Klusch et al. (Eds.): MATES 2016, LNAI 9872, pp. 147–154, 2016.
DOI: 10.1007/978-3-319-45889-2_11

The two factors depend on the size of the robots, and the robots themselves are not the only equipment that may be needed. There may also arise the need for maintenance parts and refuel equipment to keep the agents moving in the field. Additionally a mobile control center or headquarter is needed. These are some fixed costs that will be included but usually not mentioned in every search and rescue process. As a result each additional robot will add itself and some maintenance overhead to the load out.

Current algorithms do not define a specific number for the agents used by them. Depending on the method (e.g. [5]) there may be further robots used just to create a possible communication network between the agents. Thus increasing the number of agents that are needed to successfully run the algorithm.

As a consequence to keep the cost low and the size of the matter that needs to be transported small, a lower number of robots would be better than a higher number. This in turn means that an algorithm is preferred that uses lesser robots but is still good enough to return a result in a meaningful time frame. As a result the cost-value-ratio that needs to be optimized is the ratio between the number of agents or robots used that are needed to complete the algorithm in a successful way and the time it takes to complete the algorithm. These values are often neglected, as previous work focused more on the cost of communication and cooperation between the agents and/or between the agents and the human team members [8,10].

The number of agents that will be needed also influences the planning of the deployment centers, where the robots will be stationed. City planners will need at least an estimate, if not definitive numbers, of needed agents to implement a multi-agent method for search and rescue processes. For example a new fire station is planned and it should be equipped with a robotic search and rescue team, how many robots should this team contain? How many of these robots can be feasible brought to the disaster area in the shortest time possible?

The following section will contain a description of the current state of the art of various existing multi-agent algorithms. In the third section we will present our experimental simulation setup using the Multi-Agent Flood algorithm. The fourth section will demonstrate the results followed by a conclusion in the fifth section.

2   State of the Art

There are various robots and algorithms available already, which may be able to search for victims in a search and rescue process. The first examples are single robots, which give an idea of the used hardware and the different sizes of the robots, as most multi-agent algorithms do not specify a specific hardware.

One of the better known robots is *Quince* [12,13], which was used in the Fukushima nuclear disaster. This robot has a length of 0.71 m, a width of 0.48 m and a height of 0.21 m. It weights about 27 kg. Another example of a single robot is the *IUB Rugbot* [3]. This tracked robot has a footprint of about 0.5 m × 0.5 m and a weight of about 35 kg.

Existing multi-agent algorithms include for example the Rapid Exploration algorithm from Ferranti et al. [7]. This algorithm does not really specify how many agents should be used. But simulations on the older variant, the *Brick and Mortar* algorithm [6], in [1] show that at least about 20 agents should be used to achieve comparable results.

Another current multi-agent algorithm is the *Rendezvous* algorithm from de Hoog et al. and the newer version from Spirin et al. (respectively [5] and [14]). This method introduced an additional type of robot, which acts as a relay point to allow a continuous communication of the robots. If one applies the number of the agents from the *Brick and Mortar* algorithm and splits them up accordingly then this method would use about five to ten agents for searching around one relay agent, multiplied by said number of agents necessary for the relay network.

In our work we have presented the Multi-Agent Flood algorithm (MAF, [1,2, 4]) as a new method for the search process in a search and rescue scenario. This method allows for a start of the rescue process in parallel with the search process. To achieve this the agents will immediately inform the headquarter about any victims found and will provide the current shortest known path available to the robots to the rescue team. Current versions of the algorithm still work on a grid, which simplifies the movement pattern of the agents. This in turn means, that a cell in the grid can contain a victim, a robot, or either traversable space or an obstacle.

The agents of the MAF algorithm will usually explore the unknown terrain at random and will try to keep away from any already explored areal. While exploring the scenario agents will mark the already visited territory. These markings also provide information about the current known shortest path from the marked position back to the headquarter. Previous versions of the algorithm were only able to communicate and cooperate through these markings, resulting in an indirect communication structure. The current version, which will be used in this work, enables the agents to use also direct communication via WiFi, as long as the communicating robots have a line of sight connection. The direct type of data transfer will be used in addition to the indirect means of communication. Resulting in a robust communication method, which allows the algorithm to still run, if a radio connection is not possible due to external influences from the terrain. If a robot encounters a point of interest, respectively a victim, it will try to use the shortest known path back to the headquarter. The information about the shortest known path comes either from the markings on the floor or from the internal map, which results from the robots own sensors and the exchanged data through direct communication from the other agents. At the headquarter it will share the available information with the rescue team. The return can also be used for the maintenance of the robot. Afterwards the agent will start to search again for other victims.

None of the aforementioned methods investigated the number of agents that is needed to successfully terminate the corresponding algorithm and thus resulting in usable results. This in turn implies that no numbers exists or no suggestion exists on how many agents should be used in real world applications.

As mentioned above in the introduction the sole availability of a search algorithm may not be sufficient and additionally, if a method should be implemented in the real world, planners and decision makers should have at least a recommendation at hand on how many robots should be deployed, as this number will influence the size of the volume and mass that needs to be housed and in case of a disaster to be transported to the site of the catastrophe.

In the following section we will take a look at the number of agents that may be required to successfully use the MAF algorithm in different typical scenarios. Current experiments show that at least 20 agents should be used, as this number offers a good trade-off between number of agents and time it takes to finish the simulated search process.

3   Experimental Simulation Setup

The experimental setup used for the simulations is similar to the setup used in [4]. Four different scenarios were used to test the algorithms: House, Office, Park, and Cubicles. Three of those scenarios have a size of 500×500 pixel and one has the size of 1000×1000 pixel. Whereas each pixel or cell can have one of the following states: open area or obstacle. Agents and points of interest currently can occupy any pixel which is represented by the open area.

Each scenario depicts a possible disaster area, for example a house, an office, or a park. Each map contains ten or 15 points of interest or victims uniformly distributed, depending on the size of the map. These numbers where chosen to offer a sparse distribution of the points of victims through the map and to minimize the chance of clustering.

The length of the simulation is measured in steps, were one step is the time frame in which each agent is able to move from one cell to another. The algorithm will terminate if either 95 % of the terrain is explored and 95 % of the victims are found or if the maximum number of steps is reached. This maximum number depends on the size of the map. A 500×500 map has a maximum number of steps of 250.000, whereas a 1000×1000 map has a maximum number of 1.000.000. These numbers were chosen to allow a single agent to cover the whole map, ignoring any obstacles.

Each simulation run, using one algorithm on one of the maps, was repeated 250 times. The number of agents was also increased in the different runs, starting with one agent and ending with 100 agents. This combination of algorithms, maps, and configuration parameters resulted in 200.000 simulations.

4   Simulation Results

The following diagram in Fig. 1 shows the results of the experiments for the House scenario as an example. The vertical axis denotes the number of steps and the horizontal axis discloses the number of agents used in the simulation run. Additionally the 99 % confidence interval is given for each simulation run, depicted as the usual T-capped line at the data point.

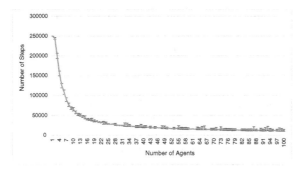

Fig. 1. House, 500×500 cells

As expected adding additional agents will decrease the number of steps it takes to finish the simulation, although the curves are not linear, showing clearly that adding additional robots after a certain point will result in a lower cost/value ratio.

To further analyse the most beneficial number of robots, that should be used in the various scenarios an *efficiency* was calculated. This calculation is based on two different functions that are aggregated together resulting in a normalized function based on the time it took to complete the algorithm and on the number of robots used.

$$C_N(r) = \begin{cases} 0, & \text{if } r \geq \frac{c_m}{c} \\ \frac{cr - c_m}{1 - c_m}, & \text{else} \end{cases} \tag{1}$$

Equation (1) represents the cost of the amount of r robots. c_m is the constant that represents the maximum amount of monetary resources that one is able or willing to offer for all robots. c is the cost of a single robot. The function will result in a number between 0 and 1. The result will be 0 if the cost of the r robots is equal or greater than the maximum allowed amount of monetary resources, c_m, whereas a result nearing 1 will mean that as least resources as possible are spent.

$$F_N(t) = \begin{cases} \frac{(m_t + \epsilon)(t - m_t - \frac{\epsilon}{2})}{(m + \frac{\epsilon}{2})(t - m_t - \epsilon)}, & \text{if } t < m_t + \frac{\epsilon}{2} \\ 0, & \text{else} \end{cases} \tag{2}$$

The second equation, Eq. (2), evaluates the time that it took the algorithm to finish. It contains two constants: m_t, which represents the maximum amount of time that the algorithm should take to terminate and ϵ, an error margin. As mentioned in the introduction, a search process should find as many victims as possible in the first 48 to 72 h, as the chance to find survivors will significantly drop, if it takes much longer (see [11]). The constant m_t with the error margin ϵ allows for this in (2). This means, that if an algorithm takes longer than $m_t + \frac{\epsilon}{2}$, its efficiency rating will decrease rapidly. The result of (2) will also be a number between 0 and 1. Whereas a result nearing 1 shows a fast run of the algorithm and a result of 0 depicts a run that took longer than the maximum allowed time or did not even finish the calculation.

$$E(r,t) = \sqrt{C_N(r)}F_N(t) \tag{3}$$

The third equation, Eq. (3), is the combination of the first and second equation. The first part also includes a square root to weight the result of the robot cost a little differently. Using the result of $\sqrt{C_N(r)}$ instead of simply $C_N(r)$ will increase the efficiency value of multiple robots and will punish the use of using only a small amount of robots.

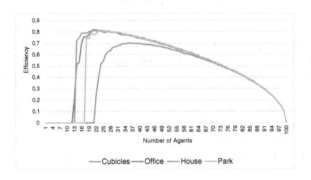

Fig. 2. 25 % of the maximum time, 5 % error margin (Color figure online)

The following values were chosen for the different constants: $c = 1$, $c_m = 100$, m_t and ϵ are percentages depending on the size of the different scenarios. The choice for c and c_m reflect that currently the cost was ignored and only the amount of robots would alter the result of the function. The diagram in Fig. 2 shows the results of $E(r,t)$ for half of the maximum time and respectively a quarter of the maximum time, ϵ was 5 % of the maximum time in both cases. This means that the maximum allowed time in a 1000 × 1000 map was 500.000 steps for the 50 % variant and 250.000 steps for the 25 % variant. In turn the maximum allowed time for the 500 × 500 scenarios was 125.000 steps and 62.500 steps. An ϵ of 5 % means an error margin of 50.000 steps in the bigger map and 12.500 steps in the smaller scenarios.

The four different lines depict the efficiency dependent on the time it took the algorithm to terminate and on the number of robots used. The blue curve represents the bigger cubicles test case, orange the office map, gray the outline of the house, and yellow the park scenario.

The diagram in Fig. 2 depicts the efficiency of the algorithm on the various maps if the maximum amount of steps is set to a quarter of the maximum allowed steps, implicating a value for m_t of 250.000 and 62.500 steps correspondingly. The different curves for the simulation on the smaller scenarios show, that only about 17 agents are needed to still achieve an efficiency of 80 %, while the simulation in the bigger terrain needs about 30 robots to deliver at least an efficiency of 70 %. Adding additional robots will decrease the efficiency as the cost goes up. As mentioned above the constants c_r and c_m, which represent the cost of a single robot and the maximum amount of money available respectively, are set to 1 and 100. Meaning that the cost does not affect the result at the moment, only the amount of agents influences the outcome. Raising the cost of a single agent or lowering the amount of monetary resources available will in turn lower the efficiency value faster.

5   Conclusion

Our studies used the Multi-Agent Flood algorithm as a base algorithm and included 200.000 simulation runs trying to find a number of agents where the cost-value-ratio between the used number of agents and the time it took to finish the algorithm was still good enough and at which point adding additional agents would not yield a significant decrease in search time. This number influences both: economy and logistics. More robots are more expensive and more agents need more transport space to get to the disaster area. As a consequence it may be more efficient to keep more smaller teams of robots around than one big team.

The experiments show that, at least for the Multi-Agent Flood algorithm, a maximum of 30 agents is quite sufficient. This number provides an acceptable trade-off between the number of agents and the time it takes to finish the search process. If the intended robots are more expensive and/or the maximum amount of monetary resources available is lower, than even a lower maximum should be considered.

Additionally we propose an approximated expression based on the results of the simulations for an estimated number of robots that maximises the search success under the constraints of available resources. These resources are split into two parts: monetary resources and cost of an individual robot, and time it takes the algorithm to finish the calculation and a maximum time span that should not be overstepped. The combined equation is independent from both the simulator used and from the type of algorithm deployed to run the simulation. As the only variables in the formula stem from the number of agents and the time it takes to complete the search process it should also be possible to utilize these equations for real robots.

Depending on the size of the robot used, city planners now should have at least a proposal at hand to calculate the estimated capacity needed for a deployment center using the Multi-Agent Flood algorithm and in turn to calculate the mass and volume that needs to be transported to the disaster area.

References

1. Becker, M., Blatt, F., Szczerbicka, H.: A multi-agent flooding algorithm for search and rescue operations in unknown terrain. In: Klusch, M., Thimm, M., Paprzycki, M. (eds.) MATES 2013. LNCS, vol. 8076, pp. 19–28. Springer, Heidelberg (2013)

2. Becker, M., Blatt, F., Szczerbicka, H.: A concept of layered robust communication between robots in multi-agent search & rescue scenarios. In: IEEE/ACM 18th International Symposium on Distributed Simulation and Real Time Applications (DS-RT), pp. 175–180. IEEE (2014)
3. Birk, A., Pathak, K., Schwertfeger, S., Chonnaparamutt, W.: The IUB rugbot: an intelligent, rugged mobile robot for search and rescue operations. In: IEEE International Workshop on Safety, Security, and Rescue Robotics (SSRR). IEEE Press (2006)
4. Blatt, F., Becker, M., Szczerbicka, H.: Optimizing the exploration efficiency of autonomous search and rescue agents using a concept of layered robust communication. In: IEEE 20th Conference on Emerging Technologies & Factory Automation (ETFA). pp. 1–6. IEEE (2015)
5. De Hoog, J., Cameron, S., Visser, A.: Selection of rendezvous points for multi-robot exploration in dynamic environments. In: International Conference on Autonomous Agents and Multi-Agent Systems (AAMAS) (2010)
6. Ferranti, E., Trigoni, N., Levene, M.: Brick & Mortar: an on-line multi-agent exploration algorithm. In: IEEE International Conference on Robotics and Automation, pp. 761–767. IEEE (2007)
7. Ferranti, E., Trigoni, N., Levene, M.: Rapid exploration of unknown areas through dynamic deployment of mobile and stationary sensor nodes. Auton. Agent. Multi-Agent Syst. $19(2)$, 210–243 (2009)
8. Hoffman, R.R., Woods, D.D.: Beyond Simon's slice: five fundamental trade-offs that bound the performance of macrocognitive work systems. IEEE Intell. Syst. $26(6)$, 67–71 (2011)
9. Kitano, H., Tadokoro, S.: Robocup rescue: a grand challenge for multiagent and intelligent systems. AI Mag. $22(1)$, 39 (2001)
10. Klein, G., Woods, D.D., Bradshaw, J.M., Hoffman, R.R., Feltovich, P.J.: Ten challenges for making automation a "team player" in joint human-agent activity. IEEE Intell. Syst. $19(6)$, 91–95 (2004)
11. Murphy, R.R., Tadokoro, S., Nardi, D., Jacoff, A., Fiorini, P., Choset, H., Erkmen, A.M.: Search and rescue robotics. In: Siciliano, B., Khatib, O. (eds.) Handbook of Robotics, pp. 1151–1173. Springer, Heidelberg (2008)
12. Nagatani, K., Kiribayashi, S., Okada, Y., Tadokoro, S., Nishimura, T., Yoshida, T., Koyanagi, E., Hada, Y.: Redesign of rescue mobile robot Quince. In: IEEE International Symposium on Safety, Security, and Rescue Robotics (SSRR), pp. 13–18. IEEE (2011)
13. Rohmer, E., Yoshida, T., Ohno, K., Nagatani, K., Tadokoro, S., Koyangai, E.: Quince: a collaborative mobile robotic platform for rescue robots research and development. In: Proceedings of International Conference on Advanced Mechatronics, pp. 225–230 (2010)
14. Spirin, V., Cameron, S.: Rendezvous through obstacles in multi-agent exploration. In: IEEE International Symposium on Safety, Security, and Rescue Robotics (SSRR), pp. 1–6. IEEE (2014)
15. Takahashi, T., Tadokoro, S., Ohta, M., Ito, N.: Agent based approach in disaster rescue simulation-from test-bed of multiagent system to practical application. In: RoboCup 2001: Robot Soccer World Cup V, pp. 63–74 (2002)

Using Models at Runtime to Adapt Self-managed Agents for the IoT

Inmaculada Ayala, Jose Miguel Horcas$^{(\boxtimes)}$, Mercedes Amor$^{(\boxtimes)}$,
and Lidia Fuentes

Departamento de Lenguajes y Ciencias de la Computación, Universidad de Málaga,
Andalucía Tech, Campus de Teatinos s/n, 29071 Málaga, Spain
{ayala,horcas,pinilla,lff}@lcc.uma.es

Abstract. One of the most important challenges of this decade is
the Internet of Things (IoT) that pursues the integration of real-world
objects in the virtual world of the Internet. One property that charac-
terises IoT systems is that they have to react to variable and continuous
changes. This means that IoT systems need to work as self-managed
systems to effectively manage context changes. The autonomy property
inherent to software agents makes them a suitable choice for developing self-managed IoT systems. By embedding agents in the devices that
compose the IoT is possible to realize a decentralized system with self-
management capacities. However, in this scenario new problems arise.
Firstly, current agent development approaches lack mechanisms to deal
with the heterogeneity present in the IoT domain. Secondly, agents
must simultaneously deal with potentially conflicting changes in their
behaviour, concerning self-management and application goals. In order to
afford these challenges we propose to use an approach based on Dynamic
Software Product Lines (D-SPL) and preference-based reasoning. The
D-SPL provides to the preference-based reasoning of the agent with the
necessary information to adapt its behaviour at runtime making a trade-
off between the self-management of the system and the accomplishment
of its application goals.

Keywords: Software Product Lines · Dynamic Software Product
Lines · Goal-oriented · Internet of Things · Preference-based reasoning

1 Introduction

One of the most important challenges of this decade is the Internet of Things
(IoT) [1], which pursues the integration of real-world objects in the virtual world
of the Internet. One property that characterizes IoT systems is that they are composed of a globally connected, highly dynamic and interactive network of physical
and virtual devices [1]. These devices have to react to variable and continuous
changes in their context. This means that IoT systems need to work as self-
managed systems to effectively manage context changes. With this requirement,

© Springer International Publishing Switzerland 2016
M. Klusch et al. (Eds.): MATES 2016, LNAI 9872, pp. 155–173, 2016.
DOI: 10.1007/978-3-319-45889-2_12

it is essential to have a decentralized solution to deal with the self-management of the system [4].

The autonomy property inherent to software agents makes them a suitable choice for developing self-managed IoT systems. By embedding agents in the devices that compose the IoT is possible to realize a decentralized system with self-management capacities. In fact, the notion of environment (i.e. the context) is a key concept in agent and Multi-Agent Systems (MASs) technology, since it strongly affects agent behavior [23,26]. The proactive and autonomous behavior of agents, usually modeled in terms of goals, means that they are able to be aware of and adapt to the particular context in which they are embedded according to a set of self-management goals. These goals endow agents in IoT systems with the ability to run continuously under different conditions such as changing environments, partial subsystem failures, and changing user needs. Often, they must run unattended with no interruption. Agents running in smart devices also need to adapt their overall system behavior to energy levels and varying quality in network connection. However, in this scenario new challenges arise. Firstly, current agent development approaches lack mechanisms to deal with the variability present in the IoT domain. Secondly, as part of self-management, agents must be able to dynamically adapt their goal-driven behaviour influenced by the current context situation, even at runtime.

Managing variability can be done during the phase of analysis and design. In a previous work, the variability imposed by IoT domain was done at the stage of analysis and design of the MASs for the IoT [3]. This solution involved using a Software Product Line (SPL) process [20] to model the variability of the IoT domain, the agent context, and its dependencies with agent internal behavior specified by means of goals. In SPLs, a variability model allows specifying commonality and variability amongst a set of similar products that are part of the same product family (seen as a collection of similar software systems derived from a shared set of software assets using a common means of production process). Therefore, variability models are a natural and suitable way to easily model context variability and their interdependencies with the agent behavior in agent-based IoT systems. This information is valuable for the self-management of agents at runtime, however SPL approaches are restricted to the development phase of the system. One solution is to foresee all the functionality or management an agent in an IoT system may require and include them in the SPL. The issue is to consider all possible variations and in addition, to reason about them at runtime. This would be unaffordable in time and computational resources for an agent embedded in a lightweight device.

Therefore, there is a need to produce software agents for the IoT capable of evolving and adapting to different system management requirements while meeting the application goal they were intended for. In order to meet this challenge we propose to use an approach based on Dynamic SPL (D-SPL) [10,11]. D-SPL is an area of research that applies the ideas of the SPL like variability modeling and automatic product derivation to the runtime. This makes to produce software capable of adapting to context variations and evolving resource constraints.

In D-SPLs, monitoring the current situation and controlling the adaptation are central tasks. The D-SPL provides the agent with the necessary information to evolve self-management at runtime taking into account how it affects agent goals. In this work we propose to use D-SPLs to adapt the behaviour of the agent. Our goal is to achieve a trade-off between application specific goals and self-management goals ensuring the agent preserves an acceptable quality of service for the IoT system. Such quality is quantified in terms of the *wellness* and *usefulness* of the agent at one point of its execution. These metrics, which are inferred from the variability model of the D-SPL, are used to select the appropriate plan for a given goal according to the current state of the agent. The wellness of the agent is defined as a general condition of the agent in terms of its internal state (such as available resources, and activated goals, scheduled plans). The usefulness is measured in terms of the goals that the agent potentially can bring about and the goals that are currently maintaining. The scope of our approach is intented to specific closed IoT scenarios where agents reasoning only takes into account the monitorized environment values and agents goals do not interfere with other agents in the MAS.

This paper is organized as follows: Sect. 2 overviews our approach. Section 3 presents our case study and provides background in variability modeling and related work. Section 4 explains our mechanism to adapt agent behavior at runtime. This mechanism is validated in Sect. 5. The paper closes with the conclusions and future work.

2   Our Approach

We propose to develop IoT applications as a population of agents embedded in IoT nodes, that interact with each other, and which are self-managed. In emerging domains such as the IoT, software is becoming increasingly complex with an extensive variation in both requirements and resource constraints. Developers are pressed to deliver high-quality software with additional functionality, on short deadlines, and more economically. In addition, IoT environments demand a higher degree of adaptability from their software systems. Computing environments, user requirements, networking and interface mechanisms between software and hardware devices such as sensors can change even at runtime. In order for agents to be embedded in devices of the IoT, while maintaining the decentralization of the self-management, the variability and self-management must be handled at the agent level. The proactive and autonomous behavior of agents, usually modeled in terms of goals, enable agents to be aware of and adapt to the particular context in which they are embedded according to a set of self-management goals. Until now, different agent technologies have been adapted or extended to provide support for some devices of the IoT (mainly sensor motes and mobile phones) [2]. In a previous contribution, we have presented an SPL process for the development of self-managed agent-based systems for the IoT that considers these issues [3]. In SPL approaches, variability is bound at development time. However, they do not support the dynamic reconfiguration of agent architectures enabling the agent self-management at runtime. In this work, the variability model is used also at runtime to drive the adaptation of the agent to changes in the environment.

In D-SPLs, monitoring the current situation and controlling the adaptation are central tasks. These tasks are activities of the commonly known as MAPE-K loop (Monitoring, Analyzing, Planning and Execution - Knowledge) of autonomous (or autonomic) systems. The agent realizes the MAPE-K cycle, qualifying the agent it-self as being an autonomous system. Because the variability model is the core artifact for guiding system adaptation, the agent must be able to consult (in one form or another) the runtime variability model to identify adaptations. Then the variability model is the typical knowledge part of a MAPE-K feedback loop. Here, we focus on heterogeneous agents at runtime and how they deal with the dynamic adaptation of their behaviour due to changes in environment according to a self-management policy using the variability model. Our approach is depicted in Fig. 1.

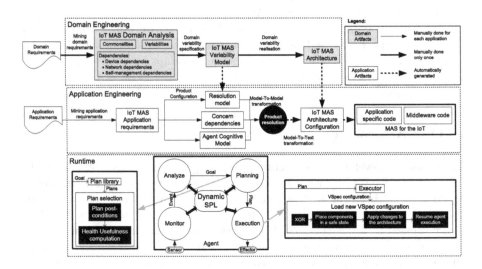

Fig. 1. SPL process for self-managed agents in the IoT.

The SPL employs two-life-cycle approach that separates domain and application engineering. While the first part, the Domain Engineering, concerns with analyzing MASs for IoT as a product line in order to produce any common (and reusable) variable parts, the second part, the Application Engineering, involves creating product-specific parts and integrating all aspects of individual products [11]. Our approach uses the information provided in the Application Engineering process to deal with the adaptation of agent behaviour using models at runtime. One of the latest steps of the Application Engineering considers the modeling of the agent cognitive concepts using CVL [12] (Agent cognitive Model box in Fig. 1). This model is used to obtain the application architecture (IoT MAS

Architecture Configuration box in Fig. 1). The MAS application architecture configuration describes the architectures of the agents of the IoT system.

As part of the Application Engineering process, the self-management policies of each agent are also selected. A self-management policy consists of a set of self-management goals, which are achieved by a set of self-management plans. The configuration of these self-management policies takes into consideration the architectural dependencies of the agent and application requirements. Plans for self-management are generated as part of the Model-To-Model (M2M) transformation that generates the application architecture. Agents continuously monitor the environment as part of their self-managed behaviour. When a change in the environment occurs, an event is thrown. These events are analysed to activate new goals that manage the new context. The agent, as part of its planning task, selects a plan to achieve the activated goal. The plan contains a set of actions that can enable or disable specific components or to change its configuration. At this point of the execution the architecture configuration is dynamically adapted. Such adaptation is addressed using an approach based on preference-based reasoning [18, 25]. Self-management for lightweight devices usually relies on common policies that can be combined in order to adapt the agent and the device where it is embedded. Agent developers must benefit from the reuse and combination of previously defined self-management policies taking into account the requirements of the application and the dependencies with the agent architecture. Changes in the agent behaviour are required when the environment changes and the self-management policy being applied adapts to the variation. The application of a self-management policy carries out the activation of a set of self-management goals, and the selection of plans to achieve both application and self-management goals are influenced by this change. As part of self-management, the agent must be able to deal with adaptation dynamically and in an autonomous manner. The ideal solution is to make a trade-off between these goals, ensuring the achievement of agent application goals, while maintaining the agent in the best conditions as long as possible with an acceptable quality of service whenever possible.

At runtime, in order to implement the aforementioned trade-off, the activation of self-management goals is driven by the *wellness* and *usefulness* of the agent. These properties quantify different concerns of the agent. Wellness is concerned with the quality or state of being healthy. The wellness of the agent is defined as a general condition of the agent in terms of its internal state (such as available resources, and activated goals, scheduled plans). More specifically wellness is related to self-management policies that are contained in its architecture. The usefulness is measured in terms of the goals that the agent potentially can bring about and the goals that are currently maintaining. In general (but not in all cases), plans that increase or emphasize agent usefulness are going to erode its wellness. Both metrics are inferred from the current configuration of the agent architecture and are used in the selection of plans. Then plans are tagged by their contribution to agent wellness and usefulness. The reasoning mechanism of our agent chooses plans to achieve its goals taking into account these factors.

When wellness factor is good, the agent tends to choose those plans (to achieve application and self-management goals) that increase its usefulness in spite of its well-being. When the wellness of the agent gets worse, it behaves conservatively to maintain its current state although its usefulness decreases.

3 Background

This section presents the case study that will be used to illustrate our proposal, additionally provides the background in CVL and related work.

3.1 Case Study

In order to illustrate our proposal, we use, as a case study a smart shopping centre. The case study focus in a shop endowed with IoT devices intended to enhance the shopping experience.

This system uses different technologies to improve the shopping experience of customers through an *active environment*. To become an active environment, the physical space is endowed with a set of small devices, namely beacons [27], that can send signals to smartphones and other personal devices entering their immediate vicinity. Signals, which contain information about the context, are sent via Bluetooth Low Energy Technology (BLE for short) [9]. BLE is a part of the Bluetooth 4.0 specification released back in 2010. It has a different set of protocols from "classic" Bluetooth, and devices are not backwards-compatible. Accordingly, you can now encounter three types of Bluetooth support: Bluetooth (devices supporting only the "classic mode"; Bluetooth Smart Ready (devices supporting both "classic" and LE modes); and Bluetooth Smart (devices supporting only the LE mode). Beaconing can be applied in all kinds of valuable ways. To put it simpler, beacons transmit data to devices that are in range to enable transmission (immediate, near or far), allow the user to be located in places where GPS is not as useful, for example, in a museum, park or shopping centre. For shopping centres in particular, beacons are important because they allow a more precise targeting of customers in a premises. For example, a customer approaching a store, could receive a message from a battery-powered beacon installed there, offering information or a promotion that relates specifically to products displayed there. In a different area or location of the same store, another beacon transmits a different message. Before beacons, marketers used geofencing technology, so that a message, advertisement, or coupon could be sent to consumers when they were within a certain range of a geofenced area, such as within a one-block radius of a store. However, that technology typically relies on GPS tracking, which only works well outside the store. With beaconing, marketers can lead and direct customers to specific areas and products within a particular store or the shopping centre itself.

Our case study focuses on a single store (see Fig. 2), BLE Beacons are scattered and spread over the shop space, linked to the different furniture elements. These elements contain are associated with specific categories of products and

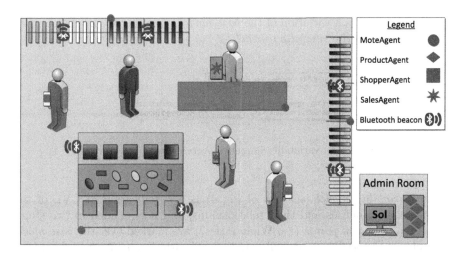

Fig. 2. Overview of the multi-agent system of the smart shopping centre.

special offers. The information loaded in each BLE Beacon is related to this category of product or special offer. Then, when a customer with a smartphone is close to a beacon (and also a category of products or a special offer), the device receives a (context-aware) recommendation. The salespeople also benefit from the technology around them. Store employees are informed of the position of customers in the store, and receive information about the environmental conditions of the shop in real time on their hand-held devices. This system has been designed as a MAS composed of agents embedded in the different devices that comprise the application. There are agents embedded in sensor motes (which provide the environmental conditions of the store), in the personal devices of the users (both customer and employees) and in the shop manager's computer. Henceforth, we use *ShopperAgent* to illustrate our approach.

3.2   The Common Variability Language

Variability of SPLs can be specified using different modeling languages. Although feature models [15] have been very popular in the SPL community over the last decade, recently the Common Variability Language (CVL) [12] has been proposed as a standard. Both variability languages can be used in our proposal, but here we opt to use CVL.

CVL is a domain-independent language for specifying and resolving variability over any instance of any language defined using a MOF-based metamodel (e.g. UML) which is called the *base model*. In a CVL process (see Fig. 3) all the variations of the *base model* are specified using the *variability model*. Each possible variation expressed in the *variability model* is called a *resolution model*. When one of the *resolution models* is selected, the CVL tool is executed and obtains the *resolved model*, a product model, fully described in the MOF-based metamodel, which is a variation of the *base model* according to the choices that have been made in the *resolution model.*

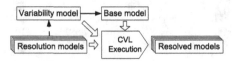

Fig. 3. Common variability language overview as specified in [12].

The *variability model* (see top of Fig. 4) is a specification in CVL of the base model variabilities and their relationships, and it is defined in two steps. Firstly, the *variation points* (i.e. What varies?) are marked over the *base model* (see center of Fig. 4). There are different types of variation points: to indicate the *existence* of an element; for the *substitution* of a particular part of the base model; for the *value assignment* of a particular slot of the model; or to set a domain specific variability associated with objects. Additionally, a set of variation points can be grouped in *Configurable Units.*

Secondly, to complete the *variability model* the CVL process specifies, separately from the base model, *Variability Specifications* (VSpec). These entities are specifications of abstract variability that are organised in tree structures (VSpec trees) representing logical constraints on their resolutions (see Fig. 4). The sub-tree under a VSpec means that the resolution (i.e. the selection of a particular variability decision) of this VSpec imposes certain constraints on the resolutions of the VSpecs in its sub-tree. Additionally, it is possible to specify explicit constraints that are also known as *crosstree constraints* (e.g. *not(Color)* in Fig. 4). A VSpec tree can be composed of different VSpecs that have different meanings. In the modeling that is shown in following sections we use *choices,* variability classifier (*VClassifier*), *value assignments, CVSpec* and *group multiplicities. Choices* represents yes/no decisions or features that can appear in the base model or not (e.g. *BothSides*). *VClassifiers* mean having to create instances and then providing per-instance resolution for the VSpec in its sub-tree. *Variable* requires providing a value of its specified type (e.g. *speed:Integer*). *CVSpecs* are used to encapsulate sections of the VSpec tree and their resolution requires resolving the VSpecs inside it. *Group multiplicities* are used to apply restrictions over the number of children of a VSpec that can be chosen (e.g. *Type* and its children *Color* and *BW*). Furthermore, the appearance of VSpecs in a selection can be optional (linked by dashed lines as *BothSides*) or mandatory (linked by solid lines as *Type*). Formally, a VSpec tree is defined as follows:

Definition 1. *A **VSpec tree** is a tuple $VST = (V, E, F, G, C)$, where V is a finite set of VSpecs, $E \subseteq V \times V$ is a set of directed child-parent edges; F is set of logic formulas over V in Conjunctive Normal Form (CNF); $G \subseteq 2^E$ are non-overlapping sets of edges participating in group multiplicities; and $C : G \to N_0 \times N_0$ is a mapping from a group to a pair denoting the cardinality of the group.*

The following well-forcedness constraints hold in VST: (i) (V,E) is a rooted tree;
(ii) all edges in a group multiplicity shares the same parent, so if $g \in G$ and
$(f_1, f_2), (f_3, f_4) \in g$ then $f_2 = f_4$; and (iii) $\forall(m,n) \in range(C), m \leq n$.

Definition 1 states that mandatory VSpecs are represented by logic formulas
in the form *parent $\wedge$ child* (e.g. *Scanner $\wedge$ Type*). A VSpec tree can be translated
to propositional logic if we interpret VSpecs as variable names. To do so, we
use the function $t(\cdot)$ and $GM_{m,n}(\dots)$. Given boolean variables $f_1, \dots, f_k$ and
$0 \leq m \leq n \leq k$, $GM_{m,n}(f_1, \dots, f_k)$ holds iff at least m and at most n of
$f_1, \dots, f_k$ are true. In addition, we assume that variables are logic variables that
are always true. Formally, the function $t(\cdot)$ is defined as follows:

Definition 2. *For a VSpec tree $VST = (V, E, F, G, C)$ define:*

$$t(VST) = \bigwedge_{(c,p)\in E} (c \to p) \wedge \bigwedge_{g\in F} g \wedge$$

$$\bigwedge_{\substack{g \in G, \\ (m,n) \in C(g), \\ g=(f_1,f),\dots,(f_k,f)}} (f \to GM_{(m,n)}(f_1, \dots, f_k))$$

The effect of the variability model on the base model is specified by *bind-*
ing variation points (black arrows in Fig. 4), which relates the base model, the
variation points and the VSpec tree. Once the *variability model* and the *base*
model have been defined, the VSpecs of the VSpec tree are resolved taking into
account its specific type (e.g. *choices* are selected or not, values are given to
variable assignments,...). As stated, this resolution of VSpecs is referred to as a
resolution model. A *resolution model* holds dependencies entailed by the VSpec
tree structure and the crosstree constraints of the *variability model*. Using Definition 2, a *resolution model* is formally defined as follows:

Definition 3. *A **resolution model** $RM : V \to \{\perp, \top\}$ is an assignment of*
truth values to the propositional logic formula $t(VST)$ that makes this formula
true.

For instance one of the resolution models of the VSpec tree of Fig. 4 assigns
true to *VendingMachine*, *Type*, *BW* and assign 10 to *Speed*. Then, the resolved
model will be composed of grey rectangles shown at the bottom of Fig. 4.

3.3 Related Work

Although SPL technology has been successfully applied to different application
areas [5] that includes MAS [8,17,19], we have not found any application of
D-SPL to MAS.

Regarding SPL, the integration of the two technologies is known as MAS-
PL (Multi-Agent System Product Lines) and related works focused on different
aspects of agent development. In [8] the Gaia methodology is modified to include

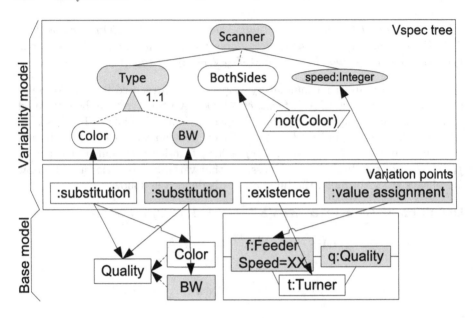

Fig. 4. Example of CVL specification extracted from [12].

SPL in the analysis and design phases of a MAS. The use of SPL allows to reduce by 48 % the design documentation time at least in the case study presented, compared to the original Gaia. MaCMAS [19] is a methodology that uses formal methods and SPL to model autonomous and self-adaptation properties of MAS. It uses SPLs to model the evolution of the system taking into account the different products contained in the SPL. The work presented in [7] focuses on the Application Engineering process by extending an existing product derivation tool for the MAS-PL domain. This proposal offers a complete SPL process with tool support to generate Jadex agents [21]. Finally, the paper [6] shows how SPL can be used to create tailor-made products based on agent platforms. However, none of these approaches consider the limitations of IoT devices where the agents are embedded.

Different works apply preference-based reasoning for controlling selection of plans in cognitive agents systems, but it has not been previously applied in the context of self-management as we do in this work [13,14,18,25]. The purpose of these works is to provide information to the agent in order to choose the appropriate plan for a given situation. In the context of the GOAL agent programming framework, this information is provided by means of linear temporal logic and is used to constraint the election of specific tasks [14]. Works [13,18] explore the use of preference in a similar way as we do in this proposal using functions that evaluate suitability of a plan. The work [13] explores the expressivity needed to specify such behaviour in the Blocks World domain, while [18] uses functions evaluated at runtime to select plan to accomplish goals with constraints. The work [25] uses summary information in order to compute preference of plans and to order the accomplishment of plan sub-goals.

In the future, the IoT will provide a large-scale environment for (intelligent) software agents. Moreover, in such open and dynamic environments, MAS need to be both self-building (able to determine the most appropriate organizational structure for the system by themselves at runtime) and adaptive (able to change this structure as their environment changes) [24]. Some works on scalability and MAS research deal with scalable architectures and applications (mostly residing in the data mining field); and algorithms and techniques for increasing scalability through change of the MAS environment.

4   Agent Adaptation by Dynamic SPL

This section explains how to compute wellness and usefulness factors that drive the agent behaviour for self-management. Wellness and usefulness are conflicting influences that a self-managed agent must take into consideration at runtime when selecting which plan is preferred to accomplish a goal. The wellness and usefuleness vary at runtime and also the goals that the agent accomplish. In order to compute these factors, we use the variability model which is included in the knowledge of the agent (see Sect. 2). The generation of this model is out of the scope of this paper and has been presented in a previous contribution [3], so, here we focus on how this model is used to compute the metrics.

As stated before, wellness describes the condition of good physical and mental health, especially when actively maintained by proper resources, activity and avoidance of risky behavior. For an agent, the function of wellness provides a quantification of the quality or state of being healthy in physical resources, especially as the result of deliberate effort. The concept of usefulness function is similar to the utility functions used in autonomic computing [16] to guide the self-management behaviour. Both functions measure the suitability of an state for an agent. However, utility focus on states that the agent wants to reach, while usefulness focus on the potential of the agent to accomplish its goals.

4.1   D-SPL of the *ShopperAgent*

The DSPL of the *ShopperAgent* (it is graphically represented in Fig. 5) contains the elements that the agent uses to interact with its user and beacons. For example, regarding the context, the value of the *Beacon received* requires that the crosstree constraint *Inside* holds. *Inside* is the child of *Shop* by means of a group multiplicity. For goals, each of these VSpecs have three children, *Activation*, *Achievement* and *Plans*, which have crosstree constraints attached that represents conditions for activation and achievement of the goals and the conjunction of plans to accomplish these goals. For example the goal *Show item information*, the constraints *Beacon received* and *Showing item information* are attached to its children. *Request text info* is an example of a plan that has a precondition that is always true.

As stated in Sect. 2, it is necessary to annotate (i.e. quantify) plans with its contributions to wellness and usefulness of the agent. The wellness is related with

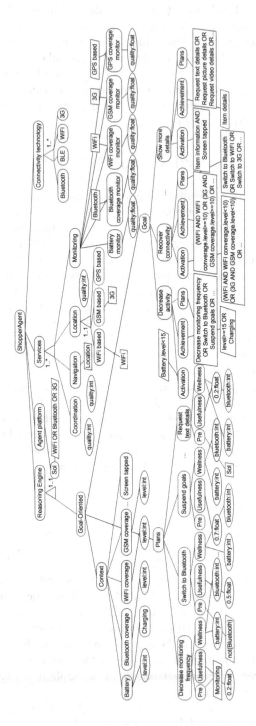

Fig. 5. Partial view of the dynamic SPL of the *ShopperAgent*.

the monitoring associated to self-management. In the case of self-management plans, the contribution to agent's wellness has been previously provided by an expert as a natural number between a range that quantifies how good or bad is the plan for agent wellness. On the other hand, the contribution of plans to agent usefulness is inferred by the resultant VSpec tree, specifically using the crosstree constraints associated with plans that state their requirements for their execution. So, if a self-management plan affects the requirement of the other plans of the agent, then it is going to negatively affect the usefulness metric. In the case of application specific plans, these values must be provided by the agent developer. Specific details of how to assess health and usefulness are provided in the following subsections. Finally, the D-SPL also includes additional information that is used for the self-management process too. Such additional information includes goals that the agent is achieving in an specific moment and the quality of the services provided.

4.2   Computation of Usefulness and Wellness

The usefulness metric captures the agent's capacity to accomplish goals and the quality of this accomplishment. This metric is computed at runtime from the information provided in the D-SPL of the agent (see Fig. 5). The D-SPL contains the number of goals that the agent can potentially accomplish in a given moment (children of VSpec *Goal* in Fig. 5) and those that are currently achieving (VSpec *Achieving*). The number of goals that the agent can accomplish could change because there is no plan that can accomplish a certain goal or they are explicitly suspended due to a self-management policy. On the other hand, children of *Services* VSpec provide a value of the quality of service of its related component in a given moment. This quality can represent an accuracy in the data provided or the frequency of a sampling or even a sum of these two values. Nonetheless, the maximum quality provided by a service is rated as 100 and the minimum is 0. To calculate agent usefulness we use (1).

$$Usefulness(A) = \sum_{i=1}^{\|Go\|} Go_i + achieving + \sum_{i=1}^{\|Ser\|} Quality(Ser_i) \qquad (1)$$

The usefulness of an agent is bounded and its maximum value is denoted by $Usefulness_{max}$. Usefulness of plans considers two factors, the direct effect on the agent architecture and the *perceived usefulness* of the plan. The effects in the agent architecture are explicitly annotated in the plan as a post-condition. In the case of plans for self-management the effects can be a decrease of the quality of a specific service or the removing or addition of a feature of the system. These modifications in the agent architecture can require the addition or removing of other components. For example, if we have a plan that disables the *Bluetooth Connectivity Technology*, then *Bluetooth coverage monitor*, *Bluetooth coverage* and *Switch to Bluetooth* will be removed too (see Fig. 5).

With regard to plans that come from the cognitive model, the effect on the agent architecture is usually an increment of the number of goals that the agent is currently achieving. On the other hand, the *perceived usefulness* is a subjective value that the developer gives to each plan for each goal that it can accomplish. For example, when the mobile phone is close to a beacon associated with a specific product of the shop, *ShopperAgent* can request information of the item from the *ProductAgent* that stands for this specific product in different formats (see Fig. 5), a piece of text (*Request text info*), a picture (*Request picture info*) or a video (*Request video info*). So, the agent developer considers that the plans with the maximum quality is *Request video info*, followed by *Request picture info* and then the *Request text info*. The value of the perceived usefulness is between 0 and 100, and it is used to compare the different plans that can be used to accomplish a specific goal. Formally, plan usefulness is defined as follows:

Definition 4. *The **usefulness of a plan** P to accomplish the goal Go of the agent A is defined as $Usefulness(P, A, Go) = Usefulness(Conf(A, P)) + Q(P, Go)$ where $Conf(A, P)$ is the VST of the agent A after the modifications that perform P, and $Q(P, Go)$ is how the user rates the accomplishment of the goal G using P.*

Agent wellness is based on the agent internal state, which comprises different factors that can be monitored for self-management activities in the VSpec. The *variables level* that are attached to the children of *Self-management* (see Fig. 5) are located in D-SPL of the agent. Formally, it is defined as follows:

Definition 5. *The **agent wellness** is an n-tuple $Wellness(A) = (h_1, ..., h_n)$ where h_i is the value of the level variable of the i-th children of the Self-management VSpec.*

Agent wellness evolves at runtime due to changes in the context and also in the configuration of the agent architecture. For example, if *WiFi* is disabled, then *WiFi coverage* will be disabled accordingly and this value will be not part of the agent wellness. In order to compute plan wellness, plan specifications must include the contribution of the plan to each of these values. Of course, they are estimations, as due to the heterogeneity present in the IoT domain, even for hand-held devices, it is difficult to provide an exact value. So, within the post-conditions and the quality of accomplishment, agent programmers must provide an n-tuple that represents the contribution of the plan for each element that comprise the agent wellness. As for the computation of usefulness, these values are predefined for self-management and must be provided by agent developers in plans of the cognitive agent model. Then, in execution time the effect of the plan on agent wellness is computed as the direct substraction between agent wellness and the effect of the plan in agent wellness.

Definition 6. *The **effect of plan** P on the health of agent A is an n-tuple $(e_1, ..., e_n)$ defined as $Effect(P, A) = Health(A) - Contribution(P)$, where $e_i \in \mathbb{R}$ and $e_i > 1$, and $Contribution(P)$ is the estimated effect of P on $Health(A)$.*

To compute preference, we work with $SE(P, A) = \sum_{i=1}^{\|Effect(P,A)\|} e_i$. As usefulness, since, agent health is a bounded value, it has a maximum value denoted by $Health_{max}$.

This approach restricts reasoning about temporal aspect of proposition evaluation. For instance, reasoning about the eventuality in which a shopper agent is interested in a specific good although she is not interested now is not approached. Dealing with temporality of gathered knowledge would require non-monotonicity expressive enough to reason about properties, which would make our approach too complex for the features of the scenarios considered.

4.3 Preference-Based Reasoning to Deal with Conflicts

The reasoning loop of our goal-oriented agent (see bottom of Fig. 1) follows the classical agent reasoning loop [22]. The agent reacts to changes in the environment by generating goals, when appropriate, it plans to achieve these goals and finally executes one of these plans. The main differences are in the knowledge element (in our agent is the D-SPL) and in the behavior of components for planning and execution.

The goal of the planning component is to select the plan to accomplish a goal taking into account to the trade-off between agent wellness and usefulness. The preference cuantifies the prossibility to choose the plan taking into account current agent wellness and plan usefulness. Goals and plans are ordered by the preference. The expected effect is such that when the agent has a good wellness it prefers plans that are going to increase its usefulness despite its wellness, while when is the opposite case, it will prefer plans that are less harmful for its wellness. So, the relation between usefulness, wellness and preference is similar to a negative exponential function. In order to equilibrate the weight of these factors in the preference function, the values of plan usefulness and the effect on agent health are normalized (i.e. dividing by maximum values of health and usefulness). So, $Preference$ is defined as follows:

$$Preference(P, A, Go) = \frac{Usefulness(P, A, Go)}{Usefulness_{max}}$$
$$-\alpha * e^{-\frac{SE(P,A)}{Health_{max}}} \tag{2}$$

Plans are ordered using the value of the application of (2) and the plan that obtains the maximum value is selected for execution. Plans are executed in the *Executor* component (see Fig. 1) and in the case of self-management plans, it is likely that they lead to a new VSpec configuration. In this case, in order to calculate VSpecs that must be added or removed, an XOR between plan postconditions and the D-SPL is calculated. Restrictions and dependencies of the D-SPL ensures that the architecture is always going to evolve to a correct state. Then, with the information of the binding, related components are placed in a safe state, changed and applied to the agent architecture and finally the agent execution is resumed.

5   Validation

In order to validate our proposal, we have simulated the behaviour of our preference function (see Eq. 2) for different values of wellness and usefulness. As we stated in the introduction, our goal is to guide the election of plans to accomplish goals, so when the agent has a good wellness is likely to select plans that are going to increase its usefulness in spite of its wellness. When the health of the agent is decreased by about a certain limit, plan selection is going to take more into consideration agent wellness. So, it is necessary to check the behaviour of the preference function for different values of effect in agent wellness (see Definition 6) and obtained usefulness (see Definition def:plansusefulness). Since usefulness and wellness are bounded, we can analyze the output of the function for all possible combinations of these values.

Figures from 6 to 8 illustrates the behavior of the preference function. The *Wellness* axis illustrates the effect of a plan in agent wellness, while the *Usefulness* axis is the resultant usefulness after plan application, and the color is the output of the preference function. For different values of α, the behaviour of the preference is as we intended and there are a tradeoff between health and usefulness.

The α value enables the control of the behaviour of the preference. As it is illustrated in the figures, when this value is higher, the preference function is more similar to an exponential function. This is useful to set a threshold for the agent to start behaving in a conservative way. For example, in hand-held devices when the battery is lower than a value, the application start to decrease monitoring frequency of services.

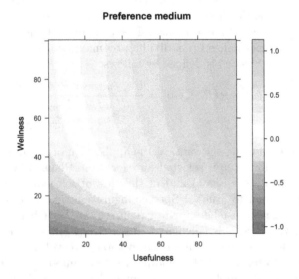

Fig. 6. Preference behaviour for a medium α.

Preference High

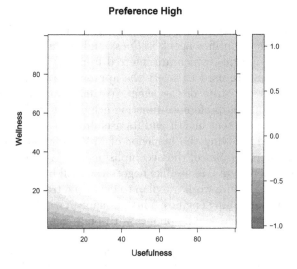

Fig. 7. Preference behaviour for high α.

Preference low

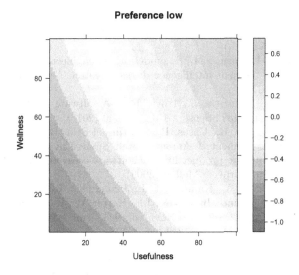

Fig. 8. Preference behaviour for low α.

6   Conclusions

In this paper we have presented an approach based on models at runtime to deal with the dynamic adaptation of agent behaviour in the IoT. In a previous contribution, we present a SPL process to generate self-managed agents in the IoT. The variability models generated in this process are used by a reasoning mechanism based on preference-based reasoning that using D-SPLs at runtime achieves a trade-off between self-management and application goals, ensuring the agent preserves an acceptable quality of service in the IoT system. This reasoning mechanism quantifies agent *wellness* and *usefulness* at one point of its execution. These metrics, which are inferred from the D-SPL are related in a *preference* function, are used to select the appropriate plan for a given goal according to the current state of the agent. We have validated our approach showing that the proposed preference function achieves a trade-off between the effect of the plan in the agent health and its usefulness.

Currently, we are studying the behavior of MAS composed of agents with this trade-off mechanisms. Since, the accomplishment of some goals is going to be influenced by other agents, issues like negotiation will be included in our reasoning mechanism. As future work, we plan to develop a trade-off mechanism for agents with reactive reasoning engines. This mechanism will be integrated in our agents for sensor motes and mobile phones with poor computational resources.

Acknowledgements. This work is supported by the project Magic P12-TIC1814 and by the project HADAS TIN2015-64841-R (co-financed by FEDER funds).

References

1. Atzori, L., Iera, A., Morabito, G.: The internet of things: a survey. Comput. Netw. **54**(15), 2787–2805 (2010)
2. Ayala, I., Amor, M., Fuentes, L.: A model driven engineering process of platform neutral agents for ambient intelligence devices. Auton. Agent. Multi-Agent Syst. **28**(2), 214–255 (2014)
3. Ayala, I., Amor, M., Fuentes, L., Troya, J.M.: A software product line process to develop agents for the IoT. Sensors **15**(7), 15640 (2015)
4. Bono-Nuez, A., Blasco, R., Casas, R., Martín-del-Brío, B.: Ambient intelligence for quality of life assessment. J. Ambient Intell. Smart Environ. **6**(1), 57–70 (2014)
5. Bosch, J.: From software product lines to software ecosystems. In: Proceedings of SPLC, pp. 111–119. Carnegie Mellon (2009)
6. Braubach, L., Pokahr, A., Kalinowski, J., Jander, K.: Tailoring agent platforms with software product lines. In: Müller, J.P., Ketter, W., Kaminka, G., Wagner, G., Bulling, N. (eds.) MATES 2015. LNCS, vol. 9433, pp. 3–21. Springer, Heidelberg (2015). doi:10.1007/978-3-319-27343-3_1
7. Cirilo, E., Nunes, I., Kulesza, U., Lucena, C.: Automating the product derivation process of multi-agent systems product lines. J. Syst. Softw. **85**(2), 258–276 (2012). Special issue with selected papers from the 23rd Brazilian Symposium on Software Engineering
8. Dehlinger, J., Lutz, R.R.: Gaia-PL: a product line engineering approach for efficiently designing multiagent systems. ACM Trans. Softw. Eng. Methodol. **20**(4), 17:1–17:27 (2011)
9. Bluetooth Special Interest Group: Bluetooth low energy 4.1. https://www.bluetooth.org/DocMan/handlers/DownloadDoc.ashx?doc_id=282159
10. Hallsteinsen, S., Hinchey, M., Park, S., Schmid, K.: Dynamic software product lines. Computer **41**(4), 93–95 (2008). http://dx.doi.org/10.1109/MC.2008.123
11. Hallsteinsen, S., Hinchey, M., Park, S., Schmid, K.: Dynamic software product lines. In: Capilla, R., Bosch, J., Kang, K.-C. (eds.) Systems and Software Variability Management, pp. 253–260. Springer, Heidelberg (2013)

12. Haugen, O.: Common variability language. Technical report ad/2012-08-05, Object Management Group, August 2012

13. Hindriks, K.V., Jonker, C.M., Pasman, W.: Exploring heuristic action selection in agent programming. In: Hindriks, K.V., Pokahr, A., Sardina, S. (eds.) ProMAS 2008. LNCS, vol. 5442, pp. 24–39. Springer, Heidelberg (2009)

14. Hindriks, K.V., van Riemsdijk, M.B.: Using temporal logic to integrate goals and qualitative preferences into agent programming. In: Baldoni, M., Son, T.C., van Riemsdijk, M.B., Winikoff, M. (eds.) DALT 2008. LNCS (LNAI), vol. 5397, pp. 215–232. Springer, Heidelberg (2009)

15. Kang, K.C., Lee, J., Donohoe, P.: Feature-oriented product line engineering. IEEE Softw. 19(4), 58–65 (2002)

16. Kephart, J., Walsh, W.: An artificial intelligence perspective on autonomic computing policies. In: IEEE POLICY, pp. 3–12, June 2004

17. Nunes, I., Lucena, C.J.P., Kulesza, U., Nunes, C.: On the development of multi-agent systems product lines: a domain engineering process. In: Gomez-Sanz, J.J. (ed.) AOSE 2009. LNCS, vol. 6038, pp. 125–139. Springer, Heidelberg (2011)

18. Padgham, L., Singh, D.: Situational preferences for BDI plans. In: Proceedings of AAMAS, pp. 1013–1020. IFAAMAS (2013)

19. Peña, J., Rouff, C.A., Hinchey, M., Ruiz-Cortés, A.: Modeling NASA swarm-based systems: using agent-oriented software engineering and formal methods. SoSyM 10(1), 55–62 (2011)

20. Pohl, K., Böckle, G., van der Linden, F.J.: Software Product Line Engineering: Foundations, Principles and Techniques, 1st edn. Springer, Heidelberg (2005)

21. Pokahr, A., Braubach, L., Lamersdorf, W.: Jadex: a BDI reasoning engine. In: Bordini, R.H., Dastani, M., Dix, J., Seghrouchni, A.E.F. (eds.) Multi-Agent Programming: Languages, Platforms and Applications, pp. 149–174. Springer, Boston (2005)

22. Russell, S., Norvig, P.: Artificial Intelligence: A Modern Approach, 3rd edn. Prentice Hall Press, Upper Saddle River (2009)

23. Sadri, F.: Ambient intelligence: a survey. ACM Comput. Surv. 43(4), 3601–3666 (2011)

24. Turner, P.J., Jennings, N.R.: Improving the scalability of multi-agent systems. In: Wagner, T.A., Rana, O.F. (eds.) AA-WS 2000. LNCS (LNAI), vol. 1887, p. 246. Springer, Heidelberg (2001)

25. Visser, S., Thangarajah, J., Harland, J., Dignum, F.: Preference-based reasoning in BDI agent systems. Auton. Agent. Multi-Agent Syst. 30(2), 291–330 (2016)

26. Weyns, D., Helleboogh, A., Holvoet, T., Schumacher, M.: The agent environment in multi-agent systems: a middleware perspective. Multiagent Grid Syst. 5(1), 93–108 (2009)

27. Wikimedia Foundation, Inc.: ibeacon. http://en.wikipedia.org/wiki/IBeacon

Dynamic (Dis-)Information in Self-adaptive Distributed Search Systems with Information Delays

Friederike Wall[✉]

Alpen-Adria-Universitaet Klagenfurt, 9020 Klagenfurt, Austria
friederike.wall@aau.at
http://www.aau.at/csu

Abstract. This paper studies the effects of self-adaptive change of distributed search systems in which imperfectly informed search agents rather loosely collaborate and pursue objective functions which are not necessarily complements to each other. The results indicate that employing learning-based self-adaptation of major features of search systems may lead to high levels of systems' performance, although the complexity of the search problem considerably tends to shape the effects of self-adaptation. The results further suggest that the selective effects of self-adaptation correspond to major features of the underlying search problem. This is of particular interest when the structure of the search problem is not known to the designer of the search system.

Keywords: Agent-based simulation · Complexity · Coordination · Imperfect information · Reinforcement learning · Self-adaptation

1   Introduction

A major question in multi-agent systems is whether agents cooperate or compete - or whether rather a combination of both, i.e. co-opetition (e.g. [8, 15]) is predominant. Depending on this, different domains of organization and control of multi-agent systems are of relevance, may it be control theory, computational organization theory or dynamic game theory to name but a few (for overviews [1, 5, 6, 24]). Moreover, with the question of cooperation or competition the predominant control mechanisms studied in the context of multi-agent systems vary - may it be, for example, coordination mechanisms (which has been differentiated into streams on consensus, formation control, task assignment, and estimation [24]) or negotiation protocols (e.g. [15]).

However, in a multi-agent system agents are not necessarily perfectly informed about the nature of their relationships within the system - neither the designer of the system has to know necessarily perfectly in advance. For these situations an interesting approach is to let a system of agents itself adapt its organization to the "nature" of the underlying problem to be solved (e.g. [7]), especially since there is some evidence that distributed search processes could

© Springer International Publishing Switzerland 2016
M. Klusch et al. (Eds.): MATES 2016, LNAI 9872, pp. 174–189, 2016.
DOI: 10.1007/978-3-319-45889-2_13

remarkably benefit from inducing organizational dynamics in the course of the search for better solutions ([20,22], see also [2]).

Building on these results, this paper studies situations where search agents - imperfectly informed about the nature of the search problem - rather loosely collaborate. In particular, though agents are not directly competing, they pursue different objective functions which are not necessarily complements to each other with respect to the entire search problem; moreover, communication and coordination between agents is rather limited. In particular, the study seeks to contribute to the following research question: *Which effects on a search system's performance result from endowing the system with capabilities to adapt some organizational features?* For this purpose, an agent-based simulation model is employed which captures two intertwined adaptive processes: (1) in the short term the search agents - operating on NK fitness landscapes [10,11] - seek to find superior levels of performance with respect to their individual objectives; (2) in the mid term they may adapt major features of the systems' structure via learning by reinforcement.

2 Outline of the Simulation Model

2.1 Overview of the Search Systems

The simulation model captures distributed search systems in which, in each time step t, M search agents (indexed by $r = 1, ...M$) seek to find superior solutions for their partial search problems which are disjoint partitions d_t^r of an overall search problem d_t. In the course of search, in each T^*-th time step, the search agents can dynamically vary the level of specialization in performing their task, i.e., the expertise in the partial search problems assigned to the search agents and their overall view of the search problem. Moreover, from time to time the search agents can alter the mode of coordination, i.e. the way in which the overall solution of the search problem is determined from the partial solutions.

The search systems do not have a "central" instance which would be able to actively intervene in the search processes. Furthermore, the M search agents do not receive a feedback on the "quality" (i.e., the performance) of the overall solution they have implemented in each time step t, but only in each T^*-th-period - just before they jointly choose the level of specialization and mode of coordination to be implemented for the next T^* periods.

2.2 Overall Search Problem

As mentioned in Sect. 1, the overall search problem for which the search systems seek to find superior solutions follows the NK framework as suggested in evolutionary biology [10,11] and - since then - employed in rather different contexts (e.g. [21]). A major advantage of the NK model is that it allows to conveniently study problems of varying complexity [14].

In each time step t of the observation period T, the search systems face an N-dimensional binary search problem, i.e., they search for a superior configuration $\boldsymbol{d_t} = (d_{1t}, ..., d_{Nt})$ with $d_{it} \in \{0, 1\}$, $i = 1, ...N$, out of 2^N different binary vectors possible. Each of the two states $d_{it} \in \{0, 1\}$ contributes with C_{it} to the overall objective $V(\boldsymbol{d_t})$ of the search system. Depending on the context of search, this overall objective might reflect the fitness of a genome as in the original NK model's context of evolutionary biology, the level of financial performance achieved by a firm or the overall service level provided by a swarm of robots.

In line with the framework of the NK model, performance contributions C_{it} are randomly drawn from a uniform distribution with $0 \leq C_{it} \leq 1$ though controlled by the complexity of the underlying search problem as captured by parameter K [14]. In particular, K reflects the number of choices d_{jt}, $j \neq i$ which also affect the performance contribution C_{it} of choice d_{it}. In case of no interactions K is 0; at a maximum level of interactions K equals $N-1$, meaning that every single option d_{it} affects contributions of all other options and vice versa. Hence, performance contribution C_{it} might not only depend on the single choice d_{it} but also on K other choices d_{jt} where $j \in \{1, ...N\}$ and $j \neq i$:

$$C_{it} = f_i(d_{it}, d_{jt, j\in\{1,...N\}, j\neq i}). \tag{1}$$

The overall performance V_t achieved in period t is defined as the normalized sum of contributions C_{it} from

$$V_t = V(\boldsymbol{d_t}) = \frac{1}{N} \sum_{i=1}^{N} C_{it}. \tag{2}$$

2.3   Search Agents and Their Choices

In the model, the N-dimensional search problem is partitioned into M disjoint partial problems $\boldsymbol{d_t^r}$ and each of these sub-problems is exclusively assigned to one search agent $r \in \{1, ..., M\}$. Hence, each search agent r has primary control over a subset with N^r single choices of the N choices; the agents' subsets are disjoint and, thus, $\sum_{r=1}^{M} N^r$ equals N. With this, the N-dimensional search problem $\boldsymbol{d_t} = (d_{1t}, ...d_{Nt})$ can also be expressed by the combination of partial search problems as $\boldsymbol{d_t} = \left[\boldsymbol{d_t^1}...\boldsymbol{d_t^r}...\boldsymbol{d_t^M}\right]$ with each agent's choices related only to its own partial search problem $\boldsymbol{d_t^r} = (d_{1t}^r, ...d_{N^r t}^r)$.

Each search agent r seeks to find a superior solution for its partial search problem - or in other words: The objective function of search agent r is not the overall performance as captured in Eq. (2) but the performance of the partial configuration which agent r is in charge of:

$$P_t^r(\boldsymbol{d_t^r}) = \frac{1}{N} \sum_{i=1+p}^{N^r} C_{it} \tag{3}$$

where $p = \sum_{s=1}^{r-1} N^s$ for $r > 1$ and $p = 0$ for $r = 1$. Hence, search agent r is focused on the performance of that partial search vector d_t^r which is in its own primary control. However, if interactions with sub-problems $d_t^q, q \neq r$ occur, choices of agent r might affect the performance of the other agents' choices, i.e.

$$P_t^{-r}(d_t^r) = \sum_{q=1,q\neq r}^{M} P_t^q \tag{4}$$

and vice versa. In each time step t, a search agent seeks to identify the best configuration for the "own" choices d_t^r while, due to a lack of information, assuming that the other agents do not alter their prior choices. For this, an agent r randomly discovers two alternatives to status quo d_{t-1}^{r*} - an alternative configuration that differs in one choice (a1) and another (a2) where two bits are flipped compared to the status quo. With this, in time step t, agent r has three options to choose from, i.e., keeping the status quo or switching to $d_t^{r,a1}$ or $d_t^{r,a2}$.

The search agents may use two different forms of "coordination": First, in a fairly "decentralized" mode, search agents decide on their partial choices d_t^r autonomously without "asking" the other search agents. Second, in a "lateral veto" mode, the search agents inform each other about their preferences and are endowed with mutual veto power. Hence, if search agent r is informed that agent $s \neq r$ intends to choose an option d_t^s that agent r suspects to have a negative impact on $P_t^r(d_t^r)$ - due to interactions across partial search problems - agent r will veto against d_t^s and vice versa. While, in fact, the "decentralized" mode does not provide any alignment of the agents' actions at all, the "lateral mode", at least, ensures that no agent is worse off with a new configuration. However, as indicated in Sect. 1, the level of collaboration is still rather low.

2.4   Search Agents' (Dis-)Information

A key feature of this study is that search agents may not be perfectly informed about their partial as well as the entire search problem. Firstly, agents do not need to perfectly know about the structure of interactions between the partial search problems (i.e., whether and, if so, how their choices affect $P_t^{-r}(d_t^r)$ or whether/how $P_t^r(d_t^r)$ is affected by other agents' choices); secondly, agents are not necessarily able to perfectly evaluate the performance P_t^r as given in Eq. (3) of their options, i.e., the agents may misjudge the options' contributions to objective $P_t^r(d_t)$. Depending on the context, these misjudgements may result from more or less specialized knowledge of human search agents (e.g. managers) or more or less effective algorithms of robots to assess performance effects of d_t^r. In the simulation model, distortions are captured by adding error terms, i.e.

$$\tilde{P}_t^r(d_t^r) = P_t^r(d_t^r) + e^r(d_t^r) \tag{5}$$

$$\tilde{P}_t^{-r}(d_t^r) = P_t^{-r}(d_t^r) + e^{-r}(d_t^r) \tag{6}$$

For the sake of simplicity, though distortions are individualized, they all are depicted as relative errors imputed to the true performance (for other functions see [13]). The error terms follow a Gaussian distribution $N(0; \sigma)$ with expected values 0 and standard deviations σ^r and σ^{-r} are assumed to be the same for search agents r; errors are assumed to be independent from each other. Hence, although for simplicity's sake the search agents operate with the same error levels, with this modeling each search agent r has a distinct view of the "true" performance landscape and, thus, agents are heterogeneous in this respect.

Imperfect information may not only be an unintentional shortcoming of, e.g., agents' information processing capacities but also may be intentionally induced: There is some evidence that imperfect information on the fitness (performance) of options could increase the effectiveness of search processes (e.g. [13,19]). This is, in particular, since false-positive evaluations of options increase the diversity of search by providing the opportunity to leave a local peak and, by that, to eventually find higher levels of performance.

2.5   Self-adaptation of (Dis-)Information and Coordination

As mentioned above, in every T^*-th period the search systems receive perfect information about the overall performance V_t according to Eq. (2) and the performance enhancements achieved within the last T^* periods. Moreover, in every T^*-th period, the search systems can alter the mode of coordination (decentralized vs. lateral veto) and the precision of the information (i.e., σ^r and σ^{-r}), the search agents have at their disposal (depending on the context of search system, for example, by switching algorithms of estimating $P_t^r(d_t^r)$). Hence, the search systems face a two-dimensional configuration problem $\phi_t = (a_t^{coord}; a_t^{prec})$ of alternative coordination modes $a^{coord} \in A^{coord}$ and of alternative levels of information precision $a^{prec} \in A^{prec}$.

In particular, for capturing some kind of self-adaptation of the search systems, the model employs a simple mode of reinforcement learning (for overviews see [9,18]) based on statistical learning: a generalized form of the Bush-Mosteller model [3,4]: The probabilities of choices of coordination mode and of information precision, respectively, are updated according to the - positive or negative - stimuli resulting from the performance enhancement ΔV of the prior configuration of the coordination mode and the information precision. Whether ΔV_t of configuration ϕ_t at time step t is regarded positive or negative, depends on whether, or not, it at least equals an aspiration level v. ΔV of configuration ϕ_t is defined as the maximal relative performance enhancement achieved within the last T^* periods of the adaptive walk, i.e.,

$$\Delta V_t(\phi_t) = \max[(V_{t-\tilde{t}} - V_{t-T^*})/V_{t-T^*}, \tilde{t} = 1, ...(T^* - 1)]. \tag{7}$$

Hence, the stimulus $\tau(t)$ is

$$\tau(t) = \begin{cases} 1 \text{ if } \Delta V_t(\phi_t) \geq v \\ -1 \text{ if } \Delta V_t(\phi_t) < v \end{cases} \tag{8}$$

Let $p(a^{prec}, t)$ denote the probability of an alternative level of information precision to be chosen at time t (with $0 \leq p(a^{prec}, t) \leq 1$ and

$\sum_{a^{prec} \in A^{prec}}(p(a^{prec},t)) = 1)$; $a^{prec}(t)$ denotes that option of set A^{prec} which is implemented in time step t. The probabilities of options $a^{prec} \in A^{prec}$ are updated according to the following rule, where λ (with $0 \le \lambda \le 1$) reflects the reinforcement strength [4]:

$$p(a^{prec},t+1) = p(a^{prec},t)$$
$$+ \begin{cases} \lambda \cdot \tau(t) \cdot (1 - p(a^{prec},t)) & \text{if } a^{prec} = a^{prec}(t) \wedge \tau(t) = 1 \\ \lambda \cdot \tau(t) \cdot p(a^{prec},t) & \text{if } a^{prec} = a_l(t) \wedge \tau(t) = -1 \\ -\lambda \cdot \tau(t) \cdot p(a^{prec},t) & \text{if } a^{prec} \ne a^{prec}(t) \wedge \tau(t) = 1 \\ -\lambda \cdot \tau(t) \cdot \frac{p(a^{prec},t) \cdot p(a^{prec}(t),t)}{1 - p(a^{prec}(t),t)} & \text{if } a^{prec} \ne a^{prec}(t) \wedge \tau(t) = -1 \end{cases} \quad (9)$$

The update of probabilities of the different coordination modes a^{coord} is made correspondingly. After the probabilities are updated as given in Eq. (9) the "next" configuration ϕ to be implemented from $t+1$ to $t+T^*$ is determined randomly according to the updated probabilities.

3 Simulation Experiments and Parameter Settings

In the simulation experiments (see Table 1 for parameter settings), after a fitness landscape is generated, the initial configuration ϕ of coordination mode and information precision of a search system is determined randomly with uniform probabilities within each dimension, i.e., $p(a^{coord}, t = 0) = \frac{1}{|A^{coord}|}$ and $p(a^{prec}, t = 0) = \frac{1}{|A^{prec}|}$. Then the search systems are "thrown" randomly in the performance landscape and observed while searching for higher levels of performance and, in each T^*-th period, updating probabilities (Eq. (9) and, eventually, altering configuration ϕ. However, to figure out whether dynamically adapting the search system is beneficial, we also conduct simulations for search systems which do not alter their coordination mode and informational precision within the observation time T (i.e., where $T^* > T$).

In order to capture the complexity of the search problem in the simulation experiments, the baseline scenarios depict two interaction structures which, in a way, represent two extremes [16]: in the *self-contained* structure the overall search problem can be segmented into M disjoint parts with maximal intense intra-sub-problem interactions (for $N = 10$ and $M = 2$ then $K = 4$) and no cross-sub-problem interactions ($K^* = 0$). In contrast, in the *full interdependent* case all single options d_i affect the performance contributions of all other choices; in consequence the intensity of interactions K is maximal (i.e., for $N = 10$ and $M = 2$ we have $K = 9$ and $K^* = 5$). Details on the self-contained and the full interdependent structure are given in [20].

For each configuration of parameter settings, 2,500 simulations are run, i.e., 5 runs on 500 distinct landscapes: For example, to study a certain type of interaction structure in the context of the further parameters settings, 500 sets of performance contributions C_i according to Eq. (1) are generated and each employed in 5 simulation experiments. With $N = 10$ for generating one landscape of, for example, a full-interdependent interaction structure (i.e., $K = 9$)

Table 1. Parameter settings

Parameter	Values/Types
Observation period	$T = 500$
Number of choices	$N = 10$
Number of search agents	$M = 2$, agent 1: $\boldsymbol{d}^1 = (d_1, ...d_5)$, agent 2: $\boldsymbol{d}^2 = (d_6, ...d_{10})$
Interaction structures	Baseline scenarios: self-contained ($K = 4, K^* = 0$; full interdependent ($K = 9, K^* = 5$) sensitivity analysis: additionally: ($K = 5, K^* = 1$); ($K = 6, K^* = 2$); ($K = 7, K^* = 3$); ($K = 8, K^* = 4$)
Alternative coordination	"Decentralized";
Modes a^{coord}	"Lateral veto"
Alternative levels of information precision a^{prec} (expertise)	As given by ($\sigma^r; \sigma^{-r}$): "OwnPerfect" (0; 0.2); "Expert" (0.025; 0.175); "Generalist" (0.075; 0.125); "Equal" (0.1; 0.1)
Interval of change	Baseline scenarios: "self-adaptive": $T^* = 20$; "no change": $T^* > T$ sensitivity analysis: $T^* \in \{10; 20; 30; 40; 50\}$
Aspiration level	$v = 0$
Learning strength	Baseline scenarios: $\lambda = 0.5$ sensitivity analysis; $\lambda \in \{0.1; 0.3; 0.5; 0.7; 0.9\}$

$N \cdot 2^{K+1} = 10,240$ different C_i have to be drawn from a uniform distribution as given by the framework of the NK model.

4 Results

In order to be clear and concise, the results of the simulations are presented in two steps: Sect. 4.1 introduces aggregate results in terms of not distinguishing between these eight configurations possible; second, the analysis goes into the detail of the (dynamically emerging) different configurations ϕ_t: With two alternative coordination modes and four alternatives of informational precision as reported in Sect. 3, eight alternative configurations ϕ_t of the search systems may occur within the course of self-adaptive search processes.

4.1 Condensed Results

Figure 1 depicts the adaptive walks for the self-contained and the full interdependent interaction structure - both for self-adapting search systems and for search systems remaining unchanged within the observation time. Table 2 displays condensed results of these scenarios. The final performance ($V_{t=500}$) achieved in the end of the observation period and the performance achieved on average in each of the 500 periods ($\bar{V}_{\{0;500\}}$) may be regarded as indicators for the effectiveness of the search processes. The same applies to the frequency of how often the global maximum is found in the final period. The ratio of different alternatives d_t selected in the course of the adaptive walks gives an indication about the diversity of search. The number of configurations ϕ_t informs about the organizational diversity employed by the search systems.

Table 2. Condensed results

Scenario of change*	Final perf. $V_{t=500}$*	Avg. perf. $\bar{V}_{\{0;500\}}$*	Frequency global max. in $t = 500$	Ratio alternations of d_t	Avg. no. of altered ϕ_t
Self-contained structure					
no change	0.9620	0.9589	31.20 %	3.81 %	0
self-adaptive	0.9752	0.9684	41.36 %	4.65 %	4.05
Full interdependent structure					
no change	0.8789	0.8556	7.16 %	12.86 %	0
self-adaptive	0.8781	0.8524	8.20 %	17.09 %	4.59

* Notes: Confidence intervals, at a confidence level of 99.9%, for $V_{t=500}$ range between 0.001 and 0.008, for $\bar{V}_{\{0;500\}}$ between 0.002 and 0.005. For parameter settings see Table 1. Each row shows the results of 2,500 adaptive walks: 500 landscapes with 5 walks on each.

These results indicate that altering the organizational set-up in the course of distributed search processes may be favorable and, with this, results are in line with prior research [2, 20, 22]: It has been argued that this is since organizational change increases the diversity of search and, thus, reduces the peril of sticking to local peaks. This is confirmed by the ratio of altered configurations d_t implemented and the frequency of how often the global maximum is found at $t = T$ as reported in Table 2.

However, results also suggest that alternating the configurations ϕ_t of how distributed search is conducted does not universally increase performance. Apparently, the complexity of the search problem affects the benefits of self-adaptation. While the performance of the self-adaptive systems in the self-contained structure goes beyond the performance level achieved under "no change" this is not the case in the full interdependent structure.

In order to closer analyze the relevance of the search problem's complexity for the beneficial effect of self-adaptation further sensitivity analyses were conducted: Fig. 2 reports results of simulations of the "self-adaptive" and the "no change" scenarios obtained for intermediate levels of complexity (for parameter settings see Table 1). The results support the hypothesis that the benefits of self-adaptation of a search system decrease with increasing complexity of the search problem. In principle, this corresponds to some prior research related to purely randomized organizational change [22], i.e. employing no learning ($\lambda = 0$).

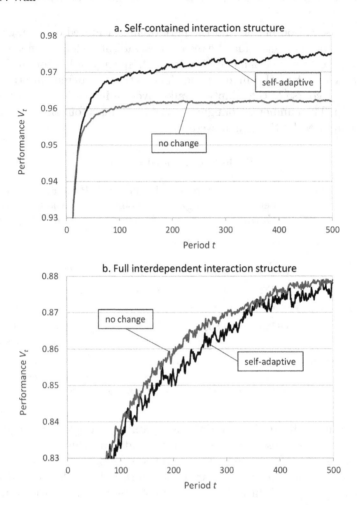

Fig. 1. Adaptive search processes for a. the self-contained and b. the full interdependent interaction structure. Each curve represents the average of 2,500 adaptive walks, i.e., 500 distinct fitness landscapes with 5 adaptive walks on each. For parameter settings see Table 1.

However, an interesting question is whether the characteristics (settings) of reinforcement learning shape this effect: Results of corresponding sensitivity analyses - reported in Fig. 3 - suggest that the full interdependent structure is particularly prone to characteristics of the learning mechanism employed. In particular, the average performance $\bar{V}_{\{0;500\}}$ increases with a higher learning strength λ (i.e., stronger learning-induced adjustment of probabilities according to Eq. (9)), and a shorter interval T^* of change. Compared to the full interdependent structure, the self-contained (i.e. decomposable) search problem is relatively insensitive towards T^* and λ. It appears helpful to study this more

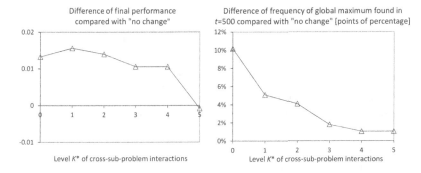

Fig. 2. Differences in final performance $V_{t=500}$ (left) and in frequency of global maximum found in $t = 500$ (right) between search processes with and without self-adaptation of the search system. Each mark represents differences of means where each subtrahend results from 2,500 adaptive walks: 500 distinct performance landscapes with 5 adaptive walks on each; for parameter settings see Table 1.

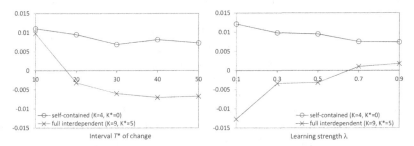

Fig. 3. Differences in average performance $\bar{V}_{\{0;500\}}$ for different intervals T^* of change (left) and different levels of learning strength λ (right) between search processes with and without self-adaptation of the search system. For further remarks see Fig. 2.

in detail in the context of analyzing the configurations ϕ_t which emerge in the self-adaptive processes as introduced subsequently.

4.2   Emerging Configurations of Search Systems

For a more detailed analysis, the simulation results obtained for the self-contained and the full interdependent structure with and without self-adaptation were grouped by that configuration $\phi_{t=500}$ that was "active" in the last period of observation (which in case of "no change" is the initial configuration $\phi_{t=0}$). Table 3 reports on the relative frequencies of the configurations for the self-adaptive search systems (in the "no change" settings frequencies are uniformly distributed).

Apparently, self-adaptation partially leads to rather different results for the two interaction structures: In the self-contained structure the two coordination modes occur with fairly similar frequency. With respect to the level of information precision, results indicate a slight tendency towards more expert-like

Table 3. Relative frequencies of configurations $\phi_{t=500}$

	Equal	Generalist	Expert	OwnPerfect	Sum
Self-contained structure					
Decentralized	9.36 %	10.80 %	12.72 %	13.64 %	46.52 %
Lateral veto	11.68 %	13.32 %	13.68 %	14.80 %	53.48 %
Sum	21.04 %	24.12 %	26.40 %	28.44 %	100 %
Full interdependent structure					
Decentralized	6.40 %	6.44 %	9.12 %	11.88 %	33.84 %
Lateral veto	15.88 %	16.44 %	15.48 %	18.36 %	66.16 %
Sum	22.28 %	22.88 %	24.60 %	30.24 %	100 %

information in both coordination modes. In the full interdependent structure - where obviously some need for coordination exists - the lateral mode which provides some horizontal coordination predominates (in around two-thirds of the 2.500 runs). Again a predominance - though not very pronounced - of more precise information occurs in both coordination modes.

Next, we turn to the final performance $V_{t=500}$ achieved with the different configurations $\phi_{t=500}$ in the "no change" and the "self-adaptive" scenarios as displayed in Figs. 3 and 4; Table 4 reports on the significance of mean differences between these scenarios according to Welch's method [12,23]. For both interaction structures, these results indicate that the lateral mode of coordination "benefits" from inducing dynamics. In most cases, final performance goes remarkably (and statistically significant) beyond that level achieved without change (up to 4.4 points of percentage). An explanation may be that with inducing change a particular pitfall of this form of coordination is mitigated:

Lateral veto power, in general, ensures that potentially detrimental effects of one agent's choices on the other agents' performance are considered [17]. In particular, lateral veto is intended to avoid false positive evaluations with regard to overall performance (i.e., false positive moves of the search system) and mitigate potentially detrimental effects of competition or conflicting objective functions. This is of particular relevance in the case of cross-sub-problem interactions (i.e. with $K^* > 0$) and may also occur even with perfect information (since agents do not know in advance which options the other agents choose). However, the lateral veto is particularly prone to inducing inertia: new configurations d_t are only implemented if no search agent perceives to be worse off than with keeping the status quo - otherwise an agent would veto. Inducing dynamics may provide a "way out" from such situations: another view of the performance landscape, i.e. switching a^{prec}, and/or altering the coordination mode, i.e. switching a^{coord}, leads to other evaluations of options and, thus, provides the chance to leave the status quo. In the same sense, rather imprecise information may lead to more diversity in the search (e.g. [13,19]). This may explain - not only but above all - why in the full interdependent structure the final performance $V_{t=500}$ achieved

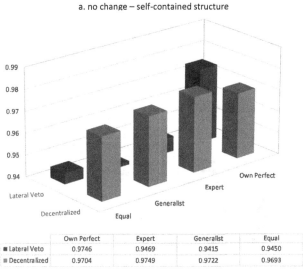

a. no change – self-contained structure

	Own Perfect	Expert	Generalist	Equal
■ Lateral Veto	0.9746	0.9469	0.9415	0.9450
■ Decentralized	0.9704	0.9749	0.9722	0.9693

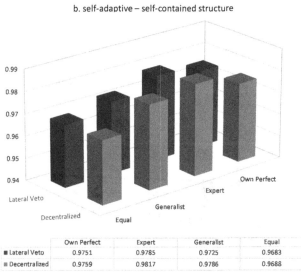

b. self-adaptive – self-contained structure

	Own Perfect	Expert	Generalist	Equal
■ Lateral Veto	0.9751	0.9785	0.9725	0.9683
■ Decentralized	0.9759	0.9817	0.9786	0.9688

Fig. 4. Final performance $V_{t=500}$ with self-adaptation and without change of the search system in the self-contained structure. For parameter settings see Table 1.

with lateral veto in combination with rather imperfect information goes beyond that level achieved with more precise information (Fig. 5).

However, a further question is why with self-adaptation in the full interdependent structure the decentralized mode combined with imprecise information apparently leads to rather inferior results (up to minus 11 points of percentage compared to "no change" as Table 4 reports): a more detailed analysis of the

a. no change – full interdependent structure

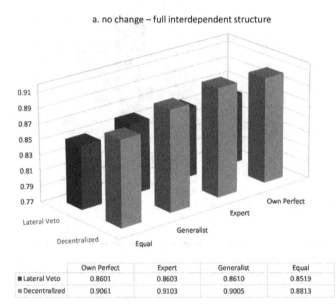

	Own Perfect	Expert	Generalist	Equal
■ Lateral Veto	0.8601	0.8603	0.8610	0.8519
■ Decentralized	0.9061	0.9103	0.9005	0.8813

b. self-adaptive – full interdependent structure

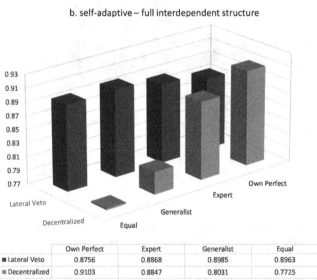

	Own Perfect	Expert	Generalist	Equal
■ Lateral Veto	0.8756	0.8868	0.8985	0.8963
■ Decentralized	0.9103	0.8847	0.8031	0.7725

Fig. 5. Final performance $V_{t=500}$ with self-adaptation and without change of the search system in the full interdependent structure. For parameter settings see Table 1.

Table 4. Mean differences and confidence intervals at a 0.99 level for all pairwise comparisons of final performance $V_{t=500}$ achieved with self-adaption versus "no change"; * indicates a significant difference

Configuration a^{coord} & a^{prec}	Self-contained structure	Full interdependent structure
Decentral-Equal	-0.0005 ± 0.0084	$-0.1088 \pm 0.0329*$
Decentral-Generalist	0.0063 ± 0.007	$-0.0974 \pm 0.0336*$
Decentral-Expert	$0.0068 \pm 0.0065*$	$-0.0256 \pm 0.0227*$
Decentral-OwnPerfect	0.0055 ± 0.0071	0.0042 ± 0.0168
Lateral Veto-Equal	$0.0233 \pm 0.0091*$	$0.0444 \pm 0.0135*$
Lateral Veto-Generalist	$0.031 \ \pm 0.0086*$	$0.0374 \pm 0.0129*$
Lateral Veto-Expert	$0.0316 \pm 0.0085*$	$0.0266 \pm 0.0139*$
Lateral Veto-OwnPerfect	0.0005 ± 0.0069	$0.0155 \pm 0.0137*$

adaptive walks reveals that in these settings the diversity of search might have been too high (with up to more than 51 %), especially since about half of the alterations of d_t are false positive ones.

5 Conclusion

The major finding of this study is that employing self-adaptation in collaborative search processes conducted by search systems with rather loosely linked search agents and information delays may lead to higher levels of performance compared to keeping the systems' configuration stable over time. However, the results also suggest that the complexity of the search problem in conjunction with the specific setting of the learning mode may considerably shape the effects of self-adaptation - which, at worst, may even be slightly harmful if compared to refraining from any alternations. This may sensitize the designer of a distributed search system to pay particular attention to figuring out the complexity of the underlying search system.

However, even with the rather simple mode of reinforcement learning employed in this study, self-adaptation may have selective effects which correspond to the characteristics of the underlying search problem: with high complexity of the search problem and, thus, high coordination need, the more intense form of coordination predominantly emerges; on the other side, when the search problem does not require coordination (i.e. coordination being obsolete though not harmful) no clear predominance of one coordination occurs. With respect to the level of informational precision things tend to be more subtle: in particular, the beneficial effect of imprecise information on mitigating inertia induced by the coordination appears to be of relevance.

Of course, these findings so far are subject to several limitations which call for further research efforts. First of all, further studies should investigate search systems facing more demanding search problems with a larger search space and consisting of a higher number of agents which also are more heterogeneous than in the study introduced (e.g., with respect to learning capabilities). Moreover, the effects of other modes of learning employed to induce self-adaptation await to be studied. Additionally, the basic search problem as captured in the NK-framework is (apart from the structure of interactions) rather unstructured in terms of randomized performance contributions; for more structured search problems learning-based self-adaptive adjustments of the search system may turn out to be even more beneficial.

References

1. Basar, T., Olsder, G.J.: Dynamic Noncooperative Game Theory, 2nd edn. Academic Press, New York (1999)
2. Baumann, O.: Distributed problem solving in modular systems: the benefit of temporary coordination neglect. Syst. Res. Behav. Sci. **32**, 124–136 (2015)
3. Bush, R.R., Mosteller, F.: Stochastic Models for Learning. Wiley, Oxford (1955). (Engl.)
4. Brenner, T.: Agent learning representation: advice on modelling economic learning. In: Tesfatsion, L., Judd, K.L. (eds.) Handbook of Computational Economics, vol. 2, pp. 895–947. Elsevier, Amsterdam (2006)
5. Carley, K.M., Gasser, L.: Computational organization theory. In: Weiss, G. (ed.) Multiagent Systems: A Modern Approach to Distributed Artificial Intelligence, pp. 299–330. MIT Press, Cambridge (1999)
6. Gross, T., Blasius, B.: Adaptive coevolutionary networks: a review. J. R. Soc. Interface **20**, 259–271 (2008)
7. Hammel, U., Bäck, T.: Evolution strategies on noisy functions how to improve convergence properties. In: Davidor, Y., Männer, R., Schwefel, H.-P. (eds.) PPSN 1994. LNCS, vol. 866, pp. 159–168. Springer, Heidelberg (1994)
8. Hu, J., Zheng, W.X.: Emergent collective behaviors on coopetition networks. Phys. Lett. A **378**(2627), 1787–1796 (2014)
9. Kaelbling, L.P., Littman, M.L., Moore, A.W.: Reinforcement learning: a survey. J. Artif. Intell. Res. **4**, 237–285 (1996)
10. Kauffman, S.A., Levin, S.: Towards a general theory of adaptive walks on rugged landscapes. J. Theor. Biol. **128**, 11–45 (1993)
11. Kauffman, S.A.: The Origins of Order: Self-organization and Selection in Evolution. Oxford University Press, Oxford (1993)
12. Law, A.M.: Simulation Modeling and Analysis, 4th edn. McGraw-Hill, New York (2007)
13. Levitan, B., Kauffman, S.A.: Adaptive walks with noisy fitness measurements. Mol. Divers. **1**, 53–68 (1995)
14. Li, R., Emmerich, M.T.M., Eggermont, J., Bovenkamp, E.G.P., Bäck, T., Dijkstra, J., Reiber, J.H.C.: Mixed-integer NK landscapes. In: Runarsson, T.P., Beyer, H.-G., Burke, E.K., Merelo-Guervós, J.J., Whitley, L.D., Yao, X. (eds.) PPSN 2006. LNCS, vol. 4193, pp. 42–51. Springer, Heidelberg (2006)
15. Reaidy, J., Massotte, P., Diep, D.: Comparison of negotiation protocols in dynamic agent-based manufacturing systems. Int. J. Prod. Econ. **99**, 117–130 (2006)
16. Rivkin, J.W., Siggelkow, N.: Patterned interactions in complex systems: implications for exploration. Manage. Sci. **53**, 1068–1085 (2007)
17. Siggelkow, N., Rivkin, J.W.: Speed and search: designing organizations for turbulence and complexity. Organ. Sci. **16**(2), 101–122 (2005)

18. Sutton, R.S., Barto, A.G.: Reinforcement Learning: An Introduction, 2nd edn. MIT Press, Cambridge (2012). (Mass.)

19. Wall, F.: The (Beneficial) role of informational imperfections in enhancingorganisational performance. In: Calzi, M.L., Milone, L., Pellizzari, P. (eds.) Progress in Artificial Economics. Lecture Notes in Economics and Mathematical Systems, vol. 645, pp. 115–126. Springer, Heidelberg (2010)

20. Wall, F.: Beneficial effects of randomized organizational change on performance. Adv. Complex Syst. **18**(05n06), 1550019 (2015)

21. Wall, F.: Agent-based modeling in managerial science: an illustrative survey and study. RMS **10**, 135–193 (2016)

22. Wall, F.: Organizational dynamics in adaptive distributed search processes: effects on performance and the role of complexity. Front. Informa. Technol. Electr. Eng. **17**(4), 283–295 (2016)

23. Welch, B.L.: The significance of the differences between two means when the population variances are unequal. Biometrika **25**, 350–362 (1938)

24. Yongcan, C., Wenwu, Y., Wei, R., Guanrong, C.: An overview of recent progress in the study of distributed multi-agent coordination. IEEE Trans. Ind. Inf. **9**, 427–438 (2013)

Multi-actor Architecture for Schedule Optimisation Based on Lagrangian Relaxation

Georg Weichhart[1,2]([✉]) and Alexander Hämmerle[1]

[1] Profactor GmbH, Steyr, Austria
{Georg.Weichhart,Alexander.Haemmerle}@Profactor.at
[2] Department of Communications Engineering - Business Informatics,
Johannes Kepler University, Linz, Austria

Abstract. In this paper an actor based approach to manufacturing scheduling is presented. It is based on a mathematical foundation, where the scheduling problem is formulated as an integer program. With lagrangian relaxation the problem is decomposed in independent sub-problems. The sub-problems can be solved concurrently, thus the mathematical foundation lends itself to a distributed computational architecture. The presented approach is discussed in the context of other distributed approaches in general and holonic manufacturing approaches in particular. The formal foundation and the computational architecture allowing its implementation are discussed.

1 Introduction

The vision of the future Enterprise as a sensing, smart and sustainable system, promotes a view of the enterprise as a complex adaptive system. This view emphasises that despite its distributed nature schedules still need to be optimised for being economically sustainable.

In the *Next-Generation Multi-Purpose Production Systems* (NgMPPS) project algorithms are developed for distributed optimisation of manufacturing schedules in production networks. A focal point is dynamic scheduling, where disruptions such as machine failures or transport delays impede the execution of planned schedules, and adapted schedules have to be calculated in real time.

The article is structured as follows. First the problem is introduced, followed by a more formal description of the problem and reformulation of the problem which allows a distributed approach. This is followed by a brief discussion of conceptual approaches and concrete distributed systems for manufacturing scheduling. An architecture is presented which allows to embed the mathematical approach and execute it in a distributed system. The last section presents the conclusions of our work in the NgMPPS project so far and next steps.

2 Flexible Job Shop Scheduling with Travel Times

Job Shop Scheduling is a computational problem which is a complex combinatorial problem, more specifically a non-deterministic polynomial-time hard ($\mathcal{NP}$-hard) problem. However, the distribution aspect of the envisioned application

© Springer International Publishing Switzerland 2016
M. Klusch et al. (Eds.): MATES 2016, LNAI 9872, pp. 190–197, 2016.
DOI: 10.1007/978-3-319-45889-2_14

scenario requires to deal with the a combinatorial optimisation problem of Flexible Job Shop Scheduling (**FJSS**) with travel times between machines (**FJSSTT**) cf. [3]:

A number of manufacturing jobs (production orders) have to be scheduled on a number of machines in one or more job shops. A job consists of a number of operations (production steps). Every operation may be executed on one or more alternative machines. The overall goal is to find an optimal assignment of operations to machines.

The optimisation problem is to be solved, respecting the following constraints:

- Processing time constraints: Every operation requires a deterministic, machine-dependent process time.
- Precedence constraints of job operations: Simple, chain-like precedence relations between operations belonging to the same job are modelled.
- Machine capacity constraints: At every time slot only one operation may be processed on a single machine.
- Operations have to be processed non-pre-emptively: Once an operation is started it may not be interrupted.

3   Problem Formulation

Due to space constraints we have to limit the presentation of the model, focusing on core concepts.

Our problem formulation is based on the integer programming formulation described in [16]. I jobs with individual due dates have to be scheduled on M available machines. We assume immediate availability of jobs. The set of jobs $\mathcal{I}$ is $\{0, 1, ..., I - 1\}$ and the set of machines $\mathcal{M}$ is $\{0, 1, ..., M - 1\}$. Job i consists of J_i non-preemptive operations, with $\mathcal{J}_i = \{0, 1, ..., J_i - 1\}$ denoting the set of operations for job i. The operation j of job i is denoted as (i, j). We regard simple, chain-like precedence constraints amongst operations belonging to the same job. The set of alternative machines for operation (i, j) is denoted as $\mathcal{H}_{ij}$, with machine-specific processing times. The scheduling horizon consists of K discrete time slots, the set of time slots $\mathcal{K}$ is $\{0, 1, ..., K - 1\}$. The beginning time of an operation is defined as the beginning of the corresponding time slot, and the completion time as the end of the time slot.

The following parameters are given with a specific problem instance as input data, whereas the decision variables span the solution space for the scheduling problem.

Parameters

$D_i, i \in \mathcal{I}$: Job due dates.
$P_{ijm}, i \in \mathcal{I}, j \in \mathcal{J}_i, m \in \mathcal{H}_{ij}$: Processing time of operation (i, j) on machine m.
$R_{mn}, m \in \mathcal{M}, n \in \mathcal{M}$: Travel time from machine m to machine n.
$W_i, i \in \mathcal{I}$: Job tardiness weight.

Variables

$\delta_{ijmk}, i \in \mathcal{I}, j \in \mathcal{J}_i, m \in \mathcal{M}, k \in \mathcal{K}$: The binary variable δ_{ijmk} is 1, if operation (i, j) is processed on machine m at time slot k, and 0 otherwise.
$b_{ij}, i \in \mathcal{I}, j \in \mathcal{J}_i$: Beginning time of operation (i, j).
$c_{ij}, i \in \mathcal{I}, j \in \mathcal{J}_i$: Completion time of operation (i, j).
$m_{ij} \in \mathcal{H}_{ij}, i \in \mathcal{I}, j \in \mathcal{J}_i$: The machine assigned to operation (i, j).
$\lambda_{mk}, m \in \mathcal{M}, k \in \mathcal{K}$: Lagrange multiplier for time slot k on machine m.

The optimisation objective is the minimisation of the weighted sum of job tardiness, the optimisation problem is then

$$\mathcal{Z} = \min_{b_{ij}, m_{ij}} \sum_{i \in \mathcal{I}} W_i * max(0, C_i - D_i), \tag{1}$$

where C_i is the completion time for job i.

Equation (1) has to be solved subject to a number of constraints. Machines have limited capacity, each time slot a machine cannot process more than one operation. Processing time constraints define the relation between beginning time and completion time of operations. The precedence constraints between operations of a job consider travel times between machines. For operations $(i, j - 1)$ and (i, j) the beginning time of (i, j) cannot be earlier than the arrival time at machine m_{ij}. We assume immediate availability of transport resources to move workpieces corresponding to jobs between machines. In a production network, the travel time between machines located in different job shops covers transport between the shops as well as shop-internal logistics activities.

Lagrangian relaxation (LR) is a well-proven method to generate high-quality solutions for hard combinatorial problems, especially when it comes to solving large problem instances. The salient point in LR is the relaxation of constraints by adding them to the objective function of the primal problem. Each relaxed constraint is multiplied with a Lagrange multiplier. In an economic interpretation these multipliers are the shadow prices of the corresponding constraints. Due to the relaxation of "nasty" constraints the relaxed problem is easier to solve than the primal problem, and an optimal solution to the relaxed problem provides a lower bound on the optimal objective value of the primal problem (for minimisation problems).

However, the simplification comes with a price: in addition to the decision variables we have to determine the values for the Lagrange multipliers. The multiplier values are determined by solving the Lagrangian dual problem, with Lagrange multipliers being the dual variables. Due to the relaxation of constraints, solutions to the dual problem are generally infeasible for the primal problem, thus a feasibility repair mechanism has to be applied.

For the FJSSTT problem there are two candidate constraint sets for relaxation: precedence constraints and machine capacity constraints. The relaxation of precedence constraints and decomposition into independent machine-level subproblems is hampered by the structure of the precedence constraints, as these couple the precedence constraints across machines. The relaxation of machine capacity constraints results in the relaxed problem

$$\mathcal{Z}_D(\lambda) = \min_{b_{ij}, m_{ij}} \sum_{i \in \mathcal{I}} W_i T_i + \sum_{m \in \mathcal{M}} \sum_{k \in \mathcal{K}} \lambda_{mk} \left[\sum_{i \in \mathcal{I}} \sum_{j \in \mathcal{J}_i} \delta_{ijmk} - 1 \right], \qquad (2)$$

where λ is the vector of Lagrange multipliers. (2) has to be solved subject to above constraints, except machine capacity constraints. For a given pair of indices m, k the term in brackets is positive if the capacity constraint for time slot k on machine m is violated. The structure of $\mathcal{Z}_D(\lambda)$ allows the decomposition into independent job-level subproblems

$$\mathcal{S}_i = \min_{b_{ij}, m_{ij}} W_i T_i + \sum_{j \in \mathcal{J}_i} \sum_{k=b_{ij}}^{c_{ij}} \lambda_{m_{ij}k}. \qquad (3)$$

$\mathcal{S}_i$ is a one job scheduling problem and can be characterised as follows, cf. [6]. A job requires the completion of a set of operations, and each operation can be performed on one of several alternative machines. The job operations must satisfy precedence constraints as well as processing time constraints. Each machine has a marginal cost for utilisation at each time slot within the scheduling horizon. The scheduling problem is to determine the machine and the completion time of each operation of the job to minimise the sum of job tardiness and the total cost of using the machines to complete the job.

The one job scheduling problem with standard precedence constraints is not $\mathcal{NP}$-hard, and it can be solved with dynamic programming, cf. [5,6,11,16].

With the introduction of subproblems $\mathcal{S}_i$, the relaxed problem can be reformulated,

$$\mathcal{Z}_D(\lambda) = \sum_{i \in \mathcal{I}} \mathcal{S}_i - \sum_{m,k} \lambda_{mk}. \qquad (4)$$

The Lagrangian dual problem, optimising the Lagrange multiplier values, is

$$\mathcal{Z}_D = \max_{\lambda} \mathcal{Z}_D(\lambda). \qquad (5)$$

It can be shown that $\mathcal{Z}_D(\lambda)$ is concave and piece-wise linear, thus hill-climbing methods like subgradient search can be applied to solve the dual problem.

Having this formal approach, an architecture is needed that supports the possibility of executing this model in a computational network that runs within the production network. In the following we are discussing distributed approaches.

4   Adaptive and Distributed Production Scheduling

A number of different approaches exist to design a distributed system for scheduling [12,14]. In the following we give a brief overview of such systems applied to the manufacturing domain.

Agent technology has been applied to manufacturing enterprise integration, supply chain management, manufacturing scheduling and control, material handling and logistics service provision. Multi Agent Systems negotiation is used as a means to reduce the number of alternative solutions and to distribute the problem solving. In several approaches, the holonic paradigm was applied to address the openness and dynamism of enterprises and enterprise networks.

An important holonic architecture for distributed manufacturing execution is the Product Resource Order Staff Architecture (*PROSA*) cooperative control reference architecture [14,15]. *PROSA* has been extended towards ensuring adaptive behaviour of agent-based manufacturing control systems by introducing adaptive staff agents [17]. Staff agents communicate across different production facilitates and modify parameters used by the other agents.

ADACOR^2 is a distributed scheduling architecture also based on a holonic modelling approach [2]. The overall problem is divided into sub-problems and sub-problems are solved taking the level of granularity into account. In ADACOR^2 each scheduler is composed from a swarm of schedulers. ADACOR^2 is capable of self-organising the macro structure based on behaviour changes of holons.

Multi Agent Systems technology is capable of realising reactive schedule execution systems. Approaches exist that support schedule execution, advanced planing and optimisation for manufacturing networks and supply chains. In the IntLogProd project [10] a distributed infrastructure has been implemented using contract net protocols for scheduling production machines and transport for simple products in a production network.

A hierarchical approach for a centralised control of distributed manufacturing systems which share (some) resources is realised by the DSCEP framework [1]. This system supports indirect cooperation between customer agents (c) and producer agents (p). Where every c represents one order and each p represents one machine or human. The overall system is controlled by a supervisor agent S. Through the introduction of virtual c and virtual p agents a distributed system may be designed.

5   Architecture

The above architectures all have their merits. However, in the current project a computational architecture for a well-defined mathematical model has to be developed. Re-using an existing architecture would require to adapt the mathematics, which potentially leads to a formally incorrect system.

Figure 1 shows the actors, their relationships and messages used for coordination.

There is a single root actor (left in Fig. 1) started by the user. It starts the resource manager actor who is responsible for starting resource actors, representing machines and transporters. The resource actors are configured with process times for particular job operations and travel times between machines. The root agent also starts the feasibility repair actor, being responsible for repairing the

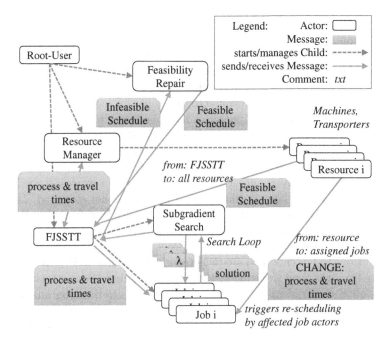

Fig. 1. NgMPPS actor based architecture

infeasible schedules resulting from solving the dual problem $\mathcal{Z}_D$. For each FJSSTT problem to be solved, a corresponding FJSSTT actor is started.

In order to solve the dual problem $\mathcal{Z}_D$, a subgradient search actor is created. The subgradient search method is an adaptation of the well-known gradient method. Due to the usage of subgradients, the method is applicable to nondifferentiable functions, like the Lagrangian dual function $\mathcal{Z}_D(\lambda)$ in Eq. (2). We have implemented two flavours of the algorithm: a standard subgradient search method requiring $\mathcal{Z}_D(\lambda)$ to be fully optimised, and a surrogate subgradient method where it is sufficient to solve $\mathcal{Z}_D(\lambda)$ approximately. For an introduction to the subgradient methods we refer to [4,7].

For each job in a FJSSTT problem a job actor is created. It is configured to use a particular subgradient search actor, and it is also introduced to resource actors knowledgeable of process and travel times. The main task of an actor representing job i is to solve a subproblem $\mathcal{S}_i$. We have implemented two problem solving methods for $\mathcal{S}_i$: (1) a dynamic programming algorithm for exact solutions, based on [16], and (2) a variable neighbourhood search for approximate solutions, allowing to solve larger problem instances than with dynamic programming. We refer to [8] for an introduction to variable neighbourhood search.

The subgradient search procedure is iterative: the vector of Lagrange multipliers λ is calculated based on the subgradients in the current iteration, and λ is communicated to the job actors. The subgradient γ_{mk}^l can be interpreted as the violation of the capacity constraint for machine m at time slot k in iteration l.

The job actors use the updated Lagrange multipliers to solve their subproblems, and send their solutions to the subgradient search actor. With the job solutions the subgradient search actor compiles the complete, generally infeasible schedule for the FJSSTT problem and calculates new subgradients.

The FJSSTT actor receives the infeasible schedule from the subgradient search actor and asks the feasibility repair actor to generate a feasible schedule. For feasibility repair we have implemented a list scheduling heuristic based on [9]. Machine actors are informed about the feasible schedule, and a machine actor is informed about the jobs that are scheduled on the machine.

When a schedule is executed, disrupting events like e.g. a border control or a machine failure may occur, leading to deviations in process/travel times. As a consequence, the planned schedule can not be further executed. *Dynamic scheduling* catches the disruptions and calculates an adapted feasible schedule: a resource actor detects a disruption and informs the job actors which are affected by the disruption. For job i, the deviating process/travel times and the reduced set of operations to be scheduled are reflected in a subproblem S'_i, with Lagrange multipliers from the final iteration of the preceding subgradient search. Affected job actors solve subproblems S'_i and send the solutions to the subgradient search actor, which starts a new subgradient search. Depending on the severity of the disruption, and the changes in job-level schedules, it is likely that in the course of the new search procedure other jobs than the initially affected are forced to re-calculate their schedules. This effect propagation of a disruption may be deliberately limited, e.g. by explicitly "freezing" the schedules of high-priority jobs.

6   Conclusions and Next Steps

We have designed and implemented a distributed architecture for scheduling in production networks. In this paper we describe the mathematical foundation of our system and the actor based computational architecture.

For executing tests at different stages of the implementation we use problem instances published by [13], suitable for considering tardiness-related optimisation criteria. These problem instances have been extended and distributed manufacturing scenarios with travel times between machines have been generated. The presented system will be improved to handle dynamic scheduling in the case of unexpected events like machine failures and travel time variations.

Acknowledgement. The research leading to these results is funded by the Austrian Ministry for Transport, Innovation and Technology www.bmvit.gv.at through the project NGMPPS-DPC: Next-Generation Multi-Purpose Production Systems – Decentralised production control based on distributed optimisation.

References

1. Archimede, B., Letouzey, A., Memon, M.A., Xu, J.: Towards a distributed multi-agent framework for shared resources scheduling. J. Intell. Manuf. **25**(5), 1077–1087 (2013). http://dx.doi.org/10.1007/s10845-013-0748-8

2. Barbosa, J., Leitão, P., Adam, E., Trentesaux, D.: Self-organized holonic multi-agent manufacturing system: the behavioural perspective. In: 2013 IEEE International Conference on Systems, Man, and Cybernetics (SMC), pp. 3829–3834, October 2013
3. Behnke, D., Geiger, M.J.: Test instances for the flexible job shop scheduling problem with work centers (2012). http://edoc.sub.uni-hamburg.de/hsu/volltexte/2012/2982/
4. Bragin, M.A., Luh, P.B., Yan, J.H., Yu, N., Stern, G.A.: Convergence of the surrogate Lagrangian relaxation method. J. Optim. Theory Appl. **164**(1), 173–201 (2014)
5. Buil, R., Piera, M.A., Luh, P.B.: Improvement of Lagrangian relaxation convergence for production scheduling. IEEE Trans. Autom. Sci. Eng. **9**(1), 137–147 (2012)
6. Chen, H., Chu, C., Proth, J.M.: An improvement of the Lagrangean relaxation approach for job shop scheduling: a dynamic programming method. IEEE Trans. Rob. Autom. **14**(5), 786–795 (1998)
7. Fisher, M.L.: The Lagrangian relaxation method for solving integer programming problems. Manage. Sci. **50**(12 Supplement), 1861–1871 (2004)
8. Hansen, P., Mladenovic, N.: Variable neighborhood search. In: Glover, F., Kochenagen, G. (eds.) Handbook of Metaheuristics, pp. 145–184. Kluwer Academic Publishers, Boston (2003)
9. Hoitomt, D.J., Luh, P.B., Pattipati, K.R.: A practical approach to job-shop scheduling problems. IEEE Trans. Rob. Autom. **9**(1), 1–13 (1993)
10. Karageorgos, A., Mehandjiev, N., Weichhart, G., Hämmerle, A.: Agent-based optimisation of logistics and production planning. Eng. Appl. Artif. Intell. **16**(4), 335–348 (2003)
11. Kaskavelis, C.A., Caramanis, M.C.: Efficient Lagrangian relaxation algorithms for industry size job-shop scheduling problems. IIE Trans. **30**(11), 1085–1097 (1998)
12. Leitão, P., Mařík, V., Vrba, P.: Past, present, and future of industrial agent applications. IEEE Trans. Industr. Inf. **9**(4), 2360–2372 (2013)
13. Mönch, L.: Problem instances for flexible job shops with due dates (2015). http://p.2schedgen.fernuni-hagen.de/index.php?id=174
14. Monostori, L., Valckenaers, P., Dolgui, A., Panetto, H., Brdys, M., Csáji, B.C.: Cooperative control in production and logistics. Ann. Rev. Control **39**, 12–29 (2015)
15. Van Brussel, H., Wyns, J., Valckenaers, P., Bongaerts, L., Peeters, P.: Reference architecture for holonic manufacturing systems: PROSA. Comput. Ind. **37**(3), 255–274 (1998). http://www.sciencedirect.com/science/article/pii/S016636159800102X
16. Wang, J., Luh, P.B., Zhao, X., Wang, J.: An optimization-based algorithm for job shop scheduling. Sadhana **22**(2), 241–256 (1997)
17. Zimmermann, J., Mönch, L.: Design and implementation of adaptive agents for complex manufacturing systems. In: Mařík, V., Vyatkin, V., Colombo, A.W. (eds.) HoloMAS 2007. LNCS (LNAI), vol. 4659, pp. 269–280. Springer, Heidelberg (2007). http://dx.doi.org/10.1007/978-3-540-74481-8_26

ASP-Driven BDI-Planning Agents in Virtual 3D Environments

André Antakli$^{(\boxtimes)}$, Ingo Zinnikus, and Matthias Klusch

German Research Center for Artificial Intelligence,
DFKI Agents and Simulated Reality Department, Saarland University Campus,
Bldg. D3.2 Stuhlsatzenhausweg 3, 66123 Saarbruecken, Germany
{andre.antakli,ingo.zinnikus,matthias.klusch}@dfki.de
http://www.dfki.de

Abstract. This paper introduces the agent platform HumanSim, a combination of the BDI-paradigm and Answer Set Programming (ASP), to simulate entities in three-dimensional virtual environments. We show how ASP can be used to (i) annotate a virtual three-dimensional world and (ii) to model the goal selection behavior of a BDI agent. Using this approach it is possible to model the agent domain and its behavior – reactive or foresighted – with ASP. To demonstrate the practical use of HumanSim, we present a three-dimensional planning and simulation application, in which worker agents are driven by HumanSim in the shop floor domain. Furthermore, we show the results of an evaluation of HumanSim in the former mentioned simulation application.

Keywords: BDI agents · Intelligent virtual agents · Virtual environments · Answer set programming · IVA architecture

1 Introduction

Applications of virtual three-dimensional environments have seen a strong growth in the last few years. One main reason is the increasing number of affordable and easy to use hardware and software by which it is possible to create and display such environments in less time, with a more realistic graphics and intuitive interaction. These technologies are not only used in the consumer section, for example in games. Moreover, those technologies enable new opportunities in research or manufacturing. Examples are the evaluation of ergonomic aspects in cars[1] or the simulation of a shop floor configuration[2] which require the (as far as possible) realistic simulation of autonomous entities. In order to use those entities in a daily routine, for example in different evaluation settings, a flexible way to model their behavior is necessary.

An often used technology to drive three-dimensional entities in virtual environments is the BDI-agent architecture (see [1,2]). This paradigm is a established

---

[1] RAMSIS Automotive http://www.human-solutions.com/.

[2] FlexSim Simulation Software, https://www.flexsim.com/flexsim/.

© Springer International Publishing Switzerland 2016
M. Klusch et al. (Eds.): MATES 2016, LNAI 9872, pp. 198–214, 2016.
DOI: 10.1007/978-3-319-45889-2_15

and well researched agent model, which has its origins in the research done by
[3]. It combines aspects of reactive and deliberative agent models. A BDI-agent
can adapt its behavior in non-deterministic environments in a resource efficient
way. The main components of a BDI-agent are *Beliefs*, *Desires* and *Intentions*.
Beliefs represent the agent knowledge about its environment and its current
situation. *Desires* are long-term goals which have to be achieved by the agent.
Intentions are the actions which have to be performed next to reach the current
goal. Agent frameworks which are using this approach are Jack [4] or Jadex [5].
An agent can only interact with its environment in an autonomous and realistic
way, if it 'understands' what it is 'seeing' by dint of its sensors. The virtual environment and thus its objects need to be annotated with semantic information,
which describe in a – for the agent – meaningful way what they are standing for.
Usually, the semantic information about the world state, the agent actions and
their potential effects are expressed in heterogeneous formalisms and languages.
In [1] for example, three-dimensional objects in a simulated virtual environment
are semantically annotated with OWL2[3]. In [6], RDF[4] is in use to describe the
3D-scene instead. The perceived semantic information can be used by the agent
to deliberate and reason about the current world state to execute specific agent
plans for reaching goals.

In this paper we present our approach to describe the BDI agent environment
and its reasoning process with a uniform declarative logical formalism, answer
set programming (ASP). The application areas of ASP, which is based on the
stable model semantics [7], are NP-hard search problems [8], typically used for
model-checking, scheduling, diagnostics and decision-making [9]. By using ASP,
on the one hand we are able to annotate the agent environment and model its
ontology. We are also in the position to endow agents with commonsense reasoning [10], to simulate reliable foresighted acting virtual humans. Furthermore,
ASP allows extending the specification of a knowledge-intensive problem domain
with additional features such as e.g. non-deterministic effects, indirect effects of
events, default reasoning or background knowledge in a uniform way. E.g. it is
possible to naturally specify and reason about transitive relations necessary for
agents in 3D environments such as reachability of locations which can be formalized in PDDL only by using *derived predicates* which are supported only by a
few PDDL planners[5]. A further motivation and requirement for using a declarative formalism is the possibility to modify and change the agent's knowledge
during the design phase of a simulation scenario without the need to recompile
the agent code after each modification. Simulation environments are used e.g. for
rapid prototyping, investigating and evaluating properties of production scenarios before they are put in place etc. In this case, the behavior of human avatars
needs to be adapted to various settings. We have integrated the ASP-based
BDI agent approach into a design and editing framework for 3D environments
which allows changing agent behaviour in a flexible way. Our approach enables

---

[3] Web Ontology Language, http://www.w3.org/TR/owl2-overview/.

[4] Resource Description Framework, https://www.w3.org/RDF/.

[5] For a discussion of the problems involved in derived predicates in PDDL cf. [11].

elaboration tolerant[6] ways of specifying human actions. If e.g. objects are duplicated in a 3D environment, logical rules can immediately be applied to these new objects without reconfiguring the agent behavior specification (which would be the case in e.g. automata based behaviour representations).

The remainder of this paper is organized as follows. In Sects. 2 and 3, we describe our layered approach and introduce the HumanSim architecture. In Sects. 4 and 5 we show, with reference to a shop floor use case example, how HumanSim can be embedded and used in a simulation environment. Section 6 describes the evaluation results and Sect. 7 shows the related work in the areas of agent description and simulation in 3D environments.

2   HumanSim: A Layered Approach

For simulating human actions in virtual worlds, we structure agents representing human avatars with a three layer architecture (see Fig. 1). Each layer is responsible for dealing with specific aspects, i.e. related to navigation and animation (bottom layer), basic actions (middle layer) and deliberation (upper layer). The navigation layer handles path finding and animation, the middle layer provides routines and recipes for executing ground actions such as e.g. walking, picking and placing objects, etc. The deliberation layer finally contains a representation of the agent's beliefs about the environment, the possible actions it might perform and their consequences, as well as the decision procedures to form an intention based on this knowledge.

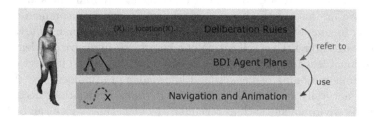

Fig. 1. The HumanSim three layer architecture.

2.1   Layered Architecture

Navigation and Animation Layer: This layer handles the basic tasks of path finding and motion generation of agents in 3D environments. Both are standard tasks in such environments supported by several game engines[7]. This

---

[6] "Elaboration tolerance is the ability to accept changes to a person's or a computer program's representation of facts about a subject without having to start all over." [12].

[7] Example of an engine which supports both tasks is unity3d: http://unity3d.com/.

layer in HumanSim represents the 3D scene, the objects as well as generating paths and motions which allow avatars to interact with the 3D scenario by avoiding collisions with objects or other avatars. The navigation and animation components are accessible for all agents and handle the motion requests and the execution of the agent motions in the 3D scene. During execution, the agents receive constant updates of their motion to control the accomplishment of a for example movement or picking task.

BDI Agent Plans: The BDI agent plans provide routines for ground actions the agents can execute in 3D environments. Ground actions include movement (walking, running, etc.), picking and placing objects as well as more fine grained tasks such as pushing buttons, locking and unlocking (doors, storages, etc.). Ground actions such as walking use the bottom layer for navigation, whereas other actions require specific animation functionality depending on the rendering environment used. Agents comprise of a set of these ground plans which according to the BDI approach are triggered when respective events are received. For selecting the ground plans, deliberation rules are used.

Deliberation Rules: HumanSim agents possess an explicitly represented, symbolic model of the world as well as knowledge about their capabilities to act and the effects of these actions. Both knowledge is expressed in ASP rules. The world model includes facts about the state of the world as well as knowledge about relationships between classes, types of objects, terminological knowledge etc. which is usually represented in ontologies. The combination is used to perform the process of intention formation, i.e. the selection of plans which allow the agent to accomplish its goals.

2.2 Logic Programs: Basic Concepts and Terminology

Due to space reasons, we refrain from a detailed introduction of the syntax and semantics of logical rules in ASP (the reader is referred e.g. to [13]). Instead we try to highlight several aspects which characterize ASP and are necessary for the understanding in the context of this paper.

A logical program P in ASP consists of a set of rules with (possibly negated) literals in the body and at most one literal in the head of a rule. Literals may be ground or contain variables. Facts are rules with empty body. The stable model semantics for a program P is based on the *Gelfond-Lifschitz* transformation [7]. Given P and a set of ground atoms S, the *reduct* P_S is obtained by deleting

1. each rule that has a negated literal **not** L in its body with $L \in S$, and
2. negated literals of the form **not** L in the bodies of the remaining rules.

The set S is a stable model of P, if the least Herbrand model $MM(P_S) = S$ (note that P_S is a definite program, i.e. does not contain negated literals). Thus, a stable model or *answer set* is a consistent set of ground literals. Intuitively, a stable model consists of the ground literals which are consistent with the rules in P and are justified by the rules (i.e. appear in the head of at least one rule). It is important to note that usually a logic program has several stable models. Answer set programming is based on the stable model semantics extended with rules for expressing e.g. choice, weights, cardinality constraints and optimization statements [14]. In the context of planning, a choice rule can be used to express that a rule may be optionally applied in a specific situation. Thus, this semantics allows expressing non-determinism in a natural way. For generating the stable models of a program, a number of efficient solvers have been developed.

2.3   Deliberation Rules for Reactive Agents

Extending the BDI reasoning cycle with deliberation rules, the logical rule set representing the agent's knowledge about the current state of the world is used for selecting the agent's intention. If a relevant event is received from the environment the belief state of the agent is changed and the reasoning process for the updated rule set is started. With respect to the usual BDI reasoning cycle, this provides a filter which interprets events in the light of the knowledge rules and as a result leads to potential intentions. Since the rule set can have several stable models, each of these models provides an option the agent might choose to achieve his goal(s). The options refer to 'ground' plans which the agent is able to perform. One implemented BDI plan is e.g. the *moveTo plan*, which will be triggered by a *moveTo(X)* predicate contained in a stable model. In the following, a random walk behavior, implemented with one rule, is shown:

```
intention(moveTo(L)) :- location(L), not agentPosition(L,T), actualTime(T).
```

This rule has the following meaning: *"Go to location L, if there is a location L and you are not at location L at time T and T is the current time."*

2.4   Look-Ahead and Planning with the Discrete Event Calculus

A general limitation of BDI agents is the limited support when accounting for the possible effects of an action while selecting an intention. The Discrete Event Calculus (DEC) is a logical formalism for expressing commonsense knowledge and enabling the reasoning about effects of events and actions, see [10]. DEC uses a sorted logic with events, fluents and timepoints. *Events* represent events or actions that can occur in a world. *Fluents* represent properties of the world which can vary over time, which is represented by *timepoints*. DEC provides axiomized predicates which allow to express the effect of events (e.g. agent actions) on fluents. Reasoning about effects of events and actions can be used to endow agents with look-ahead capabilities and planning. DEC has initially been formalised using first-order logic with circumscription (which is a second order feature) in order to cope with the frame problem. Lee and Palla [15] have shown that DEC can be represented in ASP[8] which allows the usage of state-of-the-art ASP solvers in new contexts (which indicates the close relationship between circumscription and the stable model semantics). The usage of DEC allows agents to project the knowledge about the current situation into the future, in particular to plan the course of actions in order to achieve their goals.

---

[8] DEC   ASP   Rules: http://reasoning.eas.asu.edu/ecasp/examples/foundations/ DEC.lp.

The following example shows a specification of the action *moveTo* as DEC event with effects of performing the action at timepoint T. *moveTo* can be applied to all known locations (line 1). The rule in line 2–4 specifies that a *moveTo* action can be performed under certain circumstances (e.g. the agent believes that the location is reachable at timepoint T). The DEC predicates *initiates* and *terminates* (lines 5–8) state which fluents are affected if the action is performed (the fluent *agentPosition* is modified). Finally, an ASP constraint (a rule with empty head, line 9) specifies which property must not hold after executing agent actions, i.e. the goal the agent wants to achieve (in the example: a dispenser has to be filled with units). Note that *moveTo* does not affect the fluent *needUnits*, hence by itself is not sufficient to bring about the goal condition.

```
01| event(moveTo(L)) :- location(L).
02| {happens(moveTo(L), T)} :-
03|       holdsAt(agentPosition(M),T), location(L),
04|       reachable(L, T), M!=L, time(T), T<maxtime.
05| initiates(moveTo(L),agentPosition(L),T) :- location(L),
06|       holdsAt(agentPosition(M),T), time(T), M!=L.
07| terminates(moveTo(L),agentPosition(M),T) :- location(L),
08|       holdsAt(agentPosition(M),T), time(T), M!=L.
09| :- holdsAt(needUnits(dispenser), maxtime).}
```

3 Extended BDI Architecture

The layered approach described in the previous section is embedded into a BDI-agent model and reasoning cycle in order to simulate humans in virtual three-dimensional environments by coupling several AI technologies, see Fig. 2.

Our agent model uses the BDI-model to describe the interior agent state, hence the agent model is divided into the components *Beliefs*, *Desires* and *Intentions*. The agent *Beliefs* respectively its knowledge base KB includes two different kinds of knowledge: the knowledge $K_\sigma \in KB$ of received information about the world state σ; and the knowledge $K_\beta \in KB$ about how to react to these states to reach specific goals. The set $D \subseteq Des$ represents these goals, where *Des* are all possible desires. An agent also has a subset $I \subseteq Int$ of BDI plans, where *Int* designates all possible intentions. I provides routines how to execute an atomic action $\alpha \in \Gamma$ in the agent 3D environment, where Γ denotes the set of all possible agent actions. An agent $A \subseteq Agt$ of all possible HumanSim agents has also a function φ which uses the KB of A as input to select a set of intentions I_σ at specific agent world states to reach $D \in K_\beta$. Each time φ selects I_σ, the corresponding plans out of I become the next intentions of A and atomic actions out of Γ were executed. Hereby K_σ will be updated and after processing all I_σ, φ will be executed again with the updated KB. We call φ also *reasoning cycle*, because of this cyclical execution. While receiving information δ of updated entities E in the agent environment, the old information of E will be overwritten with δ in K_σ.

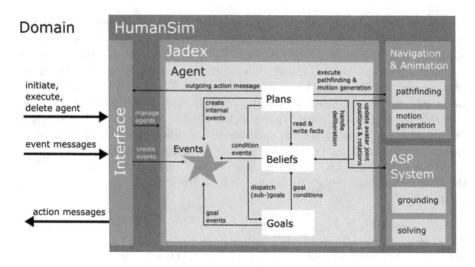

Fig. 2. HumanSim architecture overview.

3.1 Reasoning Cycle

The *reasoning cycle* φ is shown below as pseudocode by using an ASP system in our BDI-agent framework. This function will be executed if domain updates were received by the agent and no plan is currently executed.

Pseudocode of the HumanSim reasoning cycle.

reasoningCycle(*event, K_σ, K_β, I, Γ, maxtime*)

```
01 |     run := true
02 |     parallel_while true
03 |         Kσ := receiveDomainInformation()
04 |     endparallel_while
05 |     while run = true
06 |         r := getRulesets(Kσ,Kβ)
07 |         for i := 1 to maxtime do
08 |             m := GetStableModelsWithASPsystem(r,i)
09 |             if |m| ≥ 1 then break
10 |         endfor
11 |         if m = null or |m| = 0 then run := false
12 |         mx := chooseModelOutOf(m)
13 |         m'x := coverIntentionPredicates(mx,I)
14 |         if |m'x| = 0 then run := false
15 |         for s := 1 to |m'x| do
16 |             Iσ := selectIntentionBySequenceNumber(m'x,s)
17 |             success := executeActionsByIntention(Iσ,Γ,Kσ)
18 |             if success = false then break
19 |         endfor
20 |     endwhile
```

φ starts with collecting all beliefs from KB^A of agent A which is updated in a parallel process each time a updated domain information is received (line 2–4). In the next step, the ASP system will be executed (line 8) in a loop with the collected information (line 6). This loop will be passed until the ASP solver output contains a stable model or the loop number reaches $maxtime \in \mathbb{N}$. $maxtime$ is a number which can be set from outside to control the loop but also the resulting stable model. While executing the ASP system a variable defined in the rulesets is set with the current loop number, e.g. to define the maximal search depth. If no stable model has been found after $maxtime$ was reached, the *reasoning cycle* will be canceled and the agent listens to future belief changes. Otherwise one of the stable models will be chosen to cover all defined predicates which refer to available BDI plans (line 12–13). These predicates will be then transformed into agent intentions I_σ (line 16) and applied depending on the sequence number s in their predicates (line 17). While achieving a current goal, action messages were sent to perform ground actions in the agent domain. Belief updates resulting from this achievement are used to evaluate the success of the executed plan. If all intentions in the sequence are processed or the plan fails while execution, the *reasoning cycle* will be passed again (line 18).

Note that while generating the stable models, the knowledge of the agent is treated under the closed world assumption according to the stable model semantics. Nevertheless, since the environment is dynamic, the agent can acquire new knowledge (facts, but also general rules) and e.g. deliberately explore the environment to get more information[9].

4   3D Simulation Environment

The main emphasis of HumanSim is the simulation of human beings in three-dimensional virtual worlds. To create and simulate such a three-dimensional scenario we integrated our layered approach into a collaborative, web-based framework with components for creating and simulating 3D scenarios for training and evaluation issues. These components are categorized in two phases: *designtime* and *runtime*. In the *designtime* phase, a three-dimensional scenario with animated characters and the 3D models as well as their semantic information are modeled. In the *runtime* phase, the scenario designed is simulated and executed.

Designtime: To simulate a scenario it has to be created in the COMPASS web editor[10] (Fig. 3). In COMPASS it is possible to drag and drop predefined entity definitions into a scene. To define entities as agents, we use the *agent component*. With this component it is possible to model the agent behavior with ASP rules. In Fig. 4, a component which defines an agent with a 'random walk' behavior, is shown. To make ASP annotations other components are available.

---

[9] Arguably, in 3D environments considered in the context of this paper, the closed world assumption is more appropriate.

[10] COMPASS (Collaborative Modular Prototyping And Simulation Server): https://github.com/dfki-asr/compass.

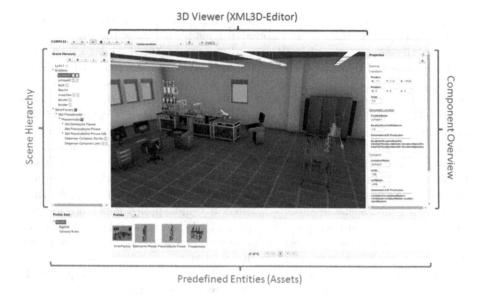

Fig. 3. COMPASS editor to model the key chain scenario.

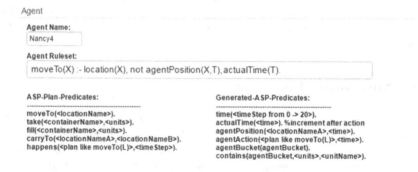

Fig. 4. Agent component to define an entity as an agent with a 'random walk' behavior.

Runtime: In the runtime phase the annotated 3D scene, modeled in COM-PASS, is simulated with the execution environment FiVES, a highly scalable synchronization platform[11]. FiVES initiates agents in HumanSim over its interface with agent information previously defined in an *agent component*. While executing agents, HumanSim sends agent information to FiVES, to interact with the simulated environment. An agent has to perceive its environment, the world state represented in FiVES, to reason about its domain. Such information is received by HumanSim (Fig. 5) through a plugin which listens to create, update or delete events of FiVES-entities. Upon receiving these events, HumanSim updates the belief base of its agents with the new information. After updating the belief

---

[11] FiVES (Flexible Virtual Environment Server): https://github.com/fives-team.

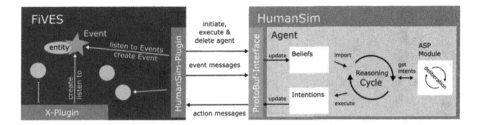

Fig. 5. FiVES-HumanSim interaction.

base the HumanSim *reasoning cycle* will be performed. While performing this
cycle, all 'perceived' information about the simulation environment and the agent
behavior is used to decide which actions have to be performed subsequently in
the simulated environment.

5   Use Case Example

In the use case scenario, a key chain manufacturing process is simulated in a
three-dimensional virtual world. In this process a single manufacturing module,
consisting of presses, two dispensers and a pick and place (PnP) arm, produces
key chains. To produce a key chain, the PnP arm has to pick all required parts
stored in the dispensers and places them into a press which finally presses all
parts together. Thus, the filling level of the dispensers decreases until their minimum filling level is reached. After reaching this level, the production stops.

A worker is present in this scenario which is in charge of maintaining the
production. The agent monitors the key chain production to react to possible
errors. The considered manufacturing fault is a reached minimum filling level
of the dispensers, while producing multiple key chains. To avoid the *key chain*
production termination, the simulated worker has to go to a storage location to
fetch new material and walk to a under filled dispenser to refill it.

5.1   Scenario Modeling

To model and simulate the *key chain* scenario, we edit the 3D scene using the
C3D-framework, in particular the COMPASS editor. Assets contained in the
scene are a *manufacturing module*, with its presses and dispensers; a *factory
model*; several *storage locations*; and also a *worker* asset. Figure 6 shows the
created 3D scene in which the *key chain* scenario will be simulated.

To annotate the three-dimensional scene, we use the *ruleset component*. With
this component, it is possible to annotate an entity with ASP rules, describing
to which classes it belongs and its initial state at the execution time. Figure 7
shows three different ASP rules which describes the minimum and maximum
filling level of an entity and the fact that entities contained are withdrawable.

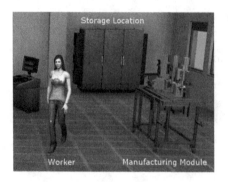

Fig. 6. 3D scenario overview.

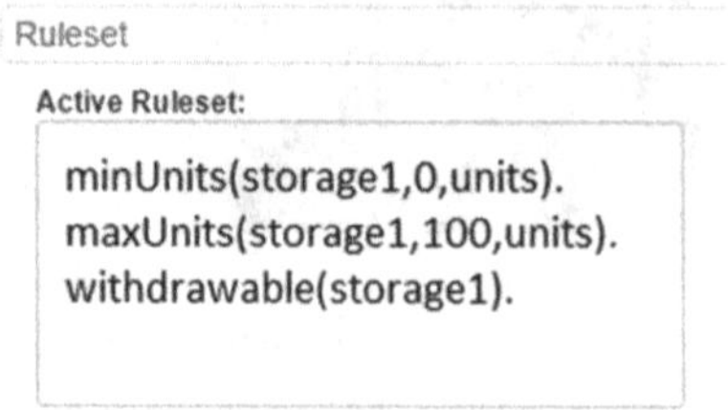

Fig. 7. Component to annotate entities by ASP rules.

5.2 Agent Description

For the *key chain* scenario we implemented in addition to the *moveTo* ground plan further BDI plans in the HumanSim framework, like the *Take* and *Fill* plan. These plans are recipes which enable an agent to interact with its environment to refill underfilled dispensers. To realize this behavior, we modeled the 'refill' behavior in two different strategies: the 'reactive' and the 'foresighted' look-ahead planning strategy.

Reactive Behavior. With this strategy, an agent assesses only its current situation and acts depending on it. This means that a 'reactive' agent has for one situation one or more action goals to reach another situation. The *take* and *fill* action rules of the 'reactive' refill agent, which are holding if the agent with no units stands beside a storage location in the first case and in the latter case, if it has enough units and stands beside the underfilled dispenser, are shown below:

```
01|  intention(take(C,U))  :- contains(C,S), withdrawable(C),
02|          needUnits(D,U), C != D, S >= U, agentPosition(C,T),
03|          agentHasUnits(B), actualTime(T), B < U, container(D).
04|  intention(fill(C,U))  :- container(C), agentPosition(C,T),
05|          agentHasUnits(B), actualTime(T), needUnits(C,U), U <= B.
```

The BDI *take* goal will be triggered if the situation from line 1–5 holds. This rule can be read as: *"If the current agent position is container C and C is withdraw able and container D needs units U and the agent does not have enough units R in its bucket B, then the agent has to take U units out of C."* Instead, the BDI *fill* goal will be triggered if the situation from line 4–5 holds.

Foresighted Behavior. As mentioned in Sect. 2, there are different ways to plan with ASP, and therefore to model foresighted agent behavior with our approach. We use the DEC axiomatisation and specify further ground actions (e.g. for *take* and *fill*) with execution conditions and effects. Unlike the 'reactive' strategy, apart from the execution conditions and effects of ground actions, only the initial situation and goal situation have to be present as rules. By defining general conditions for actions, this strategy is more flexible than the 'reactive' strategy. Moreover, it is possible to get multiple stable models and therefore multiple possible plans to solve a problem, by using this kind of strategy.

5.3   Scenario Simulation

In the *runtime* phase, the annotated *key chain* scene with the agent definition were simulated by FiVES. After initiating HumanSim, a simulated worker is driven by an agent, while receiving scenario information out of FiVES. With this information and the agent behavior modeled in ASP, the *reasoning cycle* will be performed. The execution of ground agent actions in the simulated environment depends i.a. on the used agent behavior and therefore on the predicates containing in a resulting stable model[12]. Following, the output of the ASP module at world state σ_t using the 'reactive' behavior is shown:

```
Answer: 1
intention(moveTo(storage1)) intention(moveTo(storage2))
```

We get one stable model with two *intention(moveTo(X))* predicates, if a dispenser is underfilled and the agent has to move to one of two possible storage locations to take needed units. In the next *reasoning cycle* step, one of those predicates will be chosen and a *moveTo* intention, with location X present in this predicate, apply. After achieving this goal in the simulated environment, and therefore after updating the agent belief base with the new world state `agentPosition(X)`, the *reasoning cycle* will be executed again. It is performed until no action rule is present in a stable model. This is the case when the former underfilled dispensers have enough units, after: `intention(take(X,10))`, `intention(moveTo(dispenser1))`, `intention(fill(dispenser1,5))`, `intention(moveTo(dispenser2))` and `intention(fill(dispenser2,5))` showed up in the ASP module output. The following output of the 'planning' behavior shows two of four possible stable models which hold if two dispensers are underfilled.

```
Answer: 1
intention(moveTo(storage1),1) intention(take(storage1,10),2)
intention(moveTo(dispenser1),3) intention(fill(dispenser1,5),4)
intention(moveTo(dispenser2),5) intention(fill(dispenser2,5),6)

Answer: 2
intention(moveTo(storage2),1) intention(take(storage2,10),2)
intention(moveTo(dispenser1),3) intention(fill(dispenser1,5),4)
intention(moveTo(dispenser2),5) intention(fill(dispenser2,5),6)
```

---

[12] To minimize the output of the ASP module, we use *gringo* filter statements `#show`.

In these models, the performing sequence of the BDI plan E in the *intention(E, T)* predicate, is denoted by the increasing number T. These sequences propose a way and therefore different possibilities to reach the goal state in which no dispenser is underfilled. After (e.g. randomly) selecting one sequence respectively stable model, the selected one will be performed in the virtual environment by executing the BDI intention specified for time T.

6   Evaluation

We simulated several settings for each behavior strategy: the 'reactive' and the 'foresighted' strategy. We considered multiple situations which affect the runtime of our agent system in the presented scenario domain, see Sect. 5. We assume that the execution time of selected plans is constant, thus we measured only the runtime of the agent deliberation process. To do so, we first tested two different domain situations: a 'Critical' situation where the worker has to refill two dispensers and a 'Idle' situation in which every dispenser has enough units and the worker has the goal to rest. Further aspects which influences the former mentioned process are the number of placed objects in the scene like: locations (defined by one rule), storages (defined by six rules) and dispensers (defined by five rules). We also measured the increase of the logical program complexity by defining the deliberation rules more general. While evaluating the 'foresighted' strategy, we calculate all stable models to get every possible intention for each plan step, as we receive while using the 'reactive' strategy. The evaluations were carried out with the ASP system Clingo 4.4.0 on a Windows 7 system with 16 GB memory and an Intel i7-3770k CPU.

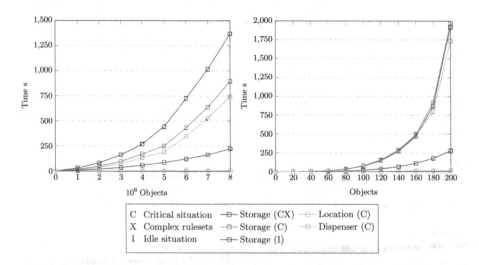

Fig. 8. Strategy runtime evaluation: 'reactive' (left); 'foresighted' (right).

In the evaluations (see Fig. 8) the number of the placed objects were increased from 1 to 8×10^6 while using the 'reactive' strategy and for the 'foresighted' strategy, 1 to 200 objects were placed. The runtime to find stable models depends i.a. on the number of evaluated rules. This relationship becomes visible while comparing both strategies for the 'Idle' setting: The ASP system needs 224.25 s to examine $\approx 48 \times 10^6$ rules to find a stable model for the 'reactive' situation. For the 'foresighted' strategy it needs 278.78 s to examine $\approx 57 \times 10^6$ rules instead. Considering the other results of the 'foresighted' program, its runtime exponentially increases, the other 'reactive' results increase polynomial instead. The strong runtime growth while using the 'foresighted' strategy depends on the search depth needed to find a stable model. In all 'Critical' situations a search depth of six is needed which is defined by *maxtime* in the agent function φ. Using the 'reactive' strategy instead, in all situations a stable model can be found with a *maxtime* of one. If placed objects do not influence the deliberation process as in the 'Location (C)' situation, their runtime effect is negligible.

7   Related Work

We use the agent paradigm to simulate human models with HumanSim. This paradigm is not just used to simulate virtual humans, as in [16], but also to control robotic systems as in [17] or in the shop floor domain as in [18]. The agent architecture used in HumanSim is the BDI approach implemented with the Jadex framework. Another BDI-agent framework is Jason[13]. Jason uses AgentSpeak(L) to describe the BDI-agent beliefs, goals and to model the decision-making process [19]. AgentSpeak(L), is a logic based programming language for modeling BDI agents such like APL3 [20] or DALI [21]. In [22] a BDI framework uses ASP to support agent belief operations. In [16] instead, the decision-making process of social virtual agents is extended with ASP. In [23] ASP modules are introduced which can be integrated in systems to describe agent "capabilities". Closer to our approach for enhancing BDI-agents with deliberation are [24–26]. While [25] focusses on incorporating plans generated from first principles into the plan library, [26] provides a detailed formal account of an extended BDI agent language and proposes to use an HTN planner to incorporate lookahead planning. Apart from the restriction on HTN planning (which again requires a different formalism and language), their theoretical focus is not oriented towards usage in practical environments.

8   Conclusion and Future Work

In this paper, we presented HumanSim, a layered BDI-agent framework for simulating human avatars in 3D environments. For intention selection, HumanSim uses logical rules expressed in ASP which incorporate knowledge about the environment as well as knowledge about the capabilities of the agent. We detailed

---

[13] Jason: http://jason.sourceforge.net/.

the extended BDI reasoning cycle with reactive and lookahead features based on the Discrete Event Calculus and described the usage of HumanSim in the context of a simulation environment for production scenarios. Finally, we evaluated the reactive and foresighted reasoning behavior with respect to solving time for different domain sizes.

One may argue that for planning purposes, PDDL could be used since highly optimised software exists. Apart from the fact that this would reintroduce another formalism as opposed to our goal of using a uniform approach, PDDL only provides the specified language constructs which are in addition not supported by all planners available. As indicated in the introduction, ASP is much more versatile and allows expressing a wide range of commonsense knowledge in an intuitive way, admittedly at the expense of efficiency.

The approach is not limited to one agent but can be applied to an open number of agents, under the condition that goals are not conflicting among agents. To coordinate agents in case of conflicting goals, standard mechanisms (protocols) could be applied. As future work, we will explore how the logical formalism used for deliberation within one agent can be used to support decisison making among a group of agents. Together with the reactive and the deliberation layer, the resulting framework would be an instantiation (with up-to-date technology) of the InteRRaP architecture [27] in which tradition we situate our approach.

Acknowledgments. The research described in this paper has been funded by the German Federal Ministry of Education and Research (BMBF) through the projects Collaborate3D and INVERSIV.

References

1. Nesbigall, S., Warwas, S., Kapahnke, P., Schubotz, R., Klusch, M., Fischer, K., Slusallek, P.: ISReal: a platform for intelligent simulated realities. In: Filipe, J., Fred, A., Sharp, B. (eds.) ICAART 2010. CCIS, vol. 129, pp. 201–213. Springer, Heidelberg (2011)
2. Davies, N.P., Mehdi, Q.: BDI for intelligent agents in computer games. In: Proceedings of CGAMES 2006, The University of Wolverhampton (2006)
3. Bratman, M.E.: Intentions, Plans, and Practical Reasoning. Cambridge University Press, Cambridge (1999)
4. Busetta, P., Ronnquist, R., Hodgson, A., Lucas, A.: JACK Intelligent Agents - Components for Intelligent Agents in Java (1999)
5. Pokahr, A., Braubach, L., Lamersdorf, W.: Jadex: a BDI reasoning engine. In: Bordini, R.H., Dastani, M., Dix, J., Seghrouchni, A.E.F. (eds.) Multi-Agent Programming: Languages, Platforms and Applications. Multiagent Systems, Artificial Societies, and Simulated Organizations, vol. 15, pp. 149–174. Springer, New York (2005)
6. Radkowski, R., Huck, W., Domik, G., Holtmann, M.: Serious games for the therapy of the posttraumatic stress disorder of children and adolescents. In: Shumaker, R. (ed.) Virtual and Mixed Reality, Part II, HCII 2011. LNCS, vol. 6774, pp. 44–53. Springer, Heidelberg (2011)

7. Gelfond, M., Lifschitz, V.: The stable model semantics for logic programming. In: 5th International Conference on Logic Programming (ICLP), pp. 1070–1080. MIT Press, Cambridge (1988)
8. Lifschitz, V.: What Is Answer Set Programming? Department of Computer Sciences, University of Texas at Austin (2008)
9. Brain, M., De Vos, M.: Answer set programming a domain in need of explanation. In: Proceeding of 3rd International Workshop on Explanation-aware Computing (ExaCat), pp. 391–403. CEUR-WS.org (2008)
10. Mueller, E.T.: Commonsense Reasoning. Elsevier Science, Amsterdam (2006)
11. Thiebaux, S., Hoffmann, J., Nebel, B.: In defense of PDDL axioms. Artif. Intell. **168**(1–2), 38–69 (2005)
12. McCarthy, J.: Elaboration Tolerance. Common-Sense 98 (1998)
13. Gelfond, M.: Answer sets. In: van Harmelen, F., Lifschitz, V., Porter, B. (eds.) Handbook of Knowledge Representation. Elsevier, Amsterdam (2007)
14. Simons, P., Niemela, I., Soininen, T.: Extending and implementing the stable model semantics. Artif. Intell. J. **138**, 181–234 (2002)
15. Lee, J., Palla, R.: Reformulating the situation calculus and the event calculus in the general theory of stable models and in answer set programming. J. Artif. Intell. Res. **43**, 571–620 (2012)
16. Lee, J.H., Li, T., De Vos, M., Padget, J.: Using social institutions to guide virtual agent behaviour. In: The AAMAS Workshop on Cognitive Agents for Virtual Environments (CAVE-2013) (2013)
17. Ryuh, Y.S., Moon, J.I.: Multi-agent control and implementation of bio-inspired underwater robots for mariculture monitoring and control. In: Robotics and Biomimetics, pp. 777–783. IEEE (2012)
18. Barenji, R.V., Barenji, A.V., Hashemipour, M.: A multi-agent RFID-enabled distributed control system for a flexible manufacturing shop. Int. J. Adv. Manuf. Technol. **71**, 1773–1791 (2014)
19. Rao, A.S.: AgentSpeak(L): BDI agents speak out in a logical computable language. In: Perram, J., Van de Velde, W. (eds.) MAAMAW 1996. LNCS, vol. 1038. Springer, Heidelberg (1996)
20. Dastani, M., van Riemsdijk, M.B., Dignum, F.P.M., Meyer, J.-J.C.: A programming language for cognitive agents goal directed 3APL. In: Dastani, M., Dix, J., El Fallah-Seghrouchni, A. (eds.) PROMAS 2003. LNCS (LNAI), vol. 3067, pp. 111–130. Springer, Heidelberg (2004)
21. Constantini, S., Tocchio, A.: DALI: An architecture for intelligent logical agents. In: Proceedings of International Workshop on Architectures for Intelligent Theory-Based Agents (AITA 2008), AAAI (2008)
22. Krümpelmann, P., Thimm, M., Ritterskamp, M., Kern-Isberner, G.: Belief operations for motivated BDI agents. In: Proceedings of Autonomous Agents and Multiagent Systems (AAMAS 2008), pp. 421–428 (2008)
23. Costantini, S.: Answer set modules for logical agents. In: de Moor, O., Gottlob, G., Furche, T., Sellers, A. (eds.) Datalog 2010. LNCS, vol. 6702, pp. 37–58. Springer, Heidelberg (2011)
24. Walczak, A., Braubach, L., Pokahr, A., Lamersdorf, W.: Augmenting BDI agents with deliberative planning techniques. In: Bordini, R.H., Dastani, M., Dix, J., Fallah Seghrouchni, A. (eds.) PROMAS 2006. LNCS (LNAI), vol. 4411, pp. 113–127. Springer, Heidelberg (2007)
25. de Silva, L., Sardina, S., Padgham, L.: First principles planning in BDI systems. In: Proceedings of Autonomous Agents and Multi-Agent Systems (AAMAS), vol. 2, pp. 1001–1008 (2009)

26. Sardina, S., Padgham, L.: A BDI agent programming language with failure recovery, declarative goals, and planning. In: Proceedings of Autonomous Agents and Multi-Agent Systems (AAMAS 2011), vol. 23, pp. 18–70 (2011)
27. Müller, J.P., Pischel, M.: The Agent Architecture InteRRaP: Concept and Application. Research Report RR-93-26, German Artificial Intelligence Research Center (DFKI), Saarbrcken, June 1993

Analysis of the Effects of Storage Capabilities Integration on Balancing Mechanisms in Agent-Based Smart Grids

Serkan Özdemir[1(✉)], Rainer Unland[1], and Wolfgang Ketter[2]

[1] DAWIS, University of Duisburg-Essen, Schützenbahn 70, 45127 Essen, Germany
{serkan.oezdemir,rainer.unland}@icb.uni-due.de
[2] RSM, Erasmus University Rotterdam, Rotterdam, Netherlands
wketter@rsm.nl

Abstract. Due to new energy transition policies fossil- and partially also nuclear based power production has been replaced by usually much more volatile renewable energy production. Volatility here means that it is substantially more difficult to keep energy production and consumption in balance. Such a challenge can be tackled by seamlessly integrating modern power storage technologies, such as batteries. This paper focuses on the role of battery storage providers to reveal their profitability and balancing potentials from the perspective of all parties, involved in the balancing process. Batteries are managed by broker agents, which are analyzed in the PowerTAC marketplace simulation environment. We first describe the Vickrey–Clarke–Groves auction mechanism to demonstrate how its pricing mechanism provides incentives for participants. Afterwards, we analyze the trading behaviors of different balancing settings to benchmark profitability levels of battery storage providers. We employ a broker agent for each setting so that variants publish a battery storage tariff with different up-regulation and down-regulation prices. The results show that battery storage providers provide extra profit for brokers if exploited strategically in the balancing market. Additionally, they help stabilizing the grid with up and down regulations.

Keywords: Balancing market · Regulation market · Autonomous trading · Agent

1 Introduction

Smart grids have not only become an exciting field for researchers but also for business, especially for new actors in this field. Some of those actors, such as electric vehicles and smart homes with their built-in batteries make it possible to store electricity in a distributed way. On the other side, recent advances in renewable technologies show that the number of renewable energy capacity will drastically increase in the near future. The California crisis at the beginning of this millennium showed that intermediate power actors (retailers, utilities and broker agencies are used interchangeably in this paper) are the most vulnerable since they have the duty of a strict financial and power management between customers and generators. Distributed storage units pose for the power regulation in the sense of producing or consuming energy, depending on the overall grid balance [2, 20].

© Springer International Publishing Switzerland 2016
M. Klusch et al. (Eds.): MATES 2016, LNAI 9872, pp. 215–230, 2016.
DOI: 10.1007/978-3-319-45889-2_16

Firstly, the paper looks at the pricing mechanism in PowerTAC's balancing market (BM). It is explained how the Vickrey–Clarke–Groves (VCG) auction algorithm clears the balancing orders of broker agents [1, 14]. Secondly, we trade in the balancing market to reveal the potentials of battery storage customers. To do that, we offer storage tariffs to attract battery storage customer. Then, those capacities are offered to BM for real-time up or down regulations. In the experiments, we use an ablation method to see the profitability level of battery storage customers from the brokers' and customers' perspective. We employ our broker agent to involve in the balancing process, in particular, creating three broker variants (AgentUDE, AgentUDEr1, AgentUDEr2, see Table 2) of AgentUDE (2015 release, see [8]). Here, each variant has a different price setting, e.g., up-regulation price, down-regulation price or no storage tariff at all. Then, we compare the profit levels of the variants, monitoring the BM results. In the experiments, we keep all the functionalities of AgentUDE (e.g., wholesale market, retail consumer market) so that these variants publish consumer tariffs and trade in the wholesale market to match its consumer demand. Thus they can generate casual imbalances [5]. The results show that a balancing market is a reasonable marketplace for all stakeholders, in terms of reliability (grid's interest) and profitability (broker's and customers' interest), thanks to its incentive-based clearing mechanism.

The experiments and their results in the paper rely on simulation data. As a framework, Power Trading Agent Competition (PowerTAC) is chosen to benchmark the proposed approaches in this paper, since it permits to study electricity markets in a competitive way [1]. See Sects. 3 and 5 for more details.

The structure of the paper is organized as follows. Related work and the Power-TAC scenario are explained in Sects. 2 and 3. The VCG mechanism is described in Sect. 4. Section 5 introduces the experimental setup and framework model while Sect. 6 presents the results. Finally, Sect. 7 concludes the paper.

2   Background and Related Work

The electricity grid has to be regulated in real-time, whenever a difference occurs in the quantity of energy production and consumption. The regulation is usually harmonized by electronic auctions, held in balancing markets. Here, generators submit offers to supply power for up-regulation, whereas consumers submit bids for down-regulation. In terms of autonomy, agent technologies are increasingly being seen as a suitable means to aggregate and act on behalf of distributed resources in decentralized markets. On the other side, demand response seems to be a strong candidate for stabilizing the electricity grid thanks to its regulation capability. Especially, batteries have significant advantages on real-time regulation since they have no ramp-up cost and starting time constraints [24–27].

Regarding the balancing and profitability potential of power storage, [22] provides an algorithm on a car-sharing fleet of electric vehicles to use the aggregated capacity of the fleet in operating reserve markets. The algorithm makes short-term decision depending on the trade-off between benefits from using the capacity for balancing the grid and renting cars for the need of native business. The algorithm tested with real metrics like charging, driving and market data. The paper concludes that using the capacity in balancing markets increases the overall profit by 7.18 %. Another storage technology is compressed air energy storage, which is studied by [23]. The paper offers a dispatch model to characterize the value of providing reserves as well as energy arbitrage. Besides, they focus on the net revenue of compressed air energy storage with several designs and performance settings. The data, used in the experiments are obtained from various Independent System Operators in USA.

The goal of this research is to employ autonomous trading agents, which control distributed battery storage customers through retail electricity tariffs and trade that aggregated capacity in PowerTAC's real-time balancing market [18, 24]. This work offers a simple business model in which brokers and customers send or receive payment in the extent of contribution to the balancing problem [7, 25]. We use our broker agent (AgentUDE) in the experiments, which is the winner of PowerTAC 2014 Finals. PowerTAC is a competitive simulation platform that models brokers in electricity markets [1, 4, 6, 18]. More will be discussed in Sect. 4.

Our work relies on a competitive benchmarking process so that our broker agent competes with other broker agents in retail, wholesale and balancing markets. On the other side, customers are also competitive as they can freely choose or change their retailers. Therefore, all approaches in the paper refer to an online decision support system and the field of competitive benchmarking.

3   The Multi-agent Smart Grid Scenario

Multi-agent-based smart grid simulations became popular after liberalized electricity markets require better resource allocations. Distributed power supplies and loads look for more autonomy as well as unifications and standards for the systematic expansion of future smart grids [21]. In the future smart grid (even now), households and EV customers may respond to electricity prices by adjusting (e.g., change speed, shift) their charging or discharging preferences. That autonomy is not only limited to batteries, but it is also needed in smart home and smart city concepts [9].

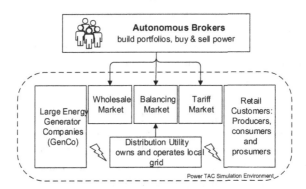

Fig. 1. High-level structure of the PowerTAC scenario. Autonomous brokers publish tariffs to attract customers. Brokers need to serve those customers by trading in the wholesale market.

Simulations aim to address those challenges to create a vision to sustainable smart grid ecosystems. PowerTAC is probably one of the most powerful and robust open-source smart grid simulation platforms. PowerTAC is a data-driven platform that brings broker and smart market concepts together [1]. Figure 1 depicts the high-level structure of PowerTAC.

The platform includes various smart grid actors such as customer models, a retail and a wholesale market, a distribution utility, and autonomous electricity brokers within a single distribution area, currently a city. The main actors within PowerTAC are:

- *Electricity Brokers* are business entities that trade as intermediaries to attain good results for their own accounts. They try to attract customers by publishing electricity tariffs in the retail market, i.e. tariff market. The so-called distribution utility closely monitors all brokers in order to evaluate their demand and supply behavior. Imbalanced energy is subject to penalties. Therefore, brokers have to trade in the wholesale market in order to cover their net demand.
- *Customers* are small and medium sized consumers and producers such as households, electric vehicles and small firms. They interact with the environment through electricity tariffs. They can buy or sell electricity, subscribing to appropriate tariffs that are described by power type, time and money domains [4].
- *Generator Companies* represent the large power generators or consumers. These actors trade in the wholesale market and manage their commitments for the next several hours up to several weeks.
- A *Distribution Utility* runs the grid and manages its imbalances in real-time. It is assumed that it owns the physical infrastructure. It charges brokers for their net distributed energy per kWh, known as distribution fee. It also manages imbalances and charges brokers for their imbalanced energy, called balancing fee.

While PowerTAC is available all year-round for all kinds of simulations, the international competition is conducted only once a year. Research institutes are encouraged to develop and pre-test their own smart energy brokers. A PowerTAC tournament consists of a collection of games, grouped in different game sizes, e.g. with three, five or seven players. The game size indicates the number of competing broker agents. In addition to these brokers, a built-in default broker is always included in the games. After all games ended, profits are summed up and normalized, based on each individual game size. The broker with the highest aggregated profit is the winner.

A PowerTAC game takes n timeslots, starting from one, cf. Fig. 2 for the activities in a timeslot. In this paper, we refer to the current timeslot t, and a future timeslot f to define the activities from the brokers' point of view:

1. Brokers receive signals at every timeslot t, e.g. current cash balance, clearing prices of timeslots $cp_t, cp_{t+1}, \ldots, cp_{t+23}$, published tariffs by all brokers.
2. Brokers receive signals at every timeslot t, e.g. current cash balance, clearing prices of timeslots $cp_t, cp_{t+1}, \ldots, cp_{t+23}$, published tariffs by all brokers.
3. Brokers ought to submit orders to the wholesale market in order to procure energy amount E^f, based on the demand patterns of their tariffs.

4. At the end of a timeslot, a broker's cash account is updated based on the profit $\sum_i T_i E_i^t - \sum_j^{24} cp_t^j E_t^j$ where T_i is the tariff price of the energy unit (kWh) and E_i^t denotes the distributed energy amount at timeslot t, under tariff i. The cost of procuring the energy amount E_t^j at timeslot n is denoted as $\sum_j^{24} cp_t^j E_t^j$. An imbalance penalty $\left(\sum_i E_i^t - \sum_j^{24} E_t^j \right) P$ is debited from the broker's cash account using the balancing fee of P (per unit). That pricing was replaced by a peak-demand assessment after the PowerTAC 1.3.1 version.

5. In addition to the tariff value, tariff activities like customer sign ups or withdrawals are subject to payment due to bonus and early withdrawal payment parameters of the according tariffs.

6. Brokers pay a distribution fee for each energy unit if market power is distributed or local power is traded in the wholesale market.

7. At the end of the timeslot brokers receive information about the net distribution and imbalance volumes as well as tariff transactions.

8. Customers initially subscribe to the default tariff. Once brokers join in they evaluate the existing tariffs based on their energy profile. Due to the tendency of a "set and forget" behavior of retail customers, an inertia factor $I_a = (1 - 2^{-n})I$ drives the motivation of customers to evaluate existing tariffs. Here, n denotes the timeslot after the latest subscription. For more details, [4] includes a comprehensive explanation of the consumption model.

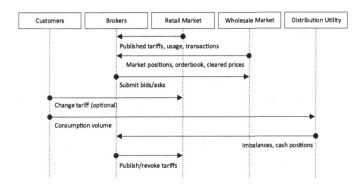

Fig. 2. Timeslot sequence diagram from brokers' horizon. Events take place from top to down.

PowerTAC relies on a number of assumptions. The simulated region has no grid constraints. Thus, line capacity related issues (e.g., congestions) do not exist. The voltage level in the region is flat; i.e., there is no voltage hierarchy. Therefore, power factor effects, phase shifts and voltage transformations are not taken into account. Transmission and distribution losses are also ignored in the simulation. The average rates of losses in Europe and USA are estimated at 3 % and 4 %, respectively [10]. Thus, the assumption is made that losses have no significant influence on the validity.

3.1 Controllable Capacities

In PowerTAC, controllable capacities are represented as customer models, which allow brokers to control their consumption or production for a specific time slot. There are two kinds of demand response events in PowerTAC:

- *Balancing Control Event:* This order targets real-time power regulations. Orders must be delivered at given time slots. Battery storage, water pumps and heat pump customers are typical models that respond to balancing control events.
- *Economic Control Event:* Interruptible customers are typical consumers or producers with the ability of shifting or curtailing power consumption or production to a future time slot. Orders must be delivered before the event. A typical example of this customer model is a smart washing machine that can be programmed intelligently. EV batteries can also be considered as interruptible since their charging or discharging speeds are adjustable.

At a timeslot, controllable capacities are characterized by the maximum and minimum rates as well as desired energy amount to be used. They share those parameters with DU at the beginning of each time slot. Thus, customers consume or produce the desired energy in kWh at the balancing order time.

Brokers may want to use controllable capacities to avoid balancing charges and reduce wholesale energy costs. Balancing orders (see next section) authorize a DU to exercise controllable capacities whereas economic control orders apply to a future time. Economic control events are out of the scope in the paper.

4 Vickrey–Clarke–Groves Auction and Balancing Process

Transmission Systems Operators (TSO, i.e., Independent System Operator in North America) closely monitor the grid to keep its frequency, voltage level and power factor stable. However, this task is getting more and more difficult as the share of partially predictable energy resources increases. In many European countries (e.g., Germany), due to guaranteed payment for renewable energy production, TSO's have to take care of produced power, feeding in from old-tech windmills, solar panels, etc. However, some of new-tech panels and windmills are not harmful for TSO's due to spinning ability [12, 15].

PowerTAC offers DU to fulfill those balancing operations. Since there is no transmission layer in the simulation (see assumptions in [1]), DU has only access to the balancing market portion of the wholesale ancillary services. Brokers may take some of the balancing responsibilities by allowing DU to exercise their controllable capacities. Brokers grant that permission by submitting a balancing order, in which a tariff, an exercise ratio and a regulation price are specified. As seen in Fig. 3, a balancing order has to target a tariff so that only the subscribers of that tariff are affected from the power regulation. If a balancing order clears, the broker is paid or pays for the exercised capacity. In most cases, brokers receive a payment. Once the capacity is exercised (consumption or production), the broker and the customer financially settle, based on the regulation rates of the tariff. Therefore, payments between brokers and DU are fully isolated from the payments between brokers and customers.

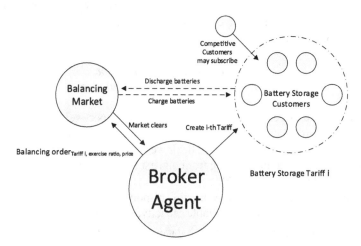

Fig. 3. Event diagram for the balancing market mechanism - brokers may ask the DU to control specified tariff, given a specific exercise ratio. Orders only apply to the relevant tariff in the extent of benefit broker will gain.

Customers also benefit from the regulation in the extent of the gap (difference of up-regulation–down-regulation price), specified as regulation rates in the subscribed tariff. In the presence of monopoly or duopoly situation, the gap is expected to be small whereas tough competitions enlarge the gap.

In principle, BM performs a non-profit balancing process, charging brokers as low as possible. Therefore, the main goal is to give an incentive to the brokers that contribute to the solution. Apart from the tariff price, BM requires a separate price to exercise balancing orders on behalf of them. The price in the balancing order is expected to be equal or less than the price in the tariff to guarantee the success of the order. Note that exercise ratio only indicates the regulation direction for battery storage customers.

$$Regulation = \begin{cases} up\text{-}regulation & if\ exerciseRatio > 0 \\ no\ regulation & if\ exerciseRatio = 0 \\ down\text{-}regulation & if\ exerciseRatio < 0 \end{cases} \quad (1)$$

Formula 1 depicts the regulation direction, given an exercise ratio. For example, given a positive exercise ratio at a time, DU assesses the balancing orders for the up regulation. Note that balancing orders remain effective until a new order arrives. If up and down regulation orders are submitted at the same time, DU exercise the one which contributes to the balancing solution, and the other one is ignored.

The Vickrey–Clarke–Groves (VCG) clearing mechanism is a sealed-bid auction that was introduced in a paper by William Vickrey, Edward H. Clarke and Theodore Groves [14]. Bidders submit orders without knowing the bids of others.

Basically, the clearing mechanism charges bidders according to the degree of the harm they cause for others.

To clear a VCG auction, BM requires to include dummy orders with an infinite capacity to represent the balancing cost at $c_0(x_{RM})$, for the traded energy amount x_{RM}. Formula 2 defines the balancing cost.

$$c_0(x_{RM}) = \begin{cases} P^+(s) + \emptyset^+ x_{RM} & \text{if up-regulation} \\ P^-(s) + \emptyset^- x_{RM} & \text{if down-regulation} \end{cases} \tag{2}$$

$\emptyset^+$ and $\emptyset^-$ are the slopes of up and down regulations respectively. P^+ and P^- refer to basis prices for up-regulation and down-regulation, respectively. For up-regulation, all balancing orders are sorted, starting from the lowest bid up to the needed amount. Likewise, down-regulation requires sorting from highest to lowest bid. Generally, the bid in the last position clears partially [15].

In addition to VCG price, brokers are also responsible for their imbalances. Let X and C be the net imbalance and controllable capacity, respectively, whereas broker b has corresponding values x_b and C_b. Then the balancing cost is denoted as $BC_X^{(C/C_b)}$, and the payment of a non-contributing broker b with an imbalance x_b is calculated through Formula 3.

$$imb_b(x_b) = \frac{BC_X^{(C/C_b)}}{X} x_b \tag{3}$$

Payment of a contributing broker b is calculated through an extra step to make sure that the payment covers the costs of non-contributing brokers B. To do that, capacities of non-contributing brokers are excluded from payment. The process is formulated in Formula 4.

$$imb_b(x_b) = \frac{BC_X^{(C/\{C_b \cup C_k : k \in B\})}}{X} x_b \tag{4}$$

At the end of a time slot, broker b pays the sum of VCG and imbalance payment.

5   Experimental Setup

In this work, we use our broker agent AgentUDE [8] and its variants to benchmark the balancing contribution of battery storage customers (cf., Table 2 for the broker settings). In default, we use all of the market functionalities of AgentUDE (serving to consumers) to generate casual imbalances. Therefore, the broker attracts customers and serves those customers by means of trading in the wholesale market. For more details, see the publication [8] that describes the algorithms used in AgentUDE. Figure 4 illustrates the model-based structure of the agent and PowerTAC environment.

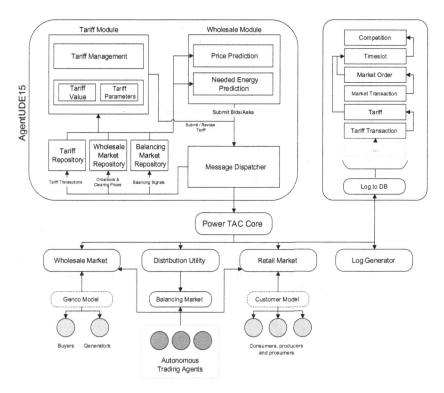

Fig. 4. Model-based structure of AgentUDE (2014 and 2015 release).

We arranged a tournament with different game variations. The following successful competitive brokers of the recent years participated in the tournament. The suffixes, at the end of the broker names indicate the year of the release:

- *AgentUDE15* (University of Duisburg-Essen, Germany) [8]
- *cwiBroker15* (CWI Amsterdam, The Netherlands) [16]
- *CrocodileAgent15* (University of Zagreb, Croatia) [11, 17]
- *Maxon15* (Westfaeliche Hochschule Muenster, Germany)
- *TacTex15* (University of Texas at Austin, United States) [3, 19]

In the tournament, all the games are defined in 3-player size in which one Agent-UDE variant is included. Therefore, 3-player actually means that AgentUDE or its variants compete with two brokers in the games. Unfortunately, few broker binaries were released in 2015. Therefore, we were unable to run 4 or 5 player games. All the brokers have the same chance to compete with AgentUDE, AgentUDEr1 and AgentUDEr2. Note that battery customers in the tournament are assumed to be captive customers. Thus, only AgentUDE publishes battery storage tariffs.

Table 1 explains the settings used in the tournament. We use a constant number of captive battery storage customers. Each customer has a 90 kW of battery storage size and maximum transfer rate of 40 kWh. Thus, the maximum charging or discharging rate is limited to 1.2 MWh whereas the full capacity is 2.7 MW. If, e.g., brokers start charging it takes 3 time slots to fully charge or discharge the batteries. Besides, batteries have an internal-discharging rate, which refers to the power loss over the time.

Table 1. Simulation settings.

Setting	Description
# of games	18 games: 6 per agent variant in Table 2
# of batteries	30 *(90 kW/each and max. transfer rate: 40 kWh/each)*
# of competing brokers	4 *(excluding default-broker and the ones in Table 2)*
Game length	1460 + 360 bootstrap time slots
Game size	3-players
PowerTAC release	1.3.1

Table 2 lists the price settings of the broker variants. As seen in the table, the same up-regulation and down-regulation prices are used in battery storage tariffs and balancing orders. AgentUDE participates in BM auctions by offering its battery capacities for up- and down-regulation. As defined in the previous section, DU may decide to use one of the orders depending on the overall imbalance. This is a fixed behavior in all the games.

Table 2. Broker variants.

Broker	BM price		Customer price	
	Up-regulation (€/kWh, BM pays)	Down-regulation (€/kWh, broker pays)	Up-regulation (€/kWh, broker pays)	Down-regulation (€/kWh, customer pays)
AgentUDE	–	–	–	–
AgentUDEr1	0.24	0.08	0.24	0.08
AgentUDEr2	0.24	0.18	0.24	0.18

In order to converge the validity of the proposed approaches many games are played. This creates a large number of log files. To deal with this challenge the open-source PowerTAC Log Analysis (PLA)[1] framework was extended to store the logs in a relational database system. Matlab R2015b is used to compute relevant output.

6   Results

Out of 18 games, 12 games were dedicated to AgentUDE's variants (AgentUDEr1 and AgentUDEr2) and 6 games were played without BM activity (AgentUDE). Therefore, we monitor the broker activities, in which AgentUDE variants compete gainst two of the brokers listed in Sect. 5. The following figure shows a snapshot of the average cumulative profits.

---

[1] PowerTAC Log Analysis, https://bitbucket.org/markuspeters/pla (13.05.2016).

Figure 5 depicts the cash positions (i.e., cumulative profit) of the brokers starting from time slot 360 and until time slot 1700. Just looking at the profit level, AgentUDEr2 seems to have a clear profit advantage over others. As noticed in the figure, there are some regular sharp decreases in the profit. The reason behind is that peak-demand assessment has been introduced in the 1.3.1 version of the PowerTAC [1], instead of fixed rate distribution fee. Now, brokers pay peak-demand charges at every 168 time slots, depending on the level of harm they cause to distribution system. Since brokers initially have no idea about the distribution costs they are expected to adjust their profit-cost balance after the peak-demand assessments.

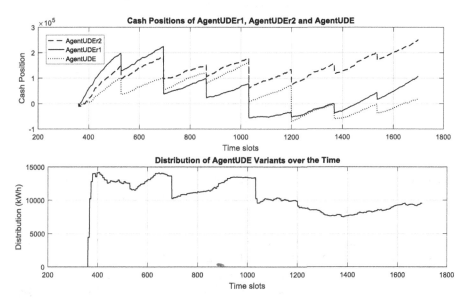

Fig. 5. Cash positions of the brokers (above) and distribution volume (below) over the time. Distribution volumes are identical for all variants since they have the same retail and wholesale market behaviors. Regulation activity has no clear contribution to the overall cash balance of AgentUDEr1 over AgentUDE.

Figure 6 illustrates the average values of imbalanced energy amount and cumulative imbalance payments. Payments graph (Fig. 6, below) show that AgentUDEr2 received the highest payment from the distribution utility. Note that the payment shown here is accounted for the net imbalance, taking the brokers' controllable capacity into account (see Formulas 3 and 4).

As noted previously, BM activities are financed in a different mechanism and therefore require balancing orders from brokers that have controllable capacities. In the variants AgentUDEr1 and AgentUDEr2, we use battery storage tariffs to use those capacities in the BM.

Figure 7 illustrates the BM payments and corresponding broker payment for the storage capacity, used in the up and down regulation. The positive or negative payments may be gained from either the BM or the customers, depending on the direction of regulation. In

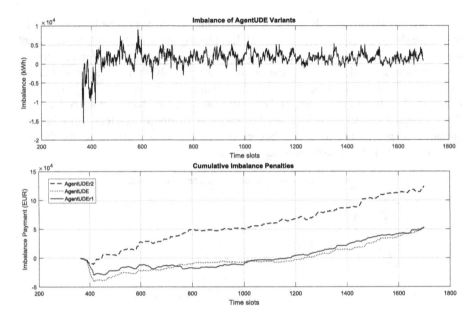

Fig. 6. Imbalanced energy amount (above) of brokers (average imbalance amounts of AgentUDE, AgentUDEr1, AgentUDEr2) and cumulative imbalance penalties (below), paid by our experimental brokers. Positive imbalance payments refer to the payment that brokers receive whereas positive imbalance denotes surplus energy that brokers procured.

most cases, brokers gain profit, which is exactly $Payment^{BM} - Payment^{Customer}$. Figure 7 shows the cost (customer payment) and balancing profit. As noticed, the cost and profit lines are close to each other since the tariff prices in the balancing order are highly customer-friendly. On the customer side, they keep getting high profit due to big gap between up-regulation and down-regulation price, as specified in the tariff.

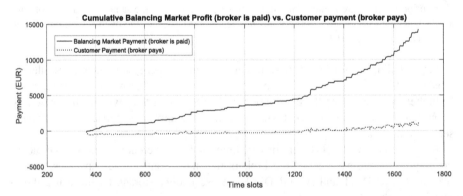

Fig. 7. Balancing transactions of AgentUDEr1, showing cumulative payments for the regulation power, traded in the balancing market (up-regulation price: 0.24 €/kWh, down-regulation price: 0.08 €/kWh). The second line (dotted) shows all associated payments to customers.

Figure 8 illustrates a similar case as in Fig. 7, this time having different prices (see the description in Fig. 8). Likewise, those prices are identical with the prices in the customer tariff. As noticed, we only changed the down-regulation price and keep the up-regulation price same as in Fig. 7. Since the gap between buy and sell price is now smaller, brokers have more opportunities to gain a decent level of profit on the downside. For example, given the clearing price for down-regulation at 0.08 €/kWh, a broker gains net 0.1 €/kWh for that regulation. On the customer side, the net customer payment still has a positive sign which shows that the regulation business is a win-win business model for brokers, customers and distribution utility (as reliability).

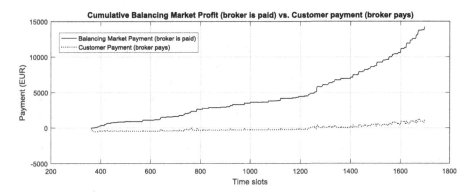

Fig. 8. Balancing transactions of AgentUDEr2, using a different pricing (up-regulation price: 0.24 €/kWh, down-regulation price: 0.18 €/kWh). The change in the tariff price has significantly changed the profit-cost balance.

7   Conclusion and Future Work

In this paper, we introduced an extended balancing mechanism for PowerTAC and its possible influence on profitability issues of brokers. We employed our broker agent and its variants to offer battery storage tariffs to use those capacities in the BM. Results showed that the balancing market provides an incentive-based clearing mechanism to satisfy all parties, which contributes to the balancing process. First goal is to keep the overall system balance stable and reliable. Apart from that, it also poses as a profitable business model from the brokers' (e.g., retailers, utilities) and customers' point of view. Even though we used a non-dynamic bidding, using fixed rate prices in the customer tariff and balancing market, balancing orders contributed to the overall cash balance of the broker.

In order to turn balancing orders into a more profitable business model from the brokers' perspectives a number of strategies will be considered in future work:

- More attractive tariff prices from the customer's point of view will influence the balancing mechanism, too.

- Using the same price on the tariffs and balancing orders can only maximize the probability of winning an auction. However, differentiating the prices may increase the profit while the probability of clearing the auction may decrease.

The use of larger capacities and strategic pricing on the balancing market and on the tariff may result in a profitable business model for the intermediary business actors. In this small experiment, we used a symbolic capacity of 2,7 MW for the total of 30 batteries. A larger storage portfolio can make the landscape clearer and provide a better guidance.

Taking the indicators found in the paper future work will be:

- Hydrogen storage customers are a typical real-world example for hydrogen refueling stations that produce hydrogen on-site and sell it to fuel-cell customers. Besides being a business on its own such customers may become very important for the electricity grid balancing. Thus, we will create a model for a hydrogen storage customer to simulate various scenarios from the transportation to the balancing processes.
- Due to energy conversion efficiencies and power storage capabilities of hydrogen storage and battery storage technologies there has been a debate between the proponents of both approaches. Our second goal is to have a closer look at the trade-off value of those storage technologies, considering balancing capabilities and economic effects.
- Economically driven usage of storage units supports the effective allocation of resources if market trends and customer demands are considered appropriately. In this context, we will implement a number of machine learning techniques to trade in the market wisely, satisfying its customers demand (e.g., fuel-cell customers).

Due to increasing renewable capacities all around the world, power storage technologies are getting more and more important to pump or dump power when the electricity grid needs it. Among storage technologies, batteries and power-to-hydrogen solutions seem to be highly promising technologies in the upcoming years, thanks to advances in battery technologies and distributed storage capability of both technologies.

References

1. Ketter, W., Collins, J., De Weerdt, M.: The 2016 power trading agent competition. ERIM Report Series Reference (2016)
2. Morris, C., Pehnt, M.: Energy Transition: The German Energiewende. Heinrich Böll Stiftung, Berlin (2014)
3. Urieli, D., Stone, P.: Tactex'13: a champion adaptive power trading agent. In: Proceedings of the 2014 International Conference on Autonomous Agents and Multi-agent Systems, pp. 1447–1448 (2014)
4. Reddy, P.P., Veloso, M.M.: Factored models for multiscale decision-making in smart grid customers. In: AAAI, July 2012
5. Vickrey, W.: Counterspeculation, auctions, and competitive sealed tenders. J. Finan. **16**(1), 8–37 (1961)

6. Ansarin, M., Ketter, W., Collins, J.: Market-based multi-agent coordination to manage energy balance in smart grids. Available at SSRN (2016)
7. Möller, C., Rachev, S.T., Fabozzi, F.J.: Balancing energy strategies in electricity portfolio management. Energy Econ. **33**(1), 2–11 (2011)
8. Ozdemir, S., Unland, R.: A winner agent in a smart grid simulation platform. In: 2015 IEEE/WIC/ACM International Conference on Intelligent Agent Technology (IAT 2015) (2015)
9. Hollands, R.G.: Will the real smart city please stand up? Intelligent, progressive or entrepreneurial? City **12**(3), 303–320 (2008)
10. US Energy Information Administration: Annual Energy Review 2010, October 2011
11. Babic, J., Podobnik, V.: An analysis of power trading agent competition 2014. In: Ceppi, S., David, E., Podobnik, V., Robu, V., Shehory, O., Stein, S., Vetsikas, I.A. (eds.) AMEC/TADA 2013 and 2014. LNBIP, vol. 187, pp. 1–15. Springer, Heidelberg (2014)
12. RES EU: Directive 2009/28/EC of the European Parliament and of the Council of 23 April 2009 on the promotion of the use of energy from renewable sources and amending and subsequently repealing Directives 2001/77/EC and 2003/30. Off. J. Eur. Comm. **5**, 16–62 (2009)
13. Vandezande, L., Meeus, L., Belmans, R., Saguan, M., Glachant, J.-M.: Well-functioning balancing markets: a prerequisite for wind power integration. Energy Policy **38**(7), 3146–3154 (2010)
14. Vickrey, W.: Counterspeculation, auctions, and competitive sealed tenders. J. Finan. **16**(1), 8–37 (1961)
15. Clarke, E.H.: Multipart pricing of public goods. Public Choice **11**(1), 17–33 (1971)
16. Liefers, B., Hoogland, J., Poutré, H.L.: A successful broker agent for power TAC. In: Ceppi, S., David, E., Podobnik, V., Robu, V., Shehory, O., Stein, S., Vetsikas, I.A. (eds.) AMEC/TADA 2013 and 2014. LNBIP, vol. 187, pp. 99–113. Springer, Heidelberg (2014)
17. Matetic, S., Babic, J., Matijas, M., Petric, A., Podobnik, V.: The CrocodileAgent 2012: negotiating agreements in smart grid tariff market. In: AT, pp. 203–204 (2012)
18. Ketter, W., Peters, M., Collins, J.: Autonomous agents in future energy markets: the 2012 power trading agent competition. In: Proceedings of the 25th Benelux Conference on Artificial Intelligence, BNAIC 2013, Delft, The Netherlands, 7–8 November 2013, Delft University of Technology (TU Delft). Under the Auspices of the Benelux Association for Artificial Intelligence (BNVKI) and the Dutch Research School for Information and Knowledge Systems (SIKS) (2013)
19. Urieli, D., Stone, P.: An MDP-based winning approach to autonomous power trading: formalization and empirical analysis. In: Workshops at the Thirtieth AAAI Conference on Artificial Intelligence (2016)
20. Joskow, P.L.: California's electricity crisis. Oxford Rev. Econ. Policy **17**(3), 365–388 (2001)
21. Derksen, C., Linnenberg, T., Unland, R., Fay, A.: Structure and classification of unified energy agents as a base for the systematic development of future energy grids. Eng. Appl. Artif. Intell. **41**, 310–324 (2015)
22. Kahlen, M., Ketter, W.: Aggregating electric cars to sustainable virtual power plants: the value of flexibility in future electricity markets. In: AAAI, pp. 665–671, January 2015
23. Drury, E., Denholm, P., Sioshansi, R.: The value of compressed air energy storage in energy and reserve markets. Energy **36**(8), 4959–4973 (2011)
24. Ramchurn, S.D., Vytelingum, P., Rogers, A., Jennings, N.: Agent-based control for decentralised demand side management in the smart grid. In: The 10th International Conference on Autonomous Agents and Multiagent Systems, vol. 1, pp. 5–12. International Foundation for Autonomous Agents and Multiagent Systems, May 2011

25. Gordijn, J., Akkermans, H.: Business models for distributed generation in a liberalized market environment. Electric Power Syst. Res. **77**(9), 1178–1188 (2007)
26. Albadi, M.H., El-Saadany, E.F.: Demand response in electricity markets: an overview. In: 2007 IEEE Power Engineering Society General Meeting, June 2007
27. Vytelingum, P., Voice, T.D., Ramchurn, S.D., Rogers, A., Jennings, N.R.: Theoretical and practical foundations of large-scale agent-based micro-storage in the smart grid. J. Artif. Intell. Res. **42**, 765–813 (2011)

A Holonic Multi-agent Control System for Networks of Micro-grids

Sajad Ghorbani[✉] and Rainer Unland

Institute for Computer Science and Business Information Systems (ICB),
University of Duisburg Essen, Essen, Germany
{sajad.ghorbani,rainer.unland}@icb.uni-due.de

Abstract. Due to the rapid growth of distributed renewable energy production in the energy markets, future power production and consumption will be more localized. As a consequence, projects and research on Micro-Grids has increased substantially in the recent years. However, the management of energy grids as such will become more complex if numerous Micro-Grids with high levels of autonomy are to be integrated. Modelling energy grids which benefit from the autonomy of the localized energy production and consumption, and at the same time, provide reliable services to the rapidly increasing energy demand seems to be a challenging issue. Combining the advantages of Holonic structures with the distributed nature of Multi-Agent Systems makes it an excellent candidate for the management of this complexity. This paper addresses the need to have autonomous management of the localized generation and consumption, as well as to increase the level of reliability, by a means of forming a Holonic control network of Micro-Grids. This holonic control approach allows the bottom-up formation of the energy grid, from the actual physical components of the grid to a network of interconnected Micro-Grids.

Keywords: Holonic Multi-Agent system · Micro-grids · Two-layer architecture · Energy agent · Energy option model

1 Introduction

The application of Micro-Grids addresses the need for more reliable power supply and localizing power production and consumption, but at the same time it makes the control issues more complex. As the participation of prosumers (an entity capable of bidirectional exchange of power) is getting higher, the power system demand to control this domination, as well as the need to provide some levels of autonomy is being increased. Moreover, the formation procedure of the Micro-Grids is bottom-up rather than the top-down formation in the main grid. Therefore, current purely centralized control, which is designed to serve the traditional unidirectional power flow, does not seem to be a feasible approach to manage the growing change in the topology of the energy grid. Coordination benefits that Holonic structure add to the decentralized MAS, makes it an appropriate solution for management of this change. The Holonic system concept was proposed to combine benefits of the decentralized control and top-down hierarchical

© Springer International Publishing Switzerland 2016
M. Klusch et al. (Eds.): MATES 2016, LNAI 9872, pp. 231–238, 2016.
DOI: 10.1007/978-3-319-45889-2_17

organization. In fact, it links the autonomous and cooperative behavior of the system in order to achieve its objectives [1]. The word Holon first used by Koestler [2], is referred to an entity which is a whole considering its sub-ordinated parts, and, at the same time, a part for a bigger entity. In the Holonic approach, agents are dynamically structured in hierarchies or so-called holarchies which can be recursively built. A popular application area for Holonic structures is in manufacturing control systems [3, 4]. Medical diagnostic systems [5], medical optimal decision making processes [6], and Holonic self-organization approaches to the design of emergent e-Logistics infra-structures [7] are also considered as important applications of Swarm Intelligence and the Holonic Multi-Agent System (Holonic MAS) paradigm.

In Holonic MAS simulation of the power grid, agents represent physical or functional components of the grid. They are able to be recursively modeled and dynamically reorganize themselves. We modelled our proposed Holonic Micro-Grids by the help of Energy Agent and Energy Option Model (EOM) [8] developed at DAWIS[1]. The Energy Agent is responsible to control any actual physical components of the Micro-Grid. The energy management of the aggregation of the entities is performed based on the detailed information about the behavior and flexibility of the system provided by EOM. In the following section, we will have a brief discussion about the related work. In Sect. 3, the concept and the main characteristics of our proposed network of Holonic Micro-Grids are introduced. Finally, in Sect. 4, we conclude and clarify the future work.

2 Related Work

One of the scaling solutions for energy grids is the local grouping of interconnected distributed generators and storages. This so-called Micro-Grid network operates both in connected to the main power grid and isolated mode. The number of Micro-Grid projects and testbeds being implemented around the world is increasing rapidly [9, 10]. In recent studies, there has been growing interest to utilize the Holonic MAS structure to simulate the control of smart grid.

There are different approaches proposed for the automation and control of the power grid, most work is still either on isolated topics only or in its preliminary phase. There are also few work proposing holonic control of the grid. These control schemes vary from homogeneous recursive control to heterogeneous multi-objective control (Table 1). In a holonic architecture for the power grid, every prosumer component (e.g. a household) can be seen as a holon [11]. Holons can cluster together to form bigger holons (e.g. a neighborhood community) in a higher aggregation level. This bottom-up aggregation continues to finally form the whole smart grid. In this approach, the homogeneous control is recursively implemented in each level. However, customers and producers may have different interests and objectives in different scales and layers of the grid, preventing the system to work with a unique control scheme. Another common drawback of the proposed MAS approaches for the control of the energy grid is that they only consider electricity and ignore the fact that energy networks are interconnected.

---

[1] https://www.dawis.wiwi.uni-due.de/en/.

Table 1. Design and control of Holonic architectures proposed for power grid.

	Holonic design	Control approach
Nageri et al. [11]	Households Neighborhood District, ...	Homogeneous Recursive Service oriented
Frey et al. [12]	Micro-Grids	Heterogeneous Multi-objective
Ounnar et al. [13]	Resource holon Energy holon Service holon	Homogeneous Multi criteria decision making
Pahwa et al. [14]	Substation network Feeder network Neighborhood network	Homogeneous Collaborative

We are trying to address the aforementioned issues by our Holonic Micro-Grid control architecture which has two layers, namely (i) *Physical Layer* and (ii) *Aggregation layer*. Depending on different interests, Holons of each layer can be competitive or collaborative. The coalition between holons can be formed by means of communication and energy profile matching. Besides, in our Holonic Multi-agent control system for the network of Micro-Grids we utilize the concept of unified Energy Agent. By so doing, not only can we model the various physical components of the grid regardless of the type of energy carrier, but also the aggregation layer which forms a network of Holonic interconnected Micro-Grids.

3   Proposed Holonic MAS Control of Micro-grids

The general scheme of the proposed two-layer Holonic control architecture is depicted in Fig. 1. In the following, the physical layer and the aggregation layer of the architecture are introduced.

3.1   Physical Layer

In the lowest layer, there are physical components that are controlled by Energy Agent interface. This unified Energy Agent is basically a specialized autonomous software system that is developed to economically manage the energy consumption, production, conversion and storage to smoothly integrate and run the potential ability of all entities (physical components) of the real world Micro-Grid system. A physical component could be as simple as a water boiler with only electricity consumption, or as complicated as a Combined Heat and Power (CHP) unit, with a natural gas consumption and electricity production. Therefore, in our model, all of the entities (holons) in the physical layer are identified by their energy profiles. This is also true for upper layer holons, as their energy profiles are the accumulation of the profiles of their sub-holons.

Electric vehicle (EV) is an example of physical components that is modeled in [8] with the help of an Energy Agent. As shown in Fig. 2, this basic EV model has three

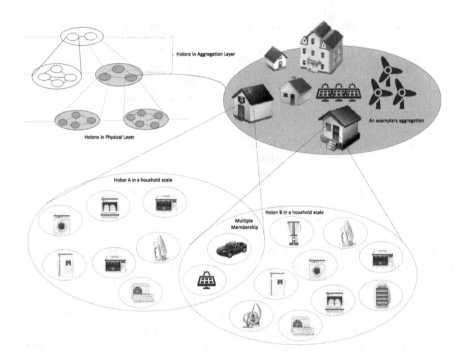

Fig. 1. Holonic architecture of micro-grids

possible system states, namely *Charge*, *Discharge* and *Idle*. The possible transition of these states and the step size, along with the state of the charge (SoC) and full charge capacity of the EV battery are also modelled.

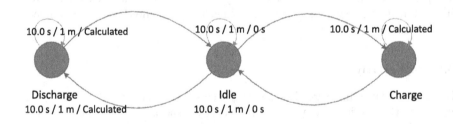

Fig. 2. Electric Vehicle (EV) basic model, system states and transitions [15]

3.2 Aggregation Layer

The second layer is composed of the aggregations of the components in the lowest layer. These aggregations are formed with the help of Energy Option Model (EOM) which provides the technical detailed information about the behavior and flexibility of the investigated system. Various possible use-cases of EOM are shown in Fig. 3. This layer is initially composed of all the (possible) combinations of existing generation and consumption units within certain Micro-Grid boundaries. Considering possible collaboration opportunities, there are different levels of aggregations in this layer. The collaboration between a single wind turbine and a storage unit is one example of the aggregations in this layer. As stated before, each entity can also have a holonic structure. Specifically, for the example mentioned above, the storage unit itself could be the result of Electric Vehicles (EVs) battery aggregation [15].

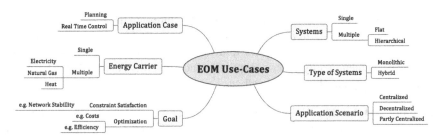

Fig. 3. Possible use-cases of EOM

The last level of aggregation is formed by the coalition of multiple Micro-Grids. Micro-Grids with various energy profiles could join together in order to exchange the power or any other energy carrier to which they are connected. The coalition could be formed based on different criteria such as economic interests, environmental, and/or reliability concerns.

3.3   Coalition Formation

Depending on being competitive or collaborative, different sorts of coalitions can be formed. Micro-grid holons with a positive energy profile are considered as *sellers*, and the one with the negative energy profile as *buyers*. An example of the collaborative power exchange between a group of Micro-Grids is the coalitions formed to decrease the power loss. Authors in [16] formulate the energy exchange between the Micro-Grids as a cooperative game. In their energy exchange model, in a set of Micro-Grids, a coalition is a group of cooperative seller and buyer Micro-Grids. The aim is to minimize the power loss during the local power exchange between a seller and a buyer, plus the power losses during the distribution from the main grid to the participated Micro-Grids. They used auction theory and matching games to optimize the problem. The collaboration between Micro-Grids is also possible and beneficial based on the fact that the Micro-grids in different locations probably have different energy profiles during the day. As the peak hours in the Micro-Grids situated in a residential area differ from the peak hours in the Micro-Grids of a commercial area [17], their energy profiles to some extent could be complementary.

As mentioned before, the aggregation between holons in our architecture could happen in each aggregation level, from the physical components aggregation to Micro-Grids coalitions. Depending on being collaborative or competitive, various matching algorithms can be used to form Holonic aggregations. To form an aggregation, first, the mapping process between the holons should be performed. The rating mechanism embedded in our Holonic model (Sect. 3.4) helps the individual holons to join or leave a holonic aggregation. This process is recursively done, whenever an energy request command is broadcasted from an upper Holon to its sub-holons.

3.4   Characteristics

Some of the most beneficial features of Holonic structures are the *Autonomy* within the boundaries of holons, *Multiple Membership*, and *Dynamic Reorganization* of holons. We also consider a *Rating Mechanism* to distinguish various energy profiles of each Holon based on their quality of service (priority and reliability degree). In the following each feature is explained in more detail.

Autonomy in Holarchy.   Holons of the aggregation layer are homogenous in the sense that they have the same inherited control mechanism, but at the same time autonomous by freedom to have multiple and conflicting objectives, leaving or joining various holons. The holons of individual Micro-Grids might be competitive, aiming to maximize their utility, and/or collaborative in the sense of satisfying common general objectives. With our two layered Holarchy, the coordination is performed by broadcasting the control decisions from a super-holon to its sub-holons, whereas autonomous operation of the Holons existing in each layer is guaranteed.

Profile Rating.   Considering various degrees of priorities and reliability, the energy needed or delivered by Holons are categorized based on their (accumulative) criticality or reliability. This categorization or, as we call it, rating mechanism could happen to each Holon, regardless of its position or scale. If the energy profile of each Holon is categorized, it may provide the potential for collaboration and resource sharing. As, for instance, the coalition between a Holon with the critical energy demand and another Holon with the high reliable energy supply is more likely to be formed.

Multiple Memberships.   The multiple memberships might happen as a means of providing the other holons with various services, such as back-up reserve. In Fig. 1, a set of solar panels in a household would join a Holon from another household to use the storage services provided by an EV battery. Another example of these multiple memberships could be found in shopping malls equipped with back-up micro-generators. These rather expensive generation facilities are used in order to provide a reliable source of energy in case of any failure in the main grid. In fact, these facilities are idle most of the time, making the owner Holon to be present in multiple bigger holons.

Dynamic Reorganization.   In each Holon of the Micro-Grid aggregation level, there is an agent representing the certain Micro-Grid. When a Micro-Grid Holon wants to enter a coalition, it receives the energy requests from the other Micro-Grids and broadcast it to its subordinated parts. Accordingly, the energy profiles of the holons in the aggregation layer are refined. This is done by means of recursively changing the existing aggregations or forming new aggregations in the way that the energy request is satisfied.

4   Conclusion and Future Work

Micro-Grids, as solutions for a better utilization of distributed renewable energy resources, are of a paramount interest in recent years. The main motivation to invest on having groups of distributed generators and storage facilities near actual loads are basically reliability issues, better resource allocation, and environmental concerns. In this paper, the concepts of a two-layered Holonic architecture for a network of Micro-Grids are introduced. We modelled our proposed Holonic Micro-Grids by the help of the unified Energy Agent and Energy Option Model (EOM), which principally enables us to aggregate and utilize the operational flexibility of any type of energy conversion process. Our control architecture consists of two layers, namely physical layer and aggregation layer. Recursive and bottom-up features of this approach enables us to model energy management of Micro-Grids in a decentralized manner, considering the comprehensive integration of prosumers in the future smarter grid. We devised a procedure in which groups of prosumers may form a coalition based on the complementarity of their energy profile. For the next steps of our work, first, the communication between the Holons in order to find proper matches of energy profiles should be described and then, the detailed negotiation mechanism between the holons to satisfy the optimum local goals as well as the general objectives of the upper layer holons ought to be described.

References

1. Fischer, K., Schillo, M., Siekmann, J.H.: Holonic multiagent systems: a foundation for the organisation of multiagent systems. In: Mařík, V., McFarlane, D.C., Valckenaers, P. (eds.) HoloMAS 2003. LNCS (LNAI), vol. 2744, pp. 71–80. Springer, Heidelberg (2003)
2. Koestler, A.: The Ghost in the Machine. Penguin Group, London (1990)
3. Brussel, H.V., Wyns, J., Valckenaers, P., Bongaerts, L., Peeters, P.: Reference architecture for holonic manufacturing systems: (PROSA). Comput. Ind. **37**, 255–274 (1998)
4. Leitão, P., Restivo, F.: ADACOR: a holonic architecture for agile and adaptive manufacturing control. Comput. Ind. **57**, 121–130 (2006)
5. Unland, R.: A holonic multi-agent system for robust, flexible, and reliable medical diagnosis. In: Meersman, R. (ed.) OTM-WS 2003. LNCS, vol. 2889, pp. 1017–1030. Springer, Heidelberg (2003)
6. Al-Qaysi, I., Othman, Z., Unland, R., Weihs, C., Branki, C.: Holonic and optimal medical decision making under uncertainty. In: 2010 IEEE EMBS Conference on Biomedical Engineering and Sciences (IECBES), pp. 295–299 (2010)
7. Ulieru, M., Unland, R.: A holonic self-organization approach to the design of emergent e-Logistics infrastructures. In: Serugendo, G.D.M., Karageorgos, A., Rana, O.F., Zambonelli, F. (eds.) Engineering Self-Organising Systems. LNCS, vol. 2977, pp. 139–156. Springer, Heidelberg (2003)
8. Derksen, C., Unland, R.: Energy agents - foundation for open future energy grids. Position Papers of the 2015 Federated Conference on Computer Science and Information Systems, 6, pp. 259–264 (2015)
9. Bayindir, R., Hossain, E., Kabalci, E., Perez, R.: A comprehensive study on microgrid technology. Int. J. Renew. Energy Res. (IJRER). **4**, 1094–1107 (2014)

10. Hatziargyriou, N., Asano, H., Iravani, R., Marnay, C.: Microgrids. IEEE Power Energy Mag. **5**, 78–94 (2007)
11. Negeri, E., Baken, N., Popov, M.: Holonic architecture of the smart grid. Smart Grid Renew. Energy **4**, 202 (2013)
12. Frey, S., Diaconescu, A., Menga, D., Demeure, I.: A holonic control architecture for a heterogeneous multi-objective smart micro-grid. In: 2013 IEEE 7th International Conference on Self-Adaptive and Self-Organizing Systems, pp. 21–30 (2013)
13. Ounnar, F., Naamane, A., Pujo, P., M'Sirdi, N.-K.: Intelligent control of renewable holonic energy systems. Energy Procedia **42**, 465–472 (2013)
14. Pahwa, A., DeLoach, S.A., Natarajan, B., Das, S., Malekpour, A.R., Shafiul Alam, S., Case, D.M.: Goal-based holonic multiagent system for operation of power distribution systems. IEEE Trans. Smart Grid **6**, 2510–2518 (2015)
15. Loose, N., Nurdin, Y., Ghorbani, S., Derksen, C., Unland, R.: Evaluation of aggregated systems in smart grids: an example use-case for the energy option model. In: Bajo, J., et al. (eds.) PAAMS 2016 Workshops. CCIS, vol. 616, pp. 369–380. Springer, Heidelberg (2016). doi:10.1007/978-3-319-39387-2_31
16. Saad, W., Han, Z., Poor, H.V.: Coalitional game theory for cooperative micro-grid distribution networks. In: 2011 IEEE International Conference on Communications Workshops (ICC), pp. 1–5. IEEE (2011)
17. Erol-Kantarci, M., Kantarci, B., Mouftah, H.T.: Reliable overlay topology design for the smart microgrid network. IEEE Netw. **25**, 38–43 (2011)

Author Index

Printed in the United States
By Bookmasters